JEFFERSON *and the* VIRGINIANS

Walter Lynwood Fleming Lectures in Southern History

JEFFERSON *and the* VIRGINIANS

Democracy, Constitutions, and Empire

PETER S. ONUF

LOUISIANA STATE UNIVERSITY PRESS
BATON ROUGE

Published with the assistance of the V. Ray Cardozier Fund

Published by Louisiana State University Press

Manufactured in the United States of America
First printing

Designer: Barbara Neely Bourgoyne
Typeface: Adobe Garamond
Printer and binder: Sheridan Books

Library of Congress Cataloging-in-Publication Data
Names: Onuf, Peter S., author.
Title: Jefferson and the Virginians : democracy, constitutions, and empire / Peter S. Onuf.
Other titles: Walter Lynwood Fleming lectures in southern history.
Description: Baton Rouge : Louisiana State University Press, [2018] | Series: Walter Lynwood Fleming lectures in southern history | Includes bibliographical references and index.
Identifiers: LCCN 2018007296 | ISBN 9780807169896 (cloth : alk. paper)
Subjects: LCSH: Jefferson, Thomas, 1743–1826—Political and social views. | Virginia—History—1775–1865. | Statesmen—Virginia—History.
Classification: LCC E332.2 .O57 2018 | DDC 973.4/6092—dc23
LC record available at https://lccn.loc.gov/2018007296

The paper in this book meets the guidelines for permanence and durability of the Committee on Production Guidelines for Book Longevity of the Council on Library Resources. ♾

to

Kristin Kirkman Onuf

Rachel Kathryn Onuf

and

Alexandra Kirkman Onuf

Contents

Preface *and* Acknowledgments

It has been a privilege spending so much time with Thomas Jefferson over the course of my career. As the essays in this book should make clear, I remain "deeply conflicted" about my subject. I reflexively resist the idea that I am his biographer, and I do not pretend or aspire to be an expert on all matters Jeffersonian. Yet I have to confess that Jefferson has increasingly engaged my sympathy as well as attention in my last efforts to make sense of his life and thought. Taking a comprehensive look at the arc of his private life and public career in the good company of my dear friend Annette Gordon-Reed may have something to do with this more accepting, less judgmental attitude toward Jefferson.

In famously invoking the principle of equality, the author of the Declaration of Independence enjoined Americans to recognize one another as fellow citizens and acknowledge the bonds of sentiment and obligation that made them a people. The book I wrote with Annette, *"Most Blessed of the Patriarchs": Thomas Jefferson and the Empire of the Imagination* (2016), represents our effort to see him across the centuries, in his own world, and so to recognize him—for all his many and all too consequential failings—as a fellow American. What does it mean to be "American"? Who are we as a "people," if we are one at all? A better understanding of Jefferson does not offer easy answers to these compelling questions. To the contrary, it has become clear to me that Jefferson himself found these questions profoundly troubling. The ultimate success of the new nation's experiment in republican self-government was by no means foreordained, and his faith in man's capacity for progress and improvement was sorely tested.

In retrospect, the failings of Jefferson and his generation are conspicuous to us. It is much harder to look *with them* toward an uncertain future, anxiously hoping that rising generations would see a way forward, animated by their own visions of progress and improvement. Jefferson's anxieties, most eloquently expressed in his retirement years, resonate with ours. In these troubled days, our faith in ourselves, in our identity and future as a people, is also being tested.

My design in this volume is to situate Jefferson in successively more capacious contexts, from Revolutionary Virginia, to the more perfect union of American state-republics, and finally to the federal republic's providential destiny as a great continental empire. In each of these contexts, I pair Jefferson with a Virginian interlocutor and focus their "conversation" on a critical theme for the future of commonwealth and continent. Jefferson's thinking about democracy was shaped by his troubled relationship with Patrick Henry, the great patriot whose stirring oratory ignited the Revolution in Virginia. Jefferson's collaboration with lifelong friend and ally James Madison shaped his constitutional thought, setting the stage for his career as leader of the Republican opposition to the Federalist administrations of George Washington and John Adams. When President Jefferson looked westward and into the future, beyond the partisan divisions that nearly destroyed the union in the 1790s, his vision of America's "empire for liberty" was grounded in an imagined, posthumous reconciliation with former Federalist foe Washington. In his Inaugural Address, Jefferson celebrated the indispensable role Washington had played in securing the independence Jefferson declared.

The erudite Jefferson's thinking drew on the books in his vast, ever-expanding library. But its deeper sources can be found in his sometimes friendly and sometimes hostile relationships with his contemporaries, including most notably and most influentially these three prominent Virginians. Jefferson does not emerge as the superior or dominant figure in the conversations I have reconstructed. But as Jefferson emerges from the isolation of his study, he becomes a more complicated, interesting, and ultimately more accessible figure.

I remain conflicted about my subject, but I am eternally grateful for the many good friends I've made in the world of Jefferson studies. A partial list includes Frank Cogliano, Christa Dierksheide, Joanne Freeman, Annette

Gordon-Reed, Matt Hale, David Konig, Csaba Levai, Jan Lewis, Armin Mattes, Johann Neem, John Ragosta, Hannah Spahn, Brian Steele, Alan Taylor, Maurizio Valsania, and George Van Cleve. Our friends Jim Horn and Andrew O'Shaughnessy, successive directors of the International Center for Jefferson Studies at Monticello, have provided a congenial setting in Charlottesville and at conferences around the world in which Jeffersonian friendships have flourished.

Frank, Annette, and John offered helpful readings of specific chapters of this book; Matt and Brian read the entire manuscript with extraordinary care. Matt's pathbreaking work on early American democracy helped spur my own thinking on that urgent and compelling theme. Brian suggested that I needed to explain what I—and my subjects—meant by "Virginia" in order to frame this book's larger argument, thus prompting me to draft the introductory essay. George's important new book *We Have Not a Government: The Articles of Confederation and the Road to the Constitution* (2017) refreshed and revised my understanding of the "critical period." Non-Jeffersonians Jon Kukla and Alan Gibson provided invaluable counsel on Patrick Henry and James Madison, respectively. Jon's fine biography, *Patrick Henry: Champion of Liberty* (2017), should change the way we all think about his subject, particularly those who have been led astray by Jefferson; Alan's mastery of the literature by and about Madison kept me pointed in the right direction, though he may think I have occasionally wandered afield. I am also grateful to Joanne Allen, my extraordinary copyeditor, who helped put the finishing touches on this book.

Andy Burstein, my first graduate student at Virginia, deserves special thanks. On behalf of the history department at Louisiana State University, Andy invited me to deliver the Fleming Lectures in Baton Rouge in March 2016. I am grateful to Department Chair Victor Slater, Bill Cooper, and their fellow historians for their warm hospitality. The lectures I gave at LSU bear faint resemblance to the essays published in this volume, with the exception of what became chapter 2, on Jefferson and Henry. But the opportunity to try out some of my preliminary thoughts before a friendly and well-informed audience of faculty and students was invaluable—and great fun too. Over the years Andy has been a constructive, encouraging critic and good friend. I have learned a great deal from his scholarship on Jefferson and many other subjects. His excellent dual biography, *Madison and Jefferson* (2010), coauthored with his partner and colleague Nancy Isenberg, was always on hand when I drafted my essay on those two great friends.

My intellectual engagement with my brother Nicholas Onuf goes back even further. Nick and I have written two books together, and he has always pressed and inspired me to think harder about the way our subjects think. For me and so many others, Nick is the model mentor, collaborator, and friend. My mentor Jack P. Greene has also been an inspiration, ever since I had the great good fortune to enroll in his graduate seminar on the American Revolution at Johns Hopkins when he was a visiting professor and I was a very young undergraduate, more than a half century ago. I thank Jack and Amy Bushnell for their friendship and support. And thanks as well to George and Margaret Billias, near neighbors and dear friends in Worcester, where I am now spending my second fellowship year at the American Antiquarian Society (the first was in 1984–85).

Happily, patriarchy is not what it used to be. I am nonetheless blessed with wonderful daughters, Rachel Kathryn Onuf and Alexandra Kirkman (Zee) Onuf. Jefferson tells us that "the earth belongs to the living," and I am comforted to know that some part of it, however small, is in their good hands. In due course, it will be time for Thomas Roscoe Lim, Zee's brilliant and beautiful son, to bring the world alive. In the meantime, I am most blessed of all to have spent the very best part of my life in the loving company of Thomas's grandmother, Rachel and Zee's mother, and my wife, Kristin Kirkman Onuf. I dedicate this last book to Kristin, Rachel, and Zee, with love.

JEFFERSON *and the* VIRGINIANS

Introduction

Thomas Jefferson loved his "country," Virginia. This fundamental fact about the author of the American Declaration of Independence is the point of departure for biographers and students of his political thought and career. Dumas Malone titled the first of the six volumes in his magisterial biography *Jefferson the Virginian,* and Jefferson would have endorsed that characterization.[1] Whenever he was away, he longed to be at home, in the bosom of his Virginia family. Monticello, the house he designed and built (and redesigned and rebuilt) on the top of a hill on land he inherited from his father, Peter Jefferson, was located at the very heart of his world, a storied place where the ambitious young man looked forward and the sentimental old man looked back.[2] Jefferson's political career was shaped by devotion to his beloved Commonwealth's vital interests, to reforming its laws and institutions, educating its citizens, and vindicating its rights. It was hardly surprising that he would be such a staunch opponent of distant cousin Chief Justice John Marshall's "consolidationist" assault on states' rights.

Yet it is not clear what Jefferson meant when he talked about his home or his country. Our understandable tendency is to interpret the history of the new nation, in the long aftermath of a devastating Civil War, in binary terms, juxtaposing localists and nationalists, Antifederalists and Federalists, South and North, Virginia and America. In this interpretative frame, federalism appears to be the great fault line. Jefferson may have straddled that line when he served the Confederation and the new federal government, but most scholars would agree that his most fundamental loyalty was to his home state.[3] From where we now stand, the great irony (or tragedy) of Jefferson's career is that this most eloquent exponent of democracy and natural rights was, to the end of his days, the owner and exploiter of enslaved people. We might blame his deeply grounded but tragically misplaced attachment to Virginia for this paradoxical state of affairs, or simply discount the hypocrite's empty rhetoric. Why didn't Jefferson press for emancipation in Virginia, or at least set an example for fellow slave owners by freeing the people he claimed to own? Why did the great reformer resign himself to such a profoundly unjust and immoral status quo? To ask these questions is to answer them: the slave-owning Jefferson and Virginia, a "slave society," are by our lights indefensible.

But what if we posed different questions? What if we looked forward *with* Jefferson into a radically uncertain future? The overarching and open-ended question that Jefferson sought to answer throughout his career and that I will explore in the following essays is so fundamental—on the face of it, so apparently self-answering—that it is rarely explicitly posed: what exactly is, or more precisely, *was* "Virginia"? There is no simple or direct answer to this question in the vast corpus of his writings. My approach is to put Jefferson into conversation with Patrick Henry, James Madison, and George Washington about the urgent and compelling questions that would define Virginia and determine its future.[4] The Old Dominion was now a new, self-constituted, self-governing Commonwealth, an "experiment" in republican government. Yet Virginians were also Americans, pledging "our lives, our fortunes, and our sacred honor" to a "common cause" and a more perfect union that transcended provincial boundaries.[5]

Jefferson and his interlocutors were all great Virginia patriots, but none could say with any authority exactly what their beloved country was, or would or should become. The break with Britain set the stage for ongoing controversy: over the identity of Virginians and Americans as a "people" or "peoples"; over Virginia's boundaries and jurisdiction within the union; and over the constitution of government in Virginia and for the states collectively. Because Virginia was part of a larger American whole, efforts to define its corporate identity and promote its collective interests inevitably entailed broader questions about the character and constitution of the Confederation and federal union.[6] Indeterminacy demanded definition, but definition promoted further controversy. The conversations I reconstruct here offer a glimpse of how influential Virginians struggled to define Virginia—and America—in the context of Revolutionary upheaval.[7] They also suggest why Thomas Jefferson's identity as a "Virginian" obscures much more than it illuminates about his thought and his career.

Jefferson is frequently charged with seeing the world in binary, black-and-white terms. He certainly betrayed Manichean tendencies during the great party battles of the 1790s, when he accused High Federalists of being "aristocrats," "monocrats," and un-American enemies of republican government. But the great political drama of his life did not revolve around vindicating Virginia's rights against the world. He had no illusions about the superior virtue of the Virginian people, nor did he idolize its 1776 constitution (which he vainly attempted to replace) or the government it authorized (which was too often dominated by political enemies). Virginian "manners" (shaped by the pernicious influence of slavery) left much to be desired, as did the wasteful ways in which his neighbors cultivated the land. The native son demonstrated his love of country by trying to reform it, to make it something it was not. He did not love Virginia with the blind devotion of a modern-day superpatriot.

For Jefferson there was nothing sacred about the Commonwealth's increasingly depleted soil. His most important contribution to the 1776 constitution, which he considered radically defective, was a provision for the future creation of new states out of its vast western territory, and his great achievement in the Confederation Congress was to complete Virginia's cession of the trans-Ohio region to the United States in 1784.[8] As an advocate of constitutional reform, Jefferson wanted to *curb* the power of state government, not consolidate or exalt its claims to "sovereignty." As a committed federalist—and opponent of nationalists who called themselves "Federalists"—he wanted to bring government home to the people through the creation of "ward republics" at the local, neighborhood level. State governments therefore could be useful barriers against encroachments from above, as they were in 1798 and as Jefferson hoped they would be against the Marshall Court in later years.[9] But they were never an end in themselves, the objects of undying devotion, terminal communities or nation-states worth dying for.

Was Virginia or any other state worth making the ultimate sacrifice? Liberty-loving patriots should "manure" the "tree of liberty" with their blood *against* unresponsive state governments (as in Shays' Rebellion in

Massachusetts), and a nation (like France in its bloody revolution) might sacrifice everything and everyone (except "an Adam and an Eve," to regenerate the race) in order to preserve its freedom and independence.[10] But Jefferson could only contemplate disunion with horror and the wish to die: the collapse of the union would be "treason against the hopes of the world," the parricidal betrayal of the precious legacy bequeathed by the Revolutionary fathers.[11]

Jefferson's patriotism was grounded in an enduring attachment to his home, and his home was connected to the nation through a "gradation of authorities," as he wrote Joseph Cabell in 1816, from "the elementary republics of the wards, [to] the county republics, the State republics, and the republic of the Union."[12] According to the conventional wisdom, patriotic attachments grew progressively weaker across space; this is why republics, whose survival depended on virtuous self-governing citizens, were supposed to be small, while great empires were governed by despotic force. Jefferson imagined a new dynamic in his vision of democratic federalism. As a "participator" in government, whether at the local or at some higher level, the patriotic republican would identify with fellow citizens elsewhere and personalize threats to liberty everywhere. Jefferson thus democratized an aristocratic sentiment traditionally associated with the ownership of great estates and dominion over the many dependents attached to them. The country Jefferson loved was not an exclusive domain or tract of land subject to the rule of a favored few but rather an expanding union of free republics destined to spread across the continent. In this dynamic world, the idea of "attachment" could be detached from particular places and projected across time and space.[13] Virginia was Jefferson's "country," but so too was the continent as a whole. As coproprietor of the great continental estate, held in stewardship for the rising generation, every good citizen would be prepared to sacrifice everything to defend the homeland: "he will let the heart be torn out of his body sooner than his power be wrested from him by a Caesar or a Bonaparte."[14]

Virginia could claim and secure its independence because of the willingness of Virginians to put their bodies on the line in the American Revolution. Throughout his political career Jefferson celebrated that willingness as the critical factor in vindicating the American experiment in republican government. The "Spirit of 1776" animated liberty-loving Anglo-Americans across the continent, enabling the "people" to demolish royal authority in their respective provinces and constitute new republican governments. In doing so, former subjects of George III in his province of Virginia made themselves into self-governing "Virginians," defining themselves against enemies at home and abroad. Of course, they were determined to vindicate the rights they had enjoyed under the British imperial old regime, including property rights in the enslaved people they claimed to own. This heightened rights-consciousness made the constitution of a self-governing commonwealth a question of the utmost urgency for Jefferson and fellow patriots, both to secure those rights for these subject-cum-citizens (making them "Virginians") and to facilitate their collective action on a continental scale (as "Americans"). The Declaration of Independence authorized (or confirmed) both processes. Or perhaps more accurately, state-making and nation-making were inextricably linked, both aspects of the *same* revolutionary process. The Declaration announced the existence of a new, American people; it was also, as Jefferson later wrote, "the fundamental act of union of these states."[15]

Revolutionary Virginia was a work in progress. This does not mean that the commonwealth Virginians created began as a blank slate. Virginians could draw on a rich array of civic and cultural resources. Their revolution, like the revolutions in the other new states, was in many ways profoundly conservative. Patriots sought to preserve a prosperous social and racial order and a provincial "constitution" that supposedly guaranteed Virginians an extraordinary degree of autonomy in the British Empire.[16] Provincial courts established an expanding regime of property rights that extended the settlement frontier into Indian country. Surveyors and mapmakers, like Jefferson's father Peter, took a leading role in promoting provincial interests in the imperial borderlands: speculators amassed vast swathes of land, preparing the way for enterprising farmers and planters. Britain's triumph over the French in the Seven Years' War (1756–63) promised to initiate a glorious new era for the empire, with Virginians in the vanguard of westward settlement. But the subsequent years of imperial reform and retrenchment dashed these expectations, exposing deepening divisions between Virginia and the other mainland provinces, on the one hand, and a distant and unresponsive metropolitan government, on the other.

Virginians became increasingly conscious of their corporate identity as

British imperial reformers sought to secure peace in the West by limiting settlement, while imposing more direct control over provincial trade and governance and drawing tax revenue from American sources to help cover the resulting administrative costs. The Virginia that Jefferson and his fellow patriots defended in the Revolution emerged *from* escalating assaults on the province's jurisdictional autonomy, territorial integrity, and customary constitutional order. That image of Virginia depended on recovering, or "inventing," a provincial history that made claims to independence seem legitimate, an unfolding origins story in which Revolutionary sons refashioned their predecessors as founding fathers.[17] Revolutionary historians synthesized the complicated history of political and constitutional struggles that periodically erupted within Virginia and among allied and opposed interests at "home," in the English and then (after the Act of Union with Scotland in 1707) British metropolis, into a straightforward linear narrative of differentiation and development.

Jefferson situated himself in a civic humanist tradition, Matthew Crow persuasively argues, in which Virginians forged a civic identity by "locating and narrating the history" of provincial government, focusing "on the constant making and remaking of legal authority through time."[18] Reconstructing history in that way erased the ambiguity and in-betweenness of the provincial situation. As Virginians invoked colonial precedents, beginning with the Crown Charter of 1609, to vindicate their extensive (and highly speculative) territorial claims, they created a civic space in which they could ultimately (and often reluctantly) reject their British connections and identity and recognize one another as Virginians and Americans. Yet much of what Revolutionary patriots hoped to defend from the British despot were legacies of British rule, of institutions that imitated or replicated metropolitan models and of a language of liberty and rights that betrayed metropolitan origins, even, or perhaps especially, when they invoked natural rights and the sanction of "Nature's God." Jefferson and his allies thus took the imaginative leap from the particular provincial contexts of political and military mobilization toward broader, more universal appeals, first to an increasingly hostile and unresponsive British political public and then to a "candid world" beyond—and against—Britain.

As they mobilized to change their worlds, Revolutionaries took their bearings from the places they called home. Britain was no longer an imagined home, and the British were no longer kin, imagined or otherwise: "we must . . . hold them," Jefferson wrote in the Declaration, "as we hold the rest of mankind, Enemies in War, in Peace Friends."[19] But if Americans now identified with all mankind, their appeals for recognition and assistance distinguished them from the other peoples and "powers of the earth." Americans made themselves into a new people, and their successful revolution confirmed their unique and exceptional character. The American continent would be their country, Jefferson promised in his First Inaugural Address, a home for Americans "to the thousandth and thousandth the generation."[20] Joining the westward flow of settlement, Virginians would become Americans. They would also make new homes and forge attachments in and to new places, so embracing new civic identities in new states.

These were the horizons of the Virginian and American patriot that Jefferson described to Joseph Cabell: the true patriot was dedicated to the defense of an expanding union of imperial dimensions as if it were the particular place he now called home. One day he, or his family, or other future members of the great American family—"our descendants" as Jefferson called them—would make a home there. A Caesar or Bonaparte would meet his match in the American patriot, for these great tyrants were merely mortal men, however puffed up by popular adulation and their God-like pretensions. But American patriots never stood alone. They represented the irresistible, inextinguishable power of a self-governing people, "the strongest government on earth."

The imperial crisis precipitated the mobilization of broadening political publics in all the colonies as embattled patriot elites sought to shore up their defenses against assaults on what they saw as their provincial constitutions. The medium would prove to be the message. In eighteenth-century Anglo-America the term "constitution" referred both to the formal organization of power in the narrow, now familiar sense and to the structure of society, or body politic as a whole.[21] When provincial governing classes turned to the governed for support against the dangerous "foreign" threat presented by Parliament, they inevitably raised fundamental questions about the boundaries of their political communities as well as about the location and legitimacy of authority within them. To excite interest in issues that did not obviously or immediately affect ordinary folk, patriot leaders had to persuade them that *their* rights were at risk when imperial officials encroached on the customary privileges and prerogatives of provincial assemblies.

The idea that property-owning Englishmen, at home and abroad, were defined by their rights was a common-sense assumption. But the claim that provinces had "constitutions" was a novelty. The challenge was to abstract and articulate fundamental principles from the poorly documented history of institutions and customary practices originally grounded in those rights. Provincial constitutions represented local versions of a shared culture and history of liberty, dating back to the Magna Carta and beyond, adapted to the distinctive circumstances of American settlements. Patriot constitutionalists thus needed to discover (or invent) the particular "peoples" whose histories they chronicled, distinguishing them from other peoples while at the same time identifying them with the English people as a whole. Only when imperial authorities refused to recognize their rights and King George III made war against his once loyal subjects would Jefferson and his congressional colleagues invoke natural-rights claims, so enabling them to identify with mankind and as "Americans."

In defense of their rights under provincial constitutions, lawyer-patriots called into question the fundamental character of—and justifications for—social and political order in their respective provinces. As they made their case for provincial rights (and an imperial "constitution" that only existed in their lawyerly imaginations), unwitting revolutionaries unleashed the power of the "people" or "peoples" they called into existence.[22] Revolutionary patriots needed the people both in theory and in practice, to define and justify the goals of resistance and mobilize their countrymen to make war and risk everything in defense of their rights. Political and military mobilization was transformative for everyone involved. Making war and declaring independence forced Anglo-Americans to make choices. But it could not resolve fundamental questions about civic identity and constitutional order that emerged with the British Empire's collapse.

What became known as the "American Revolution" was a chronicle of unintended consequences. In retrospect, the dialectical logic of British reform and American resistance seemed to lead, inexorably, to independence. But independence was no patriot's original intention. The iconic figures that dominate the conventional historical narrative—including Thomas Jefferson, Patrick Henry, James Madison, and George Washington, my subjects in this book—could not anticipate where the flow of events would carry them. However enlightened they may have been, they could not see very far into the future: they would only *become* visionary founding fathers in the eyes of their grateful children. War, to elaborate the familiar trope, generates a dense fog of indecipherable contingencies. But it may be more accurate to say in the case of the American Revolution that the outbreak of war and the fateful choices colonists were forced to make promised to *lift* the fog of a decade-long crisis that had darkened their horizons and finally immobilized their governments. Mobilization brought a kind of psychic relief, or at least cleared the immediate way forward, as the impenetrable gray fog gave way to starkly contrasting futures, black and white. "Give me liberty," as Patrick Henry importuned the God of Battles, "or give me death!"[23]

Historians of the Revolution tend to overlook the war itself, focusing instead on the power of ideas and the unfolding "logic of rebellion."[24] This is the nation-making story Americans prefer to hear, for these ideas, we like to think, were destined to triumph in America and transform the world. Nailing down "first principles" supposedly clarifies everything: these are and were ideas worth dying for. Yet clarity proved elusive, for efforts to define the "people" and to construct a new constitutional order that would secure their fundamental rights, collectively and individually, were inherently controversial. This is why I portray Jefferson and his fellow Virginians as "thinking Revolutionaries," to borrow Ralph Lerner's felicitous phrase.[25] In order to envision and secure a bright future for Commonwealth and country, they needed to negotiate a working agreement on how to proceed. The ideas they elaborated constituted bold, sometimes desperate efforts to impose order on—or discover order in—the dynamic and unpredictable course of events. As Americans stumbled from crisis to crisis the faint of heart despaired that their experiment—their leap in the dark—might well fail.

The American Revolution made Virginians conscious of themselves as a people, committed to the defense of their rights against British despotism. Civic equality and political solidarity were not the inevitable results of prior social development. Before the imperial crisis, the tendency in British America was toward an increasingly unequal distribution of wealth and power. In Virginia, a self-perpetuating oligarchy of "first families" dominated local county courts and parish vestries while defending and promoting their collective interests in the provincial House of Burgesses; dominated by great planters, the governor's council monopolized the distribution of Crown lands. White Virginians of modest means could participate in electing burgesses (the only elected officeholders), but most elections were uncontested. Civic rituals in public settings, including elections, reaffirmed elite status.[26]

In the middle decades of the eighteenth century, great planters began building big estate houses designed to represent and consolidate their social authority and cultural aspirations. They cultivated a corporate consciousness, extolling the province's distinctive history and character, but their "Virginia" was an idealized, creole version of English county society, not the egalitarian community of enlightened citizens the young Jefferson envisioned. Elite Virginians saw themselves as the "better sort," if not "born to the manner" of their metropolitan counterparts, aspiring to it. They sought to increase the social distance that separated them from their humble neighbors, not to descend from their high, well-bred horses and engage with them as equals.[27]

An Anglicizing elite presided uneasily over a dynamic and fluid society.[28] A large, ethnically diverse population of white property owners and a growing number of dissenters challenged or, more often, simply ignored the pretensions of their putative superiors. New men accumulated and exploited land and slaves, blurring social distinctions. The large number of enslaved workers, whose unrequited labor generated the province's wealth, belied elite aspirations to create a well-articulated social order in the metropolitan image. The British campaign to reform colonial administration exacerbated the dilemma of Virginia's governing class. Controversial taxes and provisions for enforcement compromised the autonomous authority of provincial grandees, threatening to subvert their "constitution" and reduce free Britons to the condition of their slaves. In the midst of the crisis precipitated by the Stamp Act of 1765, Patrick Henry and a cohort of young patriots in the Burgesses took the offensive. Virginia would resist unconstitutional encroachments on its rights, Henry warned King George III and his ministers in a set of inflammatory resolutions that pointed toward independence. Cautious burgesses repudiated the firebrand: the "Virginia" they represented recoiled from radical measures that jeopardized their status as the king's loyal subjects. But other Virginians, galvanized by Henry's speech, could envision another, much more expansive and inclusive Virginia.

The American Revolution, in Carl Becker's famous formulation, raised questions both about "home rule" and about "who should rule at home."[29] These questions were inextricably entangled, for both pivoted on the meaning of "home." To suggest that the "better sort" and common folk shared a "home" was to say that they constituted a single great family or "people." In defense of their rights, Revolutionary Virginians engaged with one another as equals, more or less reluctantly, however exalted or humble their status in the old provincial regime. Grandees donned homespun, symbolically erasing social distances and disavowing hierarchical aspirations. They could mitigate if not overcome anxieties about leveling down by embracing an enlightened, neoclassical conception of citizenship that leveled common folk up.

Elite Virginians met their humble neighbors on the common ground of citizenship, identifying with the "people" they conjured into existence in order to resist unconstitutional assaults on their liberties. Patriot leaders recognized the risks of leveling. History, as they understood it, was not necessarily on their side.[30] A few stepped back from the brink, remaining loyal to their king. Spurred by Henry, Jefferson took the leap, his faith in the future grounded in the Commonwealth's abundant resources—and in his expectation that enlightened citizens would recognize the superior merits of the "natural aristocrats" who offered to serve them. Enlightenment would lift all boats, enabling self-navigating republicans to avoid shipwreck on "the boisterous sea of liberty," while "timid men" preferred "the calm of despotism."[31]

The existence of a large enslaved population gave all white Virginians a stake in the racial order, and the opportunity to accumulate slaves as well as an abundant land supply fueled whites' aspirations for independence and improvement.[32] Jefferson envisioned a day when Virginia would be free of the incubus of slavery (a day that receded into an ever more distant future over the course of his life). The stain of slavery would be expunged when enlightened Virginians recognized the institution's injustice, emancipated and expatriated their slaves, and "declare[d] them a free and independant people."[33] But what would become of Virginia if that day did not dawn? When Jefferson contemplated the radical injustice of slavery in his *Notes on Virginia* the possibility that his world would turn upside down seemed all too real. In a passage drafted before the Peace of Paris of 1783 had been successfully negotiated and American independence was recognized by the great powers of the day, Jefferson "tremble[d] for my country." Given that his "God is just" and "considering numbers, nature, and natural means only," Jefferson acknowledged, "a revolution of the wheel of fortune, an exchange of situation" between whites and blacks, "is among possible events" and "may become probable by supernatural interference."[34] Could the wheel be made to stop, keeping open the possibility of amelioration and remediation? Or would white Virginians' "revolution" result in another revolution, a cataclysmic servile insurrection that would destroy everything Virginia's white patriots had fought for?

Anything was possible in these anxious times. Virginia was a political speculation, a "project" or "experiment," in the language of the Enlightenment. Jefferson's ambitious program of constitutional and legal reform reflected the urgency of seizing the moment and setting proper precedents for the future. Had he had his way, Jefferson would have transformed his native province, making it a model for republican reformers everywhere, making it a different place. But Jefferson was in Philadelphia, drafting the American Declaration of Independence while fellow patriots in Williamsburg were drafting the constitution that made provincial Virginia into a self-governing commonwealth. Convinced that the 1776 constitution was radically imperfect, he was haunted for the rest of his career by his absence at that founding moment. Written in haste to meet the exigencies of the moment, it was not authorized or ratified by the Virginian people as a whole: properly speaking, Jefferson became convinced, it was not a true constitution at all. And without a true constitution, it followed (in circular fashion), Virginians did not truly constitute a people.

Jefferson's misgivings about Virginia's defective founding shaped his ongoing conversation—or quarrel—with Patrick Henry about the character of the people and their presence in the government, or what we call "democracy." This was largely a one-sided conversation. Henry was impatient with Jefferson's theoretical scruples: the great orator had no doubts about the identity of the people who rallied to the Revolutionary cause in response to his stirring rhetoric, nor did he question the popular patriotic spirit that animated the 1776 constitution, whatever its supposed technical defects. Jefferson acknowledged Henry's key role in mobilizing the people, his young, highly impressionable self included. Yet he also feared (and exaggerated) Henry's supposedly demagogic influence over his followers, particularly during Jefferson's tormented tenure as governor (1779–81). Fear of demagoguery came naturally to anxious and embattled elites. What was remarkable about Jefferson's response to Henry—and what made Jefferson a "democrat"—was his recognition that the survival of republican government in Virginia and the United States as a whole depended on keeping the patriotic fires burning. Jefferson's later career as a democratic constitutionalist testifies to Henry's critically important contribution to his thought. It was a debt that Jefferson, nursing old and enduring grievances, was reluctant to acknowledge.

The constitution created the "people," Jefferson believed, raising them to civic responsibility and channeling their energies toward higher public purposes, and the people's patriotic spirit gave life to the constitution. His constitutionalism developed over the course of his career in personal exchanges and a rich and voluminous correspondence with his younger colleague and ally James Madison.[35] Theirs was a conversation between friends who could give and take criticism. In contrast to Jefferson's relationship with Henry, which was characterized by misunderstanding, Jefferson and Madison were close collaborators who worked hard to reconcile differences and understand each other. During Jefferson's years in Paris, Madison became increasingly convinced that Henry and his party (or "faction") represented the biggest obstacle to reform in Virginia. While Jefferson the diplomat was confronted with the Confederation's conspicuous weakness and recognized the need for a more energetic central government, his young ally launched his famous campaign to reconstitute the union and save Virginia and its sister republics from powerful centrifugal tendencies that seemed to threaten their very survival.

Jefferson and Madison both understood that the futures of their home state and of the union as a whole were inextricably linked. To be a "Virginian" was to be an "American," as Patrick Henry told the Continental Congress in 1774.[36] But it was not clear how the part should relate to the whole. Jefferson had wanted to be in Williamsburg in order to promote the American cause. A better state constitution would enable Virginia to bind itself to the other states in a more perfect union: commanding the loyalty of patriotic citizens, well-constituted states would constitute the foundation of a strong and enduring union. But Madison challenged this bottom-up, republican logic. Factious and parochial politics in the states, he concluded, prevented them from reforming—and perhaps even preserving—the union. The only hope for Virginia was a thorough renovation of the American system as a whole, beginning with the establishment of a federal government that would no longer be dependent on the states. The new government instead would draw its legitimacy from the American people as a whole, thus enabling it to exercise effective authority over them. Madison did not intend to abolish the states: they would retain a wide ambit of effective authority over matters of merely local interest—as most matters were. But it was essential that the federal government be distinct from and independent of the states.

The constitution the Philadelphia Convention sent out to the states for ratification was a disappointment to Madison and his fellow "nationalists." Yet despite the mixed, "partly federal, partly national" character of the new regime, Antifederalists were quick to grasp the radicalism of Madison's logic. Following Henry's lead, skeptics in Virginia looked back to the Revolution, when patriotic Americans mobilized to defend the distinct corporate rights and independence of their provinces against direct rule by an overreaching imperial government. Antifederalists were not "factious" localists dedicated to vindicating the Commonwealth's sovereignty. Like the patriots of 1776, they saw themselves as Americans *because* they were Virginians. From his perch in Paris, Jefferson was inclined to agree: Virginian and American identities were not mutually exclusive, though a failing Confederation might make them seem so. But he recognized that a comprehensive solution to systemic crisis was urgently necessary, and Madison persuaded him that the union would collapse without a proper federal constitution. Without one, Americans would not constitute a people: they would have no enduring connection with their government or with one another.

Jefferson applauded Madison's reluctant concessions at Philadelphia that brought the state governments directly or indirectly back into the government of the union. He also urged Madison to incorporate a bill of rights into the Constitution to reassure wary citizens about the republican character of the new regime. There was ample space within the Constitution's capacious frame for the two friends to collaborate. In the context of deepening partisan divisions in the 1790s, that collaboration moved them both closer to positions staked out by Henry in the Virginia debate over ratifying the Constitution. The threat Henry discerned to Virginia's vital interests and very existence from an all-powerful, neoimperial central government now became manifest in the consolidationist designs of the faction of High Federalist courtiers who gathered around the new president and dominated his administration. Yet there was no meeting of the minds between Jefferson and Henry (and certainly not between Madison and Henry). Quite to the contrary, Henry decried the factiousness of the Jeffersonian Republicans, echoing charges they had once made against him. Henry feared that their mobilization against the Washington and Adams administrations would jeopardize national unity at a critical juncture in the great geopolitical crisis unleashed by the French Revolution. Now it was the Jeffersonians who rallied around the states'-rights flag, putting Virginia first and risking the union.

George Washington, the "father of his country," was deeply distressed by the rancorous partisanship that threatened to destroy the union. As a separate state, Virginia made no sense: it would be nothing more than a "wretched fragment of Empire."[37] Washington was no less committed to the defense of American liberties than his quarrelsome younger colleagues, but his commitment to the union and its imperial destiny was foundational. Virginians could only enjoy the fruits of independence as Americans, by incorporating the vast continental domain the mother country had claimed—and forfeited—into an expanding, ever more perfect union of republican states. "Empire" was not a problematic term for Washington, as it was for orthodox republicans, who vigilantly resisted the dangerous consolidation of power in a distant and despotic central government. If Washington saw the American Revolution as a war *for* the empire that successive generations of settlers had won from the savage wilderness, liberty-loving republicans railed *against* the very idea of empire. In his second term, a few bold critics even began to criticize the revered Washington himself, portraying him as the dupe of his High Federalist advisors. Not surprisingly, Washington took such charges personally. Party divisions, he told his fellow Americans in his Farewell Address, would doom their republican experiment to failure.

"Empire" was a poorly defined, ambiguous term. Anglophobic Jeffersonians recoiled at its strong associations with British tyranny, but they did not repudiate the new nation's vast territorial domain or deny the need for a strong and enduring union. Jeffersonians organized a nationwide opposition party to capture the central government in the name of the American people (not the peoples of the states) and to vindicate the federal constitution (strictly construed) that brought that people into existence. Many contemporaries, including Washington on his deathbed, feared that the widening partisan breach was irreparable and that disunion and war were sure to follow. But all hell did not break loose in Jefferson's "Revolution of 1800." When the new president asserted that "we are all federalists, we are all republicans" in his Inaugural Address, he was playing with words in a transparent move to bury the very recent past.[38] Americans should move on, joining him as he looked forward to a glorious future unfolding in the new nation's boundless western domain. Jefferson did not use the term "empire" here and was never comfortable using it, but he offered a hopeful image of the rising empire Washington envisioned. Jefferson concluded his address with a tribute to "our first and greatest revolutionary character" and a pledge to serve the people to the best of his own "imperfect" abilities.

Jefferson and his fellow Virginians saw themselves as good Americans. But what "Virginia" and "America" meant depended on the radically changing contexts of Revolutionary and early national history. The conversations and controversies I reconstruct here were certainly shaped by and experienced in the most intimate context of personal relationships. Focusing on those relationships leads us almost irresistibly toward the familiar modes of biography and narrative history. But I have chosen instead to meet my subjects on the plane of the ideas and principles that brought them together and drove them apart. Jefferson and his contemporaries were talking about matters of profound personal importance. "Virginia" and "America" meant the world to them, signifying the people and places they knew and loved and reflecting their anxious hopes for future generations.

I never intended to be a biographer. But *Jefferson and the Virginians* is, after all, an oblique kind of biography that seeks its subject in his relationships with others. Before they make their appearance, however, I will first introduce Jefferson as a political thinker, at the moment when the new president introduced himself to the American people, on March 4, 1801, in his First Inaugural Address.

1

"Strongest Government on Earth"

THE RISE AND FALL OF JEFFERSON'S EMPIRE

Thomas Jefferson called the United States "the strongest government on earth" in his Inaugural Address as the third president of the United States on March 4, 1801. He delivered his address in "so low a tone that few" who crowded into the Senate Chamber "heard it," according to witness Margaret Bayard Smith. A notoriously poor public speaker, Jefferson spoke much more effectively to his fellow Americans through the cool medium of print. Within three weeks his text had been published in newspapers and special editions across the country, bridging the distances that separated Americans from their new capital city of Washington and bringing Jefferson closer to the people. The self-effacing Democratic-Republican was no demagogue: he did not speak *to* the people from a position of commanding authority, but instead spoke *for* them. Whether read silently or read aloud in homes, coffeehouses, or other local settings, Jefferson's words and the sentiments that animated them were given voice and brought to life by ordinary citizens. Americans were their own sovereigns, the ultimate source of the authority Jefferson was now prepared to exercise in their name.[1]

Jefferson undoubtedly would have preferred to be a more effective public speaker. The arts of persuasion were prized in an era when political leaders sought to shape public opinion and articulate the people's will; Jefferson envied the inspiring rhetoric that enabled Patrick Henry to mobilize popular support for the Revolution.[2] Yet it was also true that people like Jefferson—the elite patriot leaders and self-styled lawgivers who articulated the new regime's fundamental principles, drafted new constitutions, and assumed the deference of their humble neighbors—feared the anarchy and disorder that demagogic appeals to the people might unleash. Jefferson's solution to this problem was to refashion the role of the republican leader. By putting the right words into the mouths of the sovereign people, their humble servant could take his orders from them. Jefferson was following the script he had written for the former sovereign, in his *Summary View of the Rights of British America* (1774): Americans knew "that kings are the servants, not the proprietors of the people," he had then told George III.[3] Now, he assured his new employers, "I advance with obedience to the work, ready to retire from it whenever you become sensible how much better choices it is in your power to make."

Jefferson defined himself against the king who had betrayed his people; he also defined himself against his illustrious predecessor George Washington. "Without pretensions to that high confidence you reposed in our first and greatest revolutionary character, whose pre-eminent services had entitled him to the first place in his country's love, and destined for him the fairest page in the volume of faithful history," Jefferson asked for "so much confidence only as may give firmness and effect to the legal administration of your affairs." Washington was the "father of his country," and his dutiful children had submitted to his superior authority in the Revolution.[4] But Jefferson was only the temporary trustee of the people's business, "relying then on the patronage of your good will." The new president concluded by calling on "that infinite power, which rules the destinies of the universe" to "lead our councils to what is best, and give them a favorable issue for your peace and prosperity."

Jefferson later called his election to the presidency the "Revolution of 1800."[5] In the party struggles of the 1790s, he liked to think, the "Spirit of 1776" had been rekindled as the people came to their senses and reasserted their independence. Jefferson's Inaugural Address thus was a testimonial to the people's power. If his voice did not rise above the din of the excited crowd, the meaning of the moment was nonetheless clear. This was "one of the most interesting scenes," wrote Margaret Bayard Smith, that "a free people can ever witness," for they saw themselves—in all their majesty—ascending to power. In his address Jefferson self-consciously invoked and reaffirmed the people's Declaration of Independence. Neither document aimed at "originality of principle or sentiment." The "object" of the Declaration, as he told Henry Lee shortly before his death, was "not to find out new principles, or new arguments, never before thought of, not merely to say things which had never been said before; but to place before mankind the common sense of the subject, in terms so plain and firm as to command their assent, and to justify ourselves in the independent stand we are compelled to take." The Inaugural Address was also "intended to be an expression of the American mind," to remind his countrymen of the shared principles that bound them together and made them a single great people.[6] On neither occasion did Jefferson seek to rise above the people. To the contrary, he called on his countrymen to transcend their differences, to recognize one another as patriotic Americans, and so rise above themselves.

Bitterly opposed partisans had good reason to be skeptical. Jefferson's inauguration was preceded by rancorous partisan divisions that called the very existence of an American "people" into question. For many observers, the French Revolution seemed to change everything, at home and abroad. Pitting "aristocratic" defenders of the old regime against "democratic" insurgents, the European conflagration threatened to spread across the Atlantic in a great struggle to determine the future of the civilized world, if not its very survival.[7] The specter of disunion and war became all too frighteningly visible in the presidential succession crisis immediately preceding Jefferson's inauguration. His rhetorical challenge was to distinguish American from European politics and convince his listeners and readers that they had been fighting over means, not ends.

"It was not wonderful," Jefferson explained, that the "the throes and convulsions" of the French Revolution "should reach even this distant and peaceful shore." Yet, however much Jefferson and his followers might sympathize with the democratic revolution in Europe, they recognized—or should recognize—that it was not *their* struggle: Americans had already won their independence. And when Jefferson evoked the European scene—the "agonizing spasms of infuriated man, seeking through blood and slaughter his long-lost liberty"—he implicitly endorsed the prudential concerns of Federalists, who "felt and feared" being sucked into the vortex of the Old World's war.[8] Jefferson assured his fellow Americans that they were an exceptional people. In the heat of partisan conflict, they might forget who they were and what bound them to one another. But as Americans stood on the precipice and contemplated the prospect of disunion and war, they came to their senses and reaffirmed their national identity. "The animation of discus[s] ions and of exertions" over how to maintain the new nation's independence and steer clear of European entanglements might lead foreign observers—and even some Americans—to conclude that American partisans were proxies and pawns of European belligerents. "But every difference of opinion is not a difference of principle," Jefferson assured his countrymen. "We have called by different names brethren of the same principle," he famously intoned. "We are all republicans: we are all federalists."

The distinction between diversity of "opinion" and shared "principle" reflected Jefferson's understanding of how individuals rose to the exalted status of self-governing republican citizens. They did so by recognizing and affirming their collective identity as a free people: if republicans made the republic, the republic made republicans. Individuals escaped the state of nature when they simultaneously became conscious of their own rights and recognized those rights in others. They could then see that "all men are created equal"; this recognition was in turn the threshold of enlightened sociability and more perfect forms of union. Fearful conservatives rejected this republican logic. People needed to be governed: their natural state was anarchy, a war of all against all that could only be restrained by the imposition of a divinely sanctioned hierarchical order. Jefferson reversed this conventional formulation. The American Revolution demonstrated the civic capacity of ordinary folk mobilized in defense of their liberties. By remembering the Revolution, Americans would reinvigorate their union and reaffirm their American identity.

No good American could possibly "wish to dissolve this Union, or to change its republican form," and if a deviant few should deny their American identity by doing so, "let them stand undisturbed as monuments of the safety with which error of opinion may be tolerated, where reason is left free to combat it." For Jefferson, it was axiomatic that all Americans should uphold the principle of union, for this was what defined them *as* American: union enabled patriots to triumph in the Revolution and so establish republican governments that secured their equal rights. Union also made the American government the "strongest . . . on earth. I believe it the only one, where every man, at the call of the law, would fly to the standard of the law, and would meet invasions of the public order as his own personal concern." The power of the union thus derived from the Revolutionary republican commitment to equal rights. The choice was clear to Jefferson. "Sometimes it is said that man cannot be trusted with the government of himself. Can he then be trusted with the government of others? Or have we found angels, in the form of kings, to govern him?" It was only through self-government—and consensual union—that natural rights could be recognized and enforced. By uniting "with one heart and one mind," citizens collectively could mobilize the irresistible power of a great nation.

I. UNDER GOD

As the new century dawned, the great challenge Americans faced was to reaffirm their identity as Americans, not to preserve a federal constitution that had nearly collapsed in the recent presidential succession crisis. If a united people constituted the foundation of a durable republic, the constitution was merely its superstructure. And there was nothing sacred about a document that failed to express the will of the people and so sustain their union.[9] By the same logic, the proper alignment of foundation and superstructure—the people and a government they recognized as their own—made the United States the "strongest government on earth."

The union that Jefferson celebrated in his Inaugural Address barely survived the party conflicts of the 1790s and was only restored by the renewed patriotic commitments of the American people. He looked back to 1776 in order to promote progress toward a more perfect union that would redeem the Revolution's promise. This was not the union his friend James Madison and his fellow founders had constructed at the Philadelphia Convention in the summer of 1787.[10] The federal constitution was an elaborate mechanism designed to contain the diverse and often conflicting interests of Britain's rebellious colonies. It was certainly "more perfect" than the loose and ineffectual alliance established under the Articles of Confederation, and the Confederation was itself an improvement over the ad hoc, extraconstitutional congresses that had presided over the Revolutionary war effort. But Jefferson was less interested in contracts negotiated by lawyer-statesmen to secure the interests of their respective states than in renewing and perfecting the "spirit" or "character" of the American people.

In a letter to his friend Joseph Priestley shortly after his inauguration, Jefferson juxtaposed the weakness of the federal constitution to the power of the people, united "with one heart and one mind." Had the constitutional impasse not been resolved, Jefferson wrote, "the federal government would have been in the situation of a clock or watch run down." Yet the result would not have been anarchy, disorder, or disunion. Instead, a convention "would have been on the ground in 8 weeks" and proceeded to repair "the constitution where it was defective & wound it up again." The "mighty wave of public opinion which has rolled over" the land during the succession crisis would have guaranteed the convention's success. Recurring to "self-preservation," the first law of nature, the people would assume the role of clockmaker God, giving life to the broken constitutional mechanism. The constitutional clock could only keep accurate time if it were regularly "repaired"—amended, interpreted, and perhaps even replaced—to accord with the enlightened will of the people. "The order & good sense displayed in this recovery from delusion, and in the momentous crisis which lately arose," Jefferson concluded, "really bespeak a strength of character in our nation which augurs well for the duration of our republic, & I am much better satisfied now of it's stability, than I was before it was tried."[11]

"Nature's God" was clearly present both in Jefferson's clock metaphor and in his reference to the constitutional crisis as "the storm . . . now subsiding." The emergence of a self-governing people was something "new under the sun." Surely God intended men to stand in his light, recognizing their common humanity and ordering their affairs in accord with nature's laws. Jefferson accused his Federalist foes of attempting to keep the people in the dark, proscribing "all advances of science" as dangerous "innovations." These "barbarians" were enemies of progress who sought to turn back the clock: "we were to look backwards not forwards for improvement," to a benighted age "when ignorance put every thing into the hands of power & priestcraft." But the people had recovered from their "delusion," or what in the darkest days of the great party conflict he had called a "reign of witches."[12] An enlightened people could see more clearly—into the future and across the vast spaces of the continent.

When he addressed the American people at his inauguration, Jefferson evoked a progressive and expansive union that would enable his countrymen to overcome their differences. This "rising nation, spread over a wide and fruitful land," was "advancing rapidly to destinies beyond the reach of mortal eye."[13] Americans possessed a "chosen country, with room enough for our descendants to the thousandth and thousandth generation." Contemplating the future, Jefferson imagined the nation as a succession of generations, a "happy and a prosperous" family of families. He invited his fellow Americans to keep the "transcendent objects" of the Revolution in view as the electoral storm subsided and the "hopes of this beloved country" were renewed.

The union Americans created depended on the recognition of equal rights that flowed from their love of God. With "a due sense of our equal right to the use of our own faculties, to the acquisitions of our own industry," we earn the "honor and confidence from our fellow citizens" by "our actions and their sense of them"—not by the accidents of birth in an unequal, hierarchical society. Jefferson was not conjuring up an atomistic, libertarian fantasy of self-sovereignty. He instead envisioned a communion of equals, "enlightened by a benign religion, professed indeed and practised in various forms, yet all of them inculcating honesty, truth, temperance, gratitude and the love of man." Americans worshiped the same God in different ways, all "acknowledging and adoring an overruling providence, which by all its dispensations proves that it delights in the happiness of man here, and his greater happiness hereafter." "With all these blessings," he asked, "what more is necessary to make us a happy and a prosperous people?" The greatest blessing of all was their capacity to recognize one another as a people, to come together in "the pursuit of happiness" and thus fulfill the design of the "supreme, intelligent being" who created the world.[14]

Jefferson's religious language should not be dismissed as rhetorical cover for less exalted, secular purposes. His personal spiritual quest, undertaken in increasing earnest over the remaining years of his life, was to better understand God's design for mankind.[15] As a student of Lord Kames and other exponents of natural religion, Jefferson saw what he called "science"—or natural philosophy—as the pathway to greater enlightenment.[16] Self-appointed or state-supported religious authorities stood in the way of that quest, pretending to privileged access to the mysterious mind of God. Deploying their interpretative monopoly for self-interested purposes, "priests" set themselves and their state sponsors up as God-like intermediaries between lowly, "fallen" subjects and a deity who defied description. Jefferson thus accused conventional Christians of being man-worshiping atheists who refused to recognize the hand—and mind—of God in the laws of nature.

Conventional Christianity's original sin was the deification of Jesus in the Trinitarian conception of the Godhead. By subjecting Christians to the mystification and irrationality of a "revealed" religion that remained concealed for most of mankind, the Trinitarian heresy set the pattern for all the crimes that marred Christianity's bloody history. By deifying Jesus the man, the priestly caste obscured, distorted, and subverted his message. Enlightened by his own critical reading of the Gospels, Jefferson proclaimed himself a true, or "primitive," Christian who adhered to Jesus's original, uncorrupted teachings.[17] "Jesus embraced, with charity & philanthropy, our neighbors, our countrymen, & the whole family of mankind," President Jefferson told a correspondent in 1803.[18] Those ethical teachings—most eloquently articulated in the Sermon on the Mount—converged with and confirmed the truths that advocates of natural religion had begun to discern in their scripture, the book of nature.

Jefferson's union was grounded in the timeless principles that Jesus so eloquently articulated and that were now "self-evident" to Americans. Jefferson envisioned a bright future for enlightened republicans who returned to these first principles and threw off the shackles of old regime despotism. Kings, nobles, and priests were the enemies of the "happiness of the mass of the people," Jefferson wrote his law teacher George Wythe from Paris in 1786; "the diffusion of knowledge among the people" was the only "sure foundation . . . for the preservation of freedom."[19] In old regime France this "abandoned confederacy" sustained its rule by keeping a disunited people in the darkest ignorance. Evoking the biblical account of mankind's fall from innocence, Jefferson juxtaposed the recovery of man's original, natural rights to the descent into darkness that constituted the history of Old World monarchies. Human progress was predicated on demolishing intermediary authorities who claimed a divine mandate but instead alienated men from God, one another, and their own true natures. Enlightenment enabled the people to overcome this alienation, govern themselves, and make their own history.

History for Jefferson was a tragic chronicle of crimes against humanity.[20] The new American republic escaped the "wars and contentions" that filled "the pages of history" in an era of "constant volcanic eruption," he wrote a European correspondent in 1807. "But more blest is that nation whose silent course of happiness furnishes nothing for history to say."[21] Jefferson's naturalistic language evoked God's providential blessing on the new nation. In the enlightened exercise of their God-given powers, Americans would fulfill higher "destinies," making a different kind of history for themselves. Sustaining and perfecting the union was the only means to achieve that end and so avoid Europe's sorry fate.

In his Second Inaugural, delivered in the wake of his landslide victory in the 1804 election, Jefferson exulted in "the union of sentiment now manifested so generally, as auguring harmony and happiness to our future course." There were still some "doubting brethren," but they would eventually see the light. "In the meantime, let us cherish them with patient affection; let us do them justice, and more than justice, in all competitions of interest; and we need not doubt that truth, reason, and their own interests, will at length prevail, will gather them into the fold of their country, and will complete their entire union of opinion, which gives to a nation the blessing of harmony, and the benefit of all its strength."[22] The character of the people was a work in progress. In the fullness of time the agreement on fundamental principles that defined Americans in 1776 would give rise to a progressively more perfect union of "sentiment" and "opinion."

Jefferson believed that the success of the American experiment in republican government depended on the capacity of the people to grasp simple truths, not on the superior virtue or wisdom of great leaders or lawgivers. Because it was self-evident to them that "all men are created equal" and that they "are endowed by their Creator with certain unalienable rights," Americans would never submit to governors who claimed a higher, God-like right to rule.[23] In the idiom of the day, they were "freemen," not "slaves." It did not follow that government was unnecessary or that social order would emerge spontaneously in a state of nature. Jefferson instead insisted that man was naturally sociable, attracted and attached to his fellows as he recognized them as equals. Those attachments constituted the foundation of the "strongest government on earth," not an alternative to government. Jefferson did not envision a return to a prelapsarian state or a restoration of fallen man to primitive wholeness, but rather his progress across the generations toward the "harmony" and "strength" of ever more perfect unions.

This was the arc of the future history of an enlightened people, Jefferson's inspiring alternative to chronicles of Old World misery.

II. NATIONAL CHARACTER

Jefferson's political faith was shaped in the crucible of Revolutionary resistance to British imperial despotism. All good patriots agreed that King George's American subjects were born free, but some of Jefferson's more cautious contemporaries suspected that common folk were nonetheless born to be governed. Conservatives who feared that the destruction of the traditional monarchical order would lead to the "solitary, poor, nasty, brutish, and short" state of nature described by the philosopher Thomas Hobbes thus sought to institute a more powerful central government over the new American republics.[24] Jefferson rejected Hobbes's pessimistic account of human nature and man's natural state and therefore responded warily to the Federalist campaign to establish an "energetic" federal government. As a student of Scottish moral sense philosophy who believed in the innate human capacity for improvement, Jefferson instead relied on the character of the people.[25] The virtue and vigilance of engaged citizens constituted the only enduring foundation of their union.

John Locke and other Enlightenment theorists provided Jefferson with the language of equal rights and social contracts that he deployed on Americans' behalf in the Declaration. But ordinary Americans grasped these truths because of their shared experience, not because they read deeply in social contract theory. As Jefferson explained to Henry Lee in the year before he died, the Declaration distilled and expressed the "harmonizing sentiments of the day."[26] The people's rights-consciousness fostered solidarity, not anarchy and licentiousness. In the face of Britain's overwhelming power, the prospect of equality in subjection seemed all too immanent; recognition that Americans could so easily be reduced to slavery led them to mobilize in defense of endangered rights. This "rights talk" was later invoked *against* government, but it was precisely what enabled revolutionaries to *form* governments when the old imperial regime disintegrated.

The equality principle empowered ordinary folk who now saw themselves as the source of legitimate authority: their participation in the resistance movement and the war effort authorized the universal "sentiment" that they were "endowed" with the capacity to govern themselves. Equality also enabled newly self-conscious "Americans" to transcend the myriad differences that skeptical observers predicted would drive them apart and reduce them to anarchy. Stripped of their distinctive and distinguishing characteristics, Americans could recognize one another as fellow citizens, equal in their rights. While fearful skeptics exaggerated differences, good patriots transcended them. This leveling up through citizenship stood in stark counterpoint to the conservative caricature of democratic anarchy and mob rule: a leveling down that would reveal—and unleash—man's brutal, degenerate, ungovernable nature.[27]

Montesquieu and other "modern" students of politics emphasized the diverse influences that determined national character, from climate and natural resource endowment to the people's manners and the regime's constitution.[28] What made these "political scientists" modern was their analytical approach: if influences could be distinguished they could, at least to some limited extent, be manipulated. Climate might seem to be beyond human control, but the natural environment could be "improved," perhaps in ways that affected the climate; a nation's culture was the cumulative result of its history, but manners could become more refined and a people more polite through enlightened engagement with the larger world; wise rulers made their constitutions more legitimate by adapting law and policy to changing circumstances and thus promoting the people's welfare and happiness. Yet if political science demystified authority, emphasizing the agency of statesmen and lawgivers and the malleability of a nation's character, it also exaggerated the distance between enlightened elites and ignorant masses. Patriot leaders thus were pulled in different directions as they mobilized their countrymen for war: they relied on the people's patriotism even as they questioned their civic capacity.

The exigencies of political and military mobilization challenged patriots to redefine the traditional relationship between leaders and followers. The moral philosophers' more generous assessment of human nature pointed toward education as the obvious solution. By shifting attention away from the characteristic status markers and behaviors of common folk and emphasizing their educability, patriot leaders could imagine a republican community of equal citizens. But the Revolution could not wait for the slow and uncertain effects of schooling to enlighten the rising generation. The Declaration of Independence pointed in a more radical direction: the Revolution itself was an enlightening, educational experience that taught once loyal—and unthinking—subjects to be self-conscious, self-governing citizens. All men might be "*created* equal," but they only fulfilled their civic potential and *became* truly equal through participation in the "common cause." The Declaration recounted the "long train of abuses" that schooled people in their liberties: patriots now recognized themselves—and one another—as "Americans." Independence was the nation-defining moment when patriots forged a union based on the fundamental principles of equality and consent. "These principles form the bright constellation, which has gone before us and guided our steps through an age of revolution and reformation," Jefferson testified in his Inaugural Address. They "should be the creed of our political faith" and "the text of civic instruction."[29]

The principles were timeless abstractions, outside history and authorized by "Nature's God." But the union Americans forged was time bound, growing out of flesh and blood attachments of the "living generation" to one another and to succeeding generations.[30] Jefferson's conception of generational sovereignty juxtaposed the relentless passage of time—as one generation succeeded another—to the nation's immortality, "to the thousandth and thousandth generation." Conscious of its place in time, each generation held the common estate in "usufruct," or stewardship, for those that followed; so too, patriots pledged to sacrifice everything—"our lives, our fortunes, and our sacred honor"—in order that future generations might flourish.[31] "We threw up a few pulsations of our warmest blood" in the Revolution, Jefferson told Maria Cosway in his famous 1786 love letter: "we supplied enthusiasm against wealth and numbers: we put our existence to the hazard, when the hazard seemed against us, and we saved our country: justifying at the same time the ways of Providence, whose precept is to do always what is right, and leave the issue to him."[32]

III. CONSTITUTION

As they rose up in defense of their individual rights, citizens identified with one another and willingly sacrificed everything for the common cause. This was the paradox of patriotism: in times of crisis, the exaltation of the individual justified his annihilation. The union forged in blood sacrifice was thus made sacred. By contrast, the union Madison and his fellow founders created was the product of calculation and compromise. Prudent men sought to construct a complicated constitutional machine that secured their conflicting rights and interests. Protracted negotiations in Philadelphia and subsequent struggles over the interpretation and implementation of federal powers thus testified to what politicians were *unwilling* to sacrifice. Their union did not result from an upsurge of patriotism across the continent. The federal constitution was instead a "peace plan" that stopped time, enabling disunited states to escape an otherwise inevitable descent into anarchy.[33]

Defenders of the new federal regime called the Constitution a "miracle," emphasizing the impossibility of ever again negotiating acceptable terms of union in an era of declining patriotism. God did not appear in the text of the Constitution. But Federalists did not hesitate to warn that an angry God would wreak vengeance on an ungrateful people who failed to step back from the precipice of disunion and war. The founders miraculously had reached agreement among themselves, and skeptical voters should follow their example and submit to their superior wisdom.[34] Their God worked in mysterious ways, through them; they were "demigods" (whatever had happened behind closed doors in Philadelphia), and their handiwork should be revered as divinely sanctioned (however unseemly their compromises).[35]

Antifederalist critics of the Constitution acknowledged that the union was imperiled and reform was imperative. Most warily accepted the Constitution as an "experiment" that if properly administered and appropriately amended might provide collective security and enable a free people to flourish. Antifederalists have been aptly called "men of little faith," but this was not because they failed to believe in the capacity of the people for democratic self-government.[36] They refused to bow down before self-appointed superiors, even the sainted Washington. Their God was more like Jefferson's in the Declaration, a God who spoke to mankind through nature's laws. It was this faith in the "people" that led Jefferson and the emerging Democratic-Republican opposition to see strict construction of the Constitution as a bulwark against administration overreaching.[37] They insisted that Federalists adhere strictly to the reassuring interpretations of the Constitution that they had offered during the ratification campaign. But strict construction was not the same thing as Constitution worship.[38] Quite to the contrary, fidelity to the text was the hermeneutic means toward democratic ends, enabling opposition critics to justify their unrelenting criticism of administration measures and men. They invoked the Constitution not because it had been written by God-like lawgivers but because the people—assembled in state ratifying conventions—had approved the document, thus (as Madison later eloquently argued) becoming its true authors.[39]

The people never had approved or could approve the constructive readings—interpretations that implied "text" nowhere to be found in the Constitution—that Alexander Hamilton offered as fig leaves for bold policy innovations. To believe in Hamilton's loosely construed Constitution was to take a leap of faith, to defer to the timeless and transcendent intentions of its founder-authors as they were discerned by a privileged, priestly caste of interpreters. Republicans charged that Hamilton and his administration colleagues used their Constitution as a mystifying cover for their "aristocratic" and "monocratic" campaign to reconstruct the hierarchical old regime and destroy the people's liberties. In response, Jefferson and fellow Republicans championed a strictly construed Constitution that should be revered only because it gave voice to the will of the people at a specific historical moment. As the people became more enlightened, their will would change progressively. Over time, through their unfolding history, Americans would fulfill the Declaration's promises: successive generations would write new constitutions and find new and better ways to govern themselves.

For Jefferson, the choice was clear and momentous: Americans could cherish the union of hearts and minds that made them a people, or they could revert to a darker age when they submitted to the rule of God-like men and venerated their works. During his retirement, in 1816, Jefferson called for a new state constitution in Virginia, taking stock of what he and his Revolutionary colleagues had achieved. "Some men look at Constitutions with sanctimonious reverence," he wrote Samuel Kercheval, "& deem them, like the ark of the covenant, too sacred to be touched." But men who looked backward, ascribing "to the men of the preceding age a wisdom more than human," did not do themselves justice. Of course, the Revolutionary generation "deserved well of its country," for Jefferson and his fellow laborers first recognized one another as Americans and so initiated the nation's history. But the Revolutionaries knew very little about writing constitutions, "and 40. years of experience in government is worth a century of book-reading." Jefferson looked forward to a glorious, progressive future. As self-governing Americans became "more enlightened, as new discoveries are made, new truths disclosed, and manners and opinions change with the change of circumstances, institutions must advance also, and keep pace with the times." He likened this "progress of the human mind" to a boy's growth to manhood; constitutions were like coats, good for a season, but constantly in need of repair and replacement. "We might as well require a man to wear still the coat which fitted him when a boy, as civilised society to remain ever under the regimen of their barbarous ancestors."[40]

This was the union Jefferson cherished: the growing boy, not the threadbare coat. The nation was not an abstract idea for him. For this political sentimentalist it was instead the progressively more perfect union of like-minded individuals, attracted and attached to one another through recognition of their common humanity and drawn closer to "Nature's God" as they fulfilled the design immanent in his laws. Americans needed only to look across the ocean to see the price benighted and oppressed nations paid for resisting the tide of history. "Instead of wisely yielding to the gradual change of circumstances," he wrote Kercheval, Europe's rulers "have clung to old abuses, intrenched themselves behind steady habits, and obliged their subjects to seek, thro' blood & violence, rash & ruinous innovations, which, had they been referred to the peaceful deliberations, & collected wisdom of the nation, would have been put into acceptable and salutary forms." Americans would avoid such dreadful bloodletting as long as they sustained their faith in themselves and in their God: "let us follow no such examples, nor weakly believe that one generation is not as capable as another of taking care of itself, and of ordering it's own affairs."

IV. EMPIRE

Jefferson envisioned an ever more perfect union of Americans across the generations. This was the first self-constituted and self-governing nation in the modern world, the result of the conscious choices Revolutionary patriots made as they risked everything to win their independence. Americans faced resolutely forward, setting an inspiring example for the oppressed peoples of the world. Darkness gave way to light, human nature was vindicated, and a free people came into its birthright: it was a new order for the ages.[41]

Yet if everything changed, nothing changed. The rights Americans claimed might be universal, but they were grounded in the distinctive historical experiences of provincial Anglo-Americans. Colonists abstracted claims to natural rights from the "rights of Englishmen," or the liberties they customarily enjoyed under the "constitutions" of their largely autonomous legal regimes.[42] In *The Summary View of the Rights of British America,* Jefferson began his story of American freedom with the self-governing Saxon settlers who colonized Britain and thus set the pattern for colonization of the New World. America's settler-founders exercised the same natural right of expatriation that had brought their Saxon ancestors to Britain, and their continuing connection with the British metropolis was consensual, based on convergent interest, kinship, and allegiance to a beneficent king who protected his loyal subjects and secured their rights. The "union" Jefferson imagined in the past—through the king, among his far-flung dominions, and with fellow subjects—shaped and mirrored his hopes for the future.[43]

As he justified the break with Britain in his rough draft of the Declaration of Independence, Jefferson revealed his deep attachment to the imperial union he accused the king of betraying. By deploying "not only soldiers of our common blood, but Scotch & foreign mercenaries to invade & deluge us in blood" in order to transform freemen into slaves, George III had forfeited his right to rule and destroyed the empire. This was "the last stab to agonizing affection," Jefferson lamented, "and manly spirit bids us to renounce for ever these unfeeling brethren." The great challenge for patriots was "to forget our former love" for these British brethren. Had the imperial union been preserved, "we might have been a free & a great people together"; by the same logic, Americans could only aspire to freedom and greatness if they sustained and perfected their union *outside* the empire.[44] Clearly union was essential for prudential reasons, if patriots had any hopes of vindicating their claims on the battlefield and gaining the recognition and support of the "powers of the earth." But for Jefferson that union—the union of self-constituted state-republics—was the necessary means toward a more exalted end, the emergence of "a free & a great people" that would fulfill America's imperial promise. In declaring their independence, Americans transcended their provincial identities and embraced a common nationality. Yet they also forged an alliance of state governments. The Declaration of Independence, Jefferson insisted late in life, was the "fundamental act of union of these States."[45]

One people and many governments: this was the enduring legacy of the imperial past in the new nation's forward-looking experiment in self-government. Students of federalism—and of constitutional development more generally—have long recognized the continuities between the old imperial and new republican regimes.[46] Provincial patriots launched the resistance movement when they mobilized against efforts to reform imperial administration and relieve overburdened British taxpayers. From the outset colonists framed their responses to ministerial initiatives in constitutional terms, insisting that new revenue measures violated their fundamental rights.[47] They would cease to be liberty-loving Britons if they submitted to the will of Parliament: they would instead be "slaves." Taxes were the "free gift" of loyal subjects who pledged their allegiance in exchange for the Crown's protection. Invoking the time-honored maxims of English constitutionalism and more than a century of experience as autonomous polities in the empire, American patriots affirmed their loyalty to and love for their lawful sovereign—and their identity as Britons—by resisting radical changes in imperial governance.

Metropolitan commentators were understandably skeptical, interpreting patriot rhetoric as a smokescreen for tax avoidance. The ultimate test of loyalty, they argued, was a willingness to submit to parliamentary taxation. Parliament was the "palladium of liberty," defender of the property and rights of the people against the exactions of royal prerogative. Unruly colonists who denied that they were "virtually represented" in the imperial legislature clearly intended to throw off the shackles of government.[48] Resisting taxes was tantamount to declaring independence.[49] Colonists countered that the only "independence" they claimed was the independence or freedom of will they had always exercised under their own constitutions and according to the customary limitations of the imperial constitution. They had no intention of abjuring their allegiance to the king and being cast into an anarchic state of nature in which no rights were secure and no individual could be constitutionally independent. The long duration of the imperial crisis, from the furor over the Stamp Act in 1765–66, when all the constitutional issues had been fully and divisively aired, to the final rupture a decade later, testifies to the colonists' reluctance to break with the empire. And when the break came, the first order of business was to draft state constitutions that would secure patriots' individual and corporate rights while enabling them to sustain a protracted war effort.

The state of nature American patriots encountered in the Revolution was no abstraction. It was a state of war that they could only survive by sustaining and perfecting the constitutional union imperial reformers had sought to destroy. That union linked the individual subject-citizen to his fellow "Americans" through the jurisdictions—local and provincial—that patriots defended against unconstitutional assaults. The new republican regime was therefore federal: citizens' claims to rights were inextricably bound to the vindication of corporate rights, now ascending to the "continental" level in the "fundamental act of union" that both secured the states and transcended them as it declared the independence of a new nation.

The "independence" of the subject-cum-citizen, grounded in the deep history of common-law constitutionalism, came first in this ascending federal order, buttressing the authority (and independence) of local institutions and justifying the self-governing pretensions of provincial governments.[50] The independence of the nation as a whole came belatedly and most controversially, for Anglo-Americans could not forge effective intercolonial institutions and did not understand themselves as a distinct people until the Revolutionary crisis gave them no choice. American independence depended on the self-recognition of the American people—and many skeptical loyalists, reluctant to abjure allegiance to George III, could not see any such thing—as well as the recognition of the "powers of the earth."

Those patriots who did take the leap of faith took their bearings from their idealized vision of the British Empire, substituting Congress for king and struggling over the next decade and beyond to construct a constitutional foundation for this ad hoc, incompetent, faction-ridden and often "imbecilic" postimperial executive authority.[51] To achieve legitimacy of a recognizable sovereignty, the government of the United States depended on securing the role and rights of subordinate jurisdictions in a new regime that derived its own authority—through them—from the sovereignty of the people. American statesmen thus engaged with the same problems that had engaged and defeated their British predecessors. But if federalism defeated the British, it was the solution for Americans. A complex and expanding federal union enabled Americans to see themselves as a single people and thus to fulfill the aspiration of American imperial patriots before the Revolution, to be a "great and a free people together."

V. DEMOCRACY AND FEDERALISM

Jefferson is conventionally seen as the founding father of American democracy. His Declaration of Independence articulated the fundamental precepts of the new nation's democratic regime, beginning with the transformative premise that "all men are created equal"; he was the first exceptionalist, the forward-looking founder who broke most decisively with the past.[52] Yet it may be more historically accurate to say that "democracy"—a term he did *not* enthusiastically embrace—was the consequence, not the predicate, of Jefferson's conception of American nationhood. The idea that colonists constituted a single people grew out of the frustrated aspirations of Anglo-American imperial patriots who imagined themselves equal members of a greater British nation. Their bid for equality was based on the "rights of Englishmen" as exercised by settler-colonists over several generations, not on the abstract and universal natural rights that "all men" in theory might claim. Revolutionaries turned toward natural rights—the language of independent nations in a state of nature—only when their king refused to protect them and secure their rights as loyal subjects.[53]

When Americans began to think of themselves as a single people, they did not seek to dismantle or destroy the plurality of jurisdictions that constituted the imperial old regime. To the contrary, this radically decentralized, effectively federal regime constituted the foundation of Americans' equal-rights claims and therefore of their collective, incipiently "national" identity. The continuity between the old imperial and new republican regime was most conspicuous in the transformation of provincial liberties into states' rights and the almost seamless "reception" of the common law in new republican courts. Equality in Revolutionary America was inextricably linked to the persistence of autonomous local institutions, not to the consolidation of authority in an all-powerful central government. This was the paradox that so astonished Alexis de Tocqueville: the French Revolutionary experience had taught him that the idea of equality destroyed everything in its path, obliterating traditional social and civic relations and reducing atomized, alienated individuals to a condition of slavery. But liberty survived in democratic America. Tocqueville's great discovery was that equality and liberty could coexist because the customs and practices (or political culture) of the Anglo-American old regime had survived the Revolutionary break with Britain.[54]

The connection between democracy and federalism was particularly strong for Jefferson in his retirement years. The enduring legacy of the imperial old regime and the ongoing progress of American experiment in republican government converged in his prescriptions for constitutional reform in Virginia. The democratic constitutionalist now urged fellow reformers to jettison the 1776 state constitution and draft a new charter that would extend equal representation to all citizens of the Commonwealth. Majority rule was the master principle of a truly republican regime; it was the standard against which any constitution had to be measured, however the text or its authors might be revered. Yet even as he looked toward the future and turned his back on constitutional fetishism and ancestor worship, Jefferson celebrated the broad distribution of authority that had characterized the old empire. "Divide the counties into wards" was his mantra, and advocates of strong, participatory democracy have echoed his call ever since. "It is by dividing and subdividing these republics from the great National one down thro' all it's subordinations," he wrote Joseph C. Cabell in 1816, "until it ends in the administration of every man's farm and affairs by himself; by placing under every one what his own eye may superintend, that all will be done for the best."[55]

"The best," most democratic regime brought government (literally) home to every independent, self-governing citizen while at the same time forging a powerful link—through the ascending chain of "subordinations"—between each citizen and the citizen body. This was Jefferson's idea of union: a progressive vision of the democratic solidarity that made the United States the "strongest government on earth" conjoined with a broad distribution of authority and an expanding plurality of autonomous jurisdictions that harked back to the idealized visions of the old regime that animated liberty-loving patriots. In Jefferson's formulation, the love of liberty would be diffused throughout the population: "where every man is a sharer in the direction of his ward-republic, or of some of the higher ones," he wrote Cabell, "and feels that he is a participator in the government of affairs not merely at an election, one day in the year, but every day; when there shall not be a man in the state who will not be a member of some one of it's councils, great or small, he will let the heart be torn out of his body sooner than his power be wrested from him by a Caesar or a Bonaparte."[56] The defense of liberty was the clarion call of patriots. "Making every citizen an acting member of the government," Jefferson told Samuel Kercheval, "will attach him by his strongest feelings to the independance of his country, and it's republican constitution."[57]

For Jefferson, the body of the people was not a great, undifferentiated whole. His conception of democracy defanged the *demos,* the monstrous "beast" that gripped the fevered imaginations of embattled aristocrats in the age of revolutions. If Jefferson and like-minded "democrats" made war against old regime aristocracy, they also imaginatively obliterated old regime democracy. Every man was "the depository of the powers respecting himself," he wrote Cabell, and therefore could defend his liberty and property against assaults by fellow citizens as well as by despotic rulers. Jefferson thus preempted the class-based mobilization of the oppressed and dispossessed. In the federal "gradation of authorities, standing each on the basis of law, holding every one it's delegated share of powers," he discovered the democratic alternative to the archaic, antidemocratic constitutionalism of his tradition-bound Federalist foes. The subdivision of authority—down to the level of the farmer on his farm (or the planter on his plantation)—constituted "truly a system of fundamental balances and checks for the government," thus preempting the oligarchical concentration of power in the hands of the self-professed "better sort."[58] Patriots came together in defense of home and country because they were secure in rights as individuals and therefore free to do so. They could be united *because* they were divided.

Jefferson's rights-based conception of democracy and union was predicated on the design revealed in the works of Nature's God. "I do believe that if the Almighty has not decreed that Man shall never be free," he testified to Cabell (parenthetically noting that "it is blasphemy to believe it"), "that the secret will be found to be in making himself the depository of the powers respecting himself."[59] Man drew closer to God by being true to himself.

Legitimate authority was not imposed on an unruly, fallen, or sinful people but was instead grounded in the human nature that the moral philosophers delineated to an enlightened world. "The creator would indeed have been a bungling artist," Jefferson wrote Thomas Law in 1814, "had he intended man for a social animal, without planting in him social dispositions."[60] Deists did not banish God from the affairs of men, as earthly authorities who pretended to divine sanction charged. Quite to the contrary, relations among men were mediated through their recognition of—and responsiveness to—God's workmanship in one another. Republican revolutionaries were political Protestants who leveled earthly hierarchies by enabling "every man" to participate in his own government. Jefferson's "Creator" made "the moral principle so much a part of our constitution as that no errors of reasoning or of speculation might lead us astray from it's observance in practice." There was no mystery to republican self-government. Its fundamental principles were clearly visible to anyone with open eyes—including, and perhaps especially, his commonsensical countrymen.

VI. REPUBLICAN EXPERIMENT

Building on the axioms of natural religion, Jefferson looked to the future in the experimental spirit of natural philosophy. Federalism may now seem profoundly regressive, looking back to an idealized British Empire and enabling independent Americans to perfect and perpetuate empire-building on a continental scale. But for Jefferson the federal "gradation of authorities" offered optimal conditions for an ongoing, progressive series of experiments that would reduce his republican "creed" to practice. The people's patriotic attachments to particular local and provincial governments resulted from myriad historical contingencies, but the passage of generations made these communities "natural," revealing the innate human capacity to live together harmoniously. When the imperial crisis demystified monarchy and other artificially constructed social hierarchies, American patriots turned to one another in defense of their collective as well as individual rights. The customary veneration of traditional authority inculcated by ruling elites and established churches was *displaced* and projected across the political geography of the continent. Patriots celebrated the communities their ancestors—the first "founding fathers"—had created in the American wilderness. The Revolution was less a case of "the world turned upside down" than of a vertical or hierarchical conception of the social order flipped onto a horizontal axis. When Anglo-American patriots invoked the sanction of Nature's God, they elevated the places where they became peoples—or the greater space of the "continent," within which they recognized themselves as a single people—over the blasted pretensions of a corrupt and despotic dynasty to command the allegiance of distant subjects. The emperor had no clothes, and Americans would now, like the rising youth in Jefferson's constitutional parable, cast off "the coat which fitted him when a boy" and suit themselves.[61]

The "long train of abuses" Jefferson elaborated in the Declaration of Independence constituted a protracted, practical test of King George's rule. Monarchy failed to deliver good government. Forced to return to first principles and assert their natural rights, independent Americans now embarked on an age of experiments in republican self-government. They did not pretend to know exactly how they should—or even if they could—govern themselves. Constitution writers in the states took the lead, paying close attention to the process and progress of constructing new governments elsewhere. Centralizing "nationalists," following the lead of British advocates of parliamentary sovereignty and anticipating their French Revolutionary counterparts, sought to obliterate or at least minimize provincial distinctions. But the framers of the federal constitution quickly learned that they had to accommodate the plurality of jurisdictions inherited from the imperial old regime.

Built on the solid foundation of popular patriotism, an expansive federal superstructure would empower the people by securing their liberties. Jefferson thus promised to support the "state governments in all their rights, as the most competent administrations for our domestic concerns, and the surest bulwarks against anti-republican tendencies."[62] Far from being obstacles to the progress of republicanism, the states constituted vital, energizing links that connected Americans to one another and made them a great and powerful nation. Jefferson was not a libertarian. If a "wise and frugal Government" left citizens "free to regulate their own pursuits of industry and improvement," it also recognized their rights to regulate their collective interests at the appropriate level. The more governments the better; the more democratic they were, the more enduring their union. Jefferson admired township self-government in New England, urging reformers in Virginia to create "little republics" at the local level and democratize county government.

For Jefferson the success of democratic self-government depended on an ongoing process of experimentation. On one hand this meant that white male citizens should be fully and equally empowered to participate in their own government (enslaved people were rights-less aliens, or a "captive nation"); on the other, participation would only be meaningful and administration efficient if authority were broadly distributed across space, out to new states on the union's expanding periphery and down to the level of little, neighborhood republics.[63] Citizens and their representatives at each level claimed an autonomous sphere of action but at the same time vigilantly monitored the actions of governments at higher or lower levels. Federalism promoted the circulation of information, enabling well-informed citizens to assess their governments' performance. Did they adhere to "decisions of the majority, the vital principle of republics" and duly render "equal and exact justice to all men, of whatever state or persuasion, religious or political"?[64]

A late Enlightenment spirit of progressive improvement suffused the conception of union Jefferson developed in his prescriptions for constitutional reform in Virginia in 1816. His union would be a laboratory for experiments in implementing republican principles. The fundamental question at ascending levels of the federal system was whether the equal rights of constituent members were appropriately respected and secured. Did the federal union secure the equal rights of states that were—in terms of population, wealth, and power—unequal? Did states secure the equal rights of subordinate jurisdictions? Did local governments secure the equal rights of their citizens? Depending on where they stood, vigilant citizens were more or less well equipped to assess the experiment's success. Their ongoing assessments constituted the dynamic public opinion on which the legitimacy and effective authority of the union as a whole depended.

It was a matter of faith for Jefferson that robust popular participation in a plurality of governments would perpetuate and perfect the union. Participation fostered patriotic attachments: recognizing and respecting one another's rights, Americans would sacrifice everything in defense of the nation—a great family of families—and of the "chosen country" their ancestors had first settled, "with room enough for our descendants to the thousandth and thousandth generation."[65] Jefferson's vision of national greatness resonated with optimistic, forward-looking Americans. Yet it also did so because it was so reassuringly familiar. For Jefferson's "empire of liberty" evoked another, earlier empire: the idealized empire that had inspired Anglo-American patriots to resist the unconstitutional encroachments of a corrupt and despotic metropolitan government on their most cherished liberties.

VII. DISUNION

At first, the United States succeeded where the British Empire had so conspicuously failed. The constitutional crisis that led to independence showed American patriots that their liberties were not safe under an all-powerful central government. Efforts to reform and consolidate the empire threatened to obliterate the local and provincial governments that historically had secured their rights and identities as British subjects. This was the original "empire of liberty," the Anglo-American union that inspired provincial patriots to make such extraordinary sacrifices in the great war against France.[66] When Revolutionaries rallied in defense of rights they claimed under their provincial constitutions, they also sought to vindicate their conception of imperial union. The union Americans then created for themselves enabled imperial patriots to fulfill their colonizing destiny by establishing new and equal states on an expanding frontier of settlement. In this republican empire there would be no all-powerful metropolis. Instead, vigilant citizens would participate in their own government at every level, secure in their rights against one another and from the pretensions of supposedly superior "sovereign" authorities. Jefferson's animosity toward aristocracy, monarchy, and all forms of hierarchical power and privilege was predicated on his idealized conception of union. Federalism constituted a dynamic hierarchy of jurisdictions that secured citizens' rights and sustained their patriotic attachments.

Yet if the new United States was a more perfect version of the old British Empire, it was also destined to collapse. At the very time Jefferson was developing his ideas about democratic federalism, he was becomingly increasingly aware of ominous new threats to his cherished union. The Missouri crisis terrified Jefferson, like a "fire bell in the night." Efforts to restrict slavery in the proposed new state led to a growing rift between the slave states of the South and their free northern counterparts. "A geographical line, coinciding with a marked principle, moral and political, once conceived and held up to the angry passions of men," Jefferson warned former congressman John Holmes, "will never be obliterated; and every new irritation will mark it deeper and deeper."[67] For Jefferson (who never doubted his own antislavery credentials) the restrictionists' moralizing rhetoric about slavery's injustice was simply a cover for the "political" ambitions of northern neo-Federalists, who sought to capture the central government and reduce the southern states to the condition of subject provinces.

Anyone who heedlessly put the union at risk was guilty of a profound moral failure, committing "treason against the hopes of the world." The union was not simply or primarily an ad hoc, instrumental arrangement, calculated to secure and promote self-interest; it was, much more importantly, the ultimate end and justification of republican self-government. Good citizens, secure in their rights, recognized and loved one another as fellow Americans. Jefferson thus took the Missouri conflict personally, like a stab in the back. The struggle over slavery expansion was a kind of collective suicide, making Americans foreigners to one another. "I regret that I am now to die in the belief," an aging and demoralized Jefferson concluded, "that the useless sacrifice of themselves by the generation of 1776, to acquire self-government and happiness to their country, is to be thrown away by the unwise and unworthy passions of their sons."[68]

Jefferson's moral obtuseness seems astonishing to us. Rather than contemplate his own implication in the evil of slavery and consider ways to remedy its injustice, he once again deflected responsibility and projected blame. But Jefferson's extreme reaction illuminates what the union meant to him. Republican self-government, he supposed, was an engine of moral progress: it brought citizens closer to God and therefore to one another. Rather than contribute to the eventual resolution of the slavery problem by promoting ameliorative measures and the progressive enlightenment of public opinion, line-drawing restrictionists sought to deprive fellow citizens in Missouri of their equal rights. This, of course, was precisely what the British tried to do in the imperial crisis, and this is why Jefferson invoked the Spirit of 1776 in his belligerent response to restrictionism.

The almost irresistible temptation is to invoke reductive psychological explanations for Jefferson's apparent paranoia. Was he projecting and displacing his own sense of guilt when he questioned the good faith of northern opponents of slavery expansion? I would suggest instead that the better explanation is ideological, or perhaps even theological. Jefferson's republican faith was predicated on the capacity of enlightened citizens to see the way forward toward progressive reform and improvement. When provincial subjects of George III became independent, self-governing Americans, they initiated a new epoch in mankind's moral history. But there would be formidable obstacles to progress, internal and external. Jefferson and his followers had a ready explanation for subsequent moments of darkness like the "reign of witches" in the 1790s: their enemies were false patriots, unreconstructed loyalists who sought to subvert the republic.

High Federalist "Anglomen" favored a close alliance with, if not outright recolonization by, the former mother country. They would insidiously consolidate power and wealth, fashioning artificial distinctions and hierarchical pretensions that would alienate Americans from one another. The Jeffersonian struggle against Federalism thus was a continuation of the American Revolutionary struggle for freedom and self-government: it was a moral crusade against powerful and insidious enemies at home and abroad. And those enemies once again threatened union and republican government in the controversy over Missouri statehood. Slavery was indeed a great injustice, but destroying the union was not the solution. Under the right circumstances, enlightened slaveholders would emancipate their slaves. "The cession of that kind of property, for so it is misnamed, is a bagatelle which would not cost me a second thought," Jefferson told Holmes, "if, in that way, a general emancipation and *expatriation* could be effected; and gradually, and with due sacrifices, I think it might be."[69]

In questioning the good faith of restrictionists, Jefferson revived the specter of "English influence" that energized and justified Republican opposition to the Federalist administrations of the 1790s. For Jefferson, the mobilization of antislavery sentiment that jeopardized the union in the years after the Peace of Ghent looked like a sectionalist power grab, instigated and inspired by the British. During the Revolution and the War of 1812, the British had fomented slave insurrections in order to destroy the union; now, in an "era of good feelings" when American independence was supposedly secure, British abolitionists and their American allies (or dupes) sought to achieve the same end under the cover of a moral crusade against slavery.[70] Jefferson's "treason" charge expressed the deep conviction shared by many southerners of antislavery's alien, un-American origins.[71] He could only imagine a conflict-free, postpartisan America—a still more perfect union—when the British threat was fully and finally eliminated. The only way to end slavery was through voluntary, uncoerced, and compensated emancipation, followed by the expatriation of freedpeople; the only way to emancipate Americans from Britain's corrupt influence was to obliterate the last vestiges of Anglophile Federalism, effectively expatriating the new nation's most dangerous and insidious "internal enemy."

Yet it was impossible for Jefferson and fellow Republican patriots to deny their own British origins or extricate themselves from continuing connections with and dependency on the former metropolis. Anglophobia and Anglophilia were inextricably linked. As we have seen, Jefferson's conception of the federal union and the new republican "empire of liberty" was profoundly shaped by and continuous with the British imperial old regime. In many ways, Jefferson was more indebted to British precedents and practices than were the political enemies he vilified as "Anglomen." And no one was a more passionate or influential exponent of the "rights of Englishmen." When Jefferson invoked natural rights he did not repudiate but instead universalized those rights claims, insisting on their ancient pedigree. Americans had fought the Revolution to secure the liberties and rights that they had enjoyed as English and British subjects and that the Crown historically had secured to them. After independence, Jefferson and his fellow patriots enthusiastically embraced the imperial project that a misguided and corrupt ministry had betrayed. Fulfilling the imperial ambitions that Jefferson articulated so eloquently in his Inaugural Address depended on securing Americans' property rights in land—and their property in the labor of enslaved African Americans.[72]

The "chosen country" was so vast and fertile that it could offer landownership to the "thousandth and thousandth generation." The rejection of old regime aristocracy therefore did not require the redistribution of a limited land supply, but only prudent provisions for preempting the emergence of great estates through the abolition of primogeniture and entail. Historians may dispute the significance of land law reform in Jefferson's Virginia, but there can be no question of its world-historical significance for Jefferson.[73] A seemingly boundless hinterland enabled him to combine a deeply conservative conception of rights, grounded in the sanctity of land titles, with a progressive, uplifting vision of democratic opportunity. He acknowledged that in theory, in other places (such as old regime France) and at some future time in America (when the supply of surplus land began to diminish) it might be necessary to redistribute property through taxation or some other indirect means.[74] Yet if there was, at least for the time being, a great reservoir of free land, there was no such supply of free labor to improve it.

By the time of the Missouri controversy, it was clear that the end of the slave trade and a flood of European immigrants had not solved the labor problem in the plantation South. Jefferson might still tell Holmes that slavery only existed by convention, and under the law, as an ersatz "kind of property, for so it is misnamed." There was no absolute, natural right to landed property, and certainly not to enslaved human beings and their labor power. But for all practical purposes, the distinction between conventional and natural rights disappeared under the new republican regime. Self-governing citizens who were guided by their moral sense were answerable only to their God and to no higher human authority. This is why Jefferson, nearing death, was reduced to praying for a "revolution in public opinion." The injustice of slavery "is not to be expected in a day, or perhaps in an age; but time, which outlives all things, will outlive this evil also."[75]

In a land of "happy Mediocrity" where property was broadly distributed, Americans could identify the mass mobilization of the people in defense of their rights with the progress of democracy and enlightenment.[76] Politically active citizens could preserve their freedoms by faithful adherence to the republican principles of equal rights and majority rule; as long as they were vigilant and virtuous, they could prevent the emergence of a privileged, self-dealing ruling class. But moral progress did not naturally or necessarily follow. In slave societies, it was in the interest of ordinary, enterprising citizens to uphold property rights in slaves as well as land, and the broad distribution of authority in the new federal republic provided crucial "bulwarks" against challenges to those rights as well as "against antirepublican tendencies."[77] Jefferson imagined that his ward republics would strengthen patriotic attachments by promoting popular political participation and securing the rights of liberty-loving Americans. But his democratic federalism did not bring Americans closer together; his union did not survive a deepening sectional crisis.

Abraham Lincoln offered an eloquent tribute to Jefferson's failed union in his Inaugural Address. "We are not enemies, but friends," he assured his fellow Americans as they readied for battle in a great and devastating civil war. "We must not be enemies. Though passion may have strained, it must not break our bonds of affection. The mystic chords of memory, stretching from every battle-field, and patriot grave, to every living heart and hearthstone all over this broad land, will yet swell the chorus of the Union, when again touched, as surely they will be, by the better angels of our nature."[78] Yet those bonds were broken, chords snapped, and chorus stilled. The union had collapsed, and a new era of darkness descended. This was not because Americans had failed to defend their rights and counterrevolutionary, "antirepublican" forces were now in the ascendant. The "aristocrats" and "monocrats" who haunted Jefferson's political imagination throughout his life had *not* finally triumphed. The tragedy of Jefferson's empire was instead that it had been all too successful in fulfilling the vaulting ambitions of Anglo-American patriots. His dynamic and expansive "empire for liberty" was a new and improved version of its British predecessor, capable of harnessing the energies of a colonizing people.

The visionary Jefferson looked toward the enlightened future. As he proclaimed on his deathbed, "All eyes are opened, or opening to the rights of man."[79] But like Lincoln, he took his bearings from an idealized past. Imaginatively banishing Indians from an empty western landscape and wishing slaves away in his fantasy of emancipation and expatriation, Jefferson envisioned a republican millennium, peopled by the "better angels" Lincoln so desperately summoned in the new nation's darkest hour. Theirs would be the union of hearts and minds that Jefferson imagined and Lincoln remembered, a great nation of devoted patriots who would sacrifice everything for their country.

2

Democracy

THOMAS JEFFERSON AND PATRICK HENRY

On May 29, 1765, Patrick Henry, a newly elected member of the House of Burgesses from Hanover County, introduced a set of five resolutions condemning the Stamp Act, a controversial tax recently enacted by the British Parliament on printed material circulating in colonies, including legal documents, licenses, newspapers, and playing cards. After heated debate on the following day, the burgesses adopted his first four resolves by close votes. Forcefully developing a familiar constitutional argument for the "People's" exclusive control over taxation "derived from their own Consent, with the Approbation of their Sovereign, or his Substitute," these resolves set the stage for a still more controversial fifth resolve. By a vote of 20 to 19, the Burgesses resolved that "every Attempt to vest such Authority in any other Person or Persons whatsoever"—that is, in Parliament—"has a Manifest Tendency to destroy AMERICAN FREEDOM."[1]

Henry's defiance of Parliament—and implicitly of the King, who exercised his authority in collaboration with the Commons and the Lords as part of the great imperial legislature—sounded like treason to conservative burgesses. Henry's electrifying speech in support of his resolves dispelled any possible ambiguity. "Tarquin and Caesar had each his Brutus!," witnesses recalled him saying, "Charles the first, his Cromwell! And George the Third . . ." Radical young patriots in the House were thrilled by Henry's bold rhetoric; their conservative senior colleagues were appalled. To identify George III with such tyrants, and to ask his listeners to imagine his fate by filling in the blank, was nothing short of "Treason!," the outraged speaker of the House, John Robinson, exclaimed. Rallying their forces on May 31, conservative burgesses took advantage of dwindling attendance to rescind the fifth resolve and expunge it from the records. Lieutenant Governor Francis Fauquier made sure that none of the resolves were printed in the *Virginia Gazette.*

But the damage was done. In addition to the four (or five) resolutions adopted by the Burgesses, two additional resolves Henry had prudently withheld were reprinted throughout the colonies as if they *all* had been adopted. The sixth resolve asserted that Virginians were "not bound to yield Obedience to any Law or Ordinance whatsoever" that had not been passed by their own legislature; anyone challenging this claim, according to the seventh resolve, "shall be deemed, an Enemy to this his Majesty's Colony."[2] Whatever the burgesses had officially done, the battle lines were now clearly drawn in Virginia and across the continent. Patriots knew who they were—and they knew their enemies.

Young Thomas Jefferson was in the audience that day. "I was then but a student, & was listening at the door of the lobby," he recalled many years later. There was no disagreement about "our rights," but "all the old members whose influence in the house had, till then, been unbroken" objected to Henry's brash language. The burgesses had already made their case "in a more conciliatory form" at the "preceding session" and should wait patiently for a response from London. But "torrents of sublime eloquence from mr Henry" carried the day. "The impression made on me, at the time, was such as to fix the facts indelibly in my mind."[3]

Henry's stirring oratory marked the beginning of Jefferson's career as a Revolutionary patriot: this was the "spirit" that animated resistance to British tyranny and the movement for independence a decade later. When Albemarle County sent Jefferson to the Burgesses in 1768, the two young men forged a close relationship: "the exact conformity of our political opinions strengthened our friendship." Their friendship did not survive, but the patriotic spirit that Henry so powerfully exemplified and that so inspired Jefferson would be the touchstone of their divergent political careers long after independence had been declared and achieved. Toward different ends and in different contexts, both looked back to their joint struggle against the mother country.

Opposing ratification of the federal constitution in the Virginia Convention in 1788, Henry invoked "the spirit which predominated in the revolution"; Jefferson struck similar chords a decade later as he sought to rekindle the "Spirit of 1776" in the Democratic-Republican mobilization against High Federalist tyranny in the run-up to the "Revolution of 1800."[4] Despite his deepening animosity toward Henry in later years, Jefferson acknowledged that Henry had been the man of the moment in the Revolutionary crisis. Henry's "imagination was copious, poetical, sublime," and his "bold, grand & overwhelming eloquence" captivated auditors in Virginia and in the Continental Congress, epitomizing and unleashing the love of liberty and patriotic spirit that shaped the careers of these two provincial lawyer-politicians—and changed their world.[5] Jefferson told Daniel Webster in 1824 that Henry was "far before all in maintaining the spirit of the Revolution."[6]

I. THE SPIRIT OF 1776

Jefferson and Henry's early friendship and collaboration illuminates a critical and defining moment in an age of democratic revolutions that tax-averse defenders of Anglo-American provincial autonomy unwittingly initiated. "Democracy" was an ambiguous, protean term in 1776 and would remain so for many years thereafter.[7] When they affixed their signatures to the Declaration of Independence, patriot leaders might embrace popular sovereignty in the abstract, but this did not allay misgivings about the political presence of real people in Revolutionary politics. The "better sort" customarily defined themselves against and sought to distance themselves from the common folk, or demos. Steeped in neoclassical literature, they worried about demagogic popular tribunes and redistributionist agrarian laws; plebeian mobs, carried away by their insatiable appetites, threatened to unleash anarchy and disorder. As occasional references to the people as a mindless "beast" or "herd" made apparent, elite anxieties were not easily suppressed. Ordinary folk returned the favor, charging impolitic elites with "aristocratic" impulses, a charge that would remain potent in American politics far into the future.

The Revolutionary crisis led Americans to deploy the language of class in provincial societies that were dominated by the "middling" sort and conspicuously free of class distinctions: very few would or could self-identify as "peasants," "plebeians," or "aristocrats." Like the political ideologies that have attracted so much scholarly attention, the language of class was yet another import from the metropolis that enabled provincial Anglo-Americans to construct a new republican civic identity. Questioning their neighbors' good faith, they exaggerated differences among themselves, which they then sought to overcome through the process of political and military mobilization. Self-conscious republican citizens thus fashioned themselves as civic equals, obliterating artificial distinctions that they imputed to the imperial connection. In retrospect, this was what Americans came to call "democracy," though the term would only gain broad acceptance when it was purged of traditional associations with the lower classes. But that emergent meaning was already apparent in the complementary efforts of patriots like Henry and Jefferson to forge a new nation.

Revolutionary mobilization was predicated on defining and defending a common ground. Americans committed themselves to uphold the rights they collectively claimed as Englishmen under their provincial constitutions.[8] As they constituted their new republics, patriots transformed British provinces into independent states within a postimperial, national union. The Declaration, Jefferson later wrote, was "the fundamental act of union of these states," simultaneously affirming and transcending their separate existence.[9] In the same way, patriotic Americans from across the continent proclaimed their equal rights as independent citizens by pledging their "lives and sacred honor" to the common cause. Citizen virtue, the great French philosopher Montesquieu taught, was the animating principle of republican government.[10] In Virginia, Henry's inspiring oratory ignited "the sacred fire of freedom," setting the stage for revolution and enabling Jefferson and other key actors to perform their respective roles.[11]

Jefferson recognized the importance of persuasive speech in mobilizing popular patriotic sentiment. He acknowledged Henry's extraordinary eloquence.[12] When serving as minister to France after the war, Jefferson urged young Americans not to study abroad and so risk forfeiting their ability to communicate effectively with their countrymen.[13] Unlike many of his educated and enlightened elite counterparts, Jefferson did not reflexively assume that popular orators were pandering demagogues, despite his own recent unhappy experience with the people's representatives as Virginia's wartime governor. He instead reaffirmed his democratic conception of the republic as a community of citizen-speakers, equal in their rights. In France he was more concerned that Americans abroad would betray their country by seeking to rise above—and thus alienate themselves from and lose their influence with—their humble neighbors. Jefferson's exposure to the brutal and seductive realities of the French old regime reinforced his republican commitments; it alerted him to aristocratic temptations that *he* might be able to resist but that would jeopardize the virtue of impressionable young countrymen. Jefferson's hypersensitivity to the aristocratic threat, subsequently focused on its homegrown sources, would shape his career in American politics.

Jefferson's hostility to aristocracy largely inoculated him against the growing disenchantment with democratic politics at home that led his colleague James Madison to spearhead the movement for constitutional reform. At a time when Shays' Rebellion and other agrarian disturbances called the capacity and legitimacy of state governments into question, Jefferson celebrated the orderliness of the American republics and the good sense of the American people.[14] Looking back to 1776 and reminding himself (and Maria Cosway, his undoubtedly bemused correspondent) of the epochal significance of American independence, Jefferson wrote that the sentimental "Heart" had then taken the lead and the cool rational "Head" had followed. "You began to calculate and to compare wealth and numbers," Jefferson's Head exclaims: "we threw up a few pulsations of our warmest blood: we supplied enthusiasm against wealth and numbers: we put our existence to the hazard, when the hazard seemed against us, and we saved our country." Henry's eloquence inspired Americans to risk everything and win the new nation's independence. But if the patriotic Heart showed the way, the enlightened Head also played an important role in Jefferson's stylized history of the Revolution: republican lawmakers codified fundamental principles, framing constitutions that secured the liberty and prosperity of future generations and justified patriot sacrifices. What was crucial, as the dialogue form suggested, was that heads and hearts were engaged with each other and committed to "the ways of Providence, whose precept is to do always what is right, and leave the issue to him."[15]

Commitment to a higher cause that was sanctioned by "Nature's God" enabled patriots to overcome myriad differences and exploit their various gifts. Jefferson thus imagined a division of labor, with the Declaration he drafted for Congress articulating the new republican "creed" and inspiring writers like Thomas Paine and speakers like Patrick Henry to mobilize the masses. The medium—a shared language that subverted and transcended hierarchical distinctions—was as important as the message. Speaker and auditor, writer and reader affirmed their attachments to each other in the exchange and circulation of shared principles and sentiments. As an enlightened republican, Jefferson assaulted the bastions of aristocratic privilege and power that enabled the exalted few to dominate public life. Freedom of conscience and speech constituted fundamental challenges to the old regime, establishing a linguistic common ground where former subjects could claim and perform their equal rights as citizens. The figure of the citizen was uplifting, evoking classical conceptions of virtuous commitment to the republic.

Cast in the role of the great orator Demosthenes, Henry could be distinguished from the rabble-rousing demagogues who threatened to subvert the established social order.[16] Indeed, Henry's eloquence pointed to an entirely new conception of the social order, with vertical hierarchies of command and coercion giving way to the "natural" affinities of consenting individuals along a horizontal axis. Jefferson thus recognized that Henry contributed much more to the Revolution than mobilizing the troops. On the eve of the war's outbreak in March 1775—when, biographer William Wirt wrote, "his voice swelled to its boldest note of exclamation—'give me liberty, or give me death!'"—Henry embodied and expressed the genius of the Revolution.[17] The defense of provincial liberties that defined resistance to ministerial tyranny now gave way to a transformative conception of political community and human possibility. Americans became conscious of themselves as a people.

II. ENEMIES

Jefferson came to distrust and despise Henry, but he never denied his antagonist's crucial role in the run-up to the Revolution. Over the course of his long political career, Jefferson could convince himself that most of his enemies were "Tories," crypto-monarchists and aristocrats who were bent on reversing the Revolution's outcome. But he could not do this with regard to Henry, a fellow Virginian who commanded the love and loyalty of their countrymen. Nor was it apparent that the two patriots diverged on fundamental issues. Outraged by George III's betrayal of his loyal American subjects, both expressed a boundless faith in the people's virtue and patriotic spirit; both considered Virginia their "country" even as they embraced a neoimperial vision of America's providential destiny. The harsh assessments of Henry's character and career that Jefferson offered William Wirt and that proved so critical in shaping Henry's historical reputation thus seem gratuitously personal and mean-spirited.[18] The conclusion that Jefferson envied Henry's genius as a great republican orator and popular hero is hard to resist.

Jefferson's portrait of Henry elaborated the supposedly stark contrast between his undeniable natural gifts and his poor performance as a lawyer and statesman. Lazy and unfocused, Henry did not work well behind the scenes; he did not draft addresses during his brief stint in Congress or bills for the Virginia legislature. "He could not draw a bill on the most simple subject which would bear legal criticism," Jefferson told Wirt, "or even the ordinary criticism which looks to correctness of stile & idea." At his best in expressing "general grievances" in public settings, Henry "had the good sense to percieve that his declamation, however excellent in it's proper place, had no weight" among the "cool-headed, reflecting, judicious men" who assembled in Congress to determine the destiny of the continent. Henry "said the strongest things in the finest language, but without logic, without arrangement, desultorily." Impatient with the chores of committee work and draftsmanship, Henry was rendered "silent" in Congress, incapable of speaking in or for that august assemblage.[19]

Jefferson underscored Henry's supposed deficiencies in order to exalt his own contributions to the Revolution. Where the great orator foundered, the self-effacing Jefferson flourished. Eloquently expressing the "harmonizing sentiments of the day," the author of the Declaration of Independence coolly suppressed his own voice and exalted that of the people.[20] Indeed, Americans did not know that Jefferson had been the Declaration's draftsman until many years later.[21] By contrast, Henry's identity was inextricably linked to the passionate words that poured from him in the heat of the moment. The actual words Henry spoke were not—and apparently could not be—accurately recorded, but the powerful feelings they invoked left an indelible impression on his audiences, including the young Jefferson. Though biographer William Wirt's portrait of Henry was flattering, including many testimonies to his rhetorical brilliance, Wirt followed Jefferson's lead in explaining its sources. Henry was poorly educated: instead of his receiving a proper classical education, "the years of his youth had been wasted in idleness." Henry became "celebrated as an orator *before* he had learned to compose," Wirt claimed (wrongly, as Kevin Hayes and Jon Kukla have definitively demonstrated). Speaking from the heart, the naturally gifted Henry was in his element. But "when withdrawn from the kindling presence of the crowd" and "called upon . . . to take the pen, all the spirit and flame of his genius were extinguished."[22]

For Jefferson, the juxtaposition of nature to civilization—and of spontaneous speech to higher forms of literary expression—charted the progress of the Enlightenment. Far from seeking to deny, suppress or overcome "nature," enlightened advocates of natural law and rights sought to improve on and fulfill its immanent potential. Human nature was malleable and could be directed toward higher ends through character-forming socialization and education. Ordinary Americans had the "common sense" to resist unnatural violations of their fundamental rights in the Revolutionary crisis: "nature" itself revolted at the prospect of enslavement to a corrupt and despotic ministry and monarch. Yet, for enlightened projectors like Jefferson, the point of independence was not simply to resist change and preserve provincial Anglo-Americans in what Benjamin Franklin described as their "happy Mediocrity."[23] Jefferson's Declaration articulated the timeless truths of a new republican regime that conformed to the decrees of "Nature's God," but it also initiated an epochal new era in the history of mankind. Under the new dispensation, the people would become more and more enlightened; republicanism would be an engine for moral progress.[24]

Henry's eloquence was indispensable in the movement *toward* independence but in Jefferson's view a frustrating obstacle to moving forward *from* independence. Of course, Jefferson's interpretation of Henry's career was self-serving, reflecting his need to explain—and displace responsibility for—his own political failures, most notably as Virginia's wartime governor. But Jefferson and his allies saw an increasingly clear pattern in what they took to be Henry's seemingly reflexive opposition to constitutional and legal reforms that would eliminate antirepublican survivals of the provincial old regime. Stranded in Philadelphia in the summer of 1776, Jefferson was unable play a significant role in the new commonwealth's founding. Returning home to take a seat in the state legislature, he instead dedicated himself to a comprehensive revision of Virginia's laws. The hardworking draftsman saw himself as Henry's antitype, patiently working behind the scenes to construct a republican legal system that would be secured by a new, properly authorized and ratified state constitution.[25]

Purged of archaic and mystifying language and expressing the will of a self-governing people, Jefferson's legal code would promote their ongoing, progressive enlightenment. His proposed bills for "Establishing Religious Freedom" and for the "More General Diffusion of Knowledge" through public education would help create the informed and enlightened citizenry that the survival of republican government required; in combination with reforms in land law that guaranteed equal inheritance and abolished entail—the legal principle that perpetuated great landed estates across generations—Jefferson considered "these bills, passed or reported, as forming a system by which every fibre would be eradicated of antient or future aristocracy; and a foundation laid for a government truly republican."[26] The enlightened reformer was laying a "foundation" and looking to the future. But the representatives of the people sitting in the assembly did not see the compelling necessity—or bridled at the expense—of many of the 126 bills proposed by Jefferson's committee. The piecemeal adoption of specific bills was frustrating for Jefferson, who had a "system" in mind, and underscored a growing concern that became a lifelong obsession with more fundamental defects of the Virginia constitution of 1776.

The education bill was a notable casualty of legislators' parsimony, and though belated passage of the Bill for Religious Freedom—despite Henry's opposition—was a gratifying triumph, Jefferson feared that this and other progressive measures might be rolled back in the future. Section 3 of the bill eloquently expressed this anxiety, declaring "that the rights hereby asserted are of the natural rights of mankind" and warning future legislatures that any effort to repeal or in any way modify the bill "will be an infringement of natural right." The language of this controversial and narrowly adopted statute simply asserted its status as a higher law, notwithstanding its dubious pedigree. This was precisely what Jefferson considered so radically defective about the Virginia constitution, a stopgap measure adopted by an ad hoc, extraconstitutional Revolutionary convention that was neither authorized nor ratified by the sovereign people. Jefferson certainly hoped that section 3 would not be a mere waste of words—or what Madison later dismissively called a "parchment barrier" in reference to a federal bill of rights—but would instead be incorporated (as it was) in Virginia's customary constitution.[27] But it surely would be much better for Virginians to define and secure their fundamental rights by writing a constitution that met the high standards and followed the procedures set in Massachusetts and other states.

The mixed success of Jefferson's career as a reformer in Virginia illuminates his conception of democracy and helps explain his hostility to Henry. Republicanism was a work in progress; its ultimate survival and success depended on constituting a government and legal system that could secure the equal rights of informed and vigilant citizens. The patriotic spirit that brought Virginians together in 1776 would not guarantee the Commonwealth's future. "From the conclusion of this war we shall be going down hill," Jefferson wrote shortly after leaving the governor's office under a cloud in 1781. His *Notes on the State of Virginia* was a frustrated reformer's cry from the heart. Far from exulting in the prospect of a victorious peace, Jefferson warned that in the absence of a properly constituted government declining popular virtue portended the republic's ruin. "Is the spirit of the people an infallible, a permanent reliance?" he asked. "Is it government?" Virginia's leaders would no longer need "to resort every moment to the people for support," and they would be "forgotten . . . and their rights disregarded." More ominously still, the people "will forget themselves, but in the sole faculty of making money, and will never think of uniting to effect a due respect for their rights."[28]

Jefferson's uncharacteristically dyspeptic commentary reflected the profound damage to his reputation and self-esteem he experienced in the wake of his administration's embarrassing failure to resist the British invasion—and of his precipitous escape to his Poplar Forest estate while fleeing legislators reassembled across the Blue Ridge in Staunton.[29] Significantly, Jefferson's dire warning concluded a lengthy discussion of religion in Virginia that rehearsed the natural-rights reasoning of—but did not explicitly refer to—his Bill for Establishing Religious Freedom. Perhaps, he then feared, the bill would never pass. "It can never be too often repeated, that the time for fixing every essential right on a legal basis is while our rulers are honest, and ourselves united." The legislature's failure to "fix" this fundamental freedom was of a piece with its unwillingness to undertake comprehensive legal and constitutional reform.

When our leaders become "corrupt" and "our people careless," Jefferson predicted, "a single zealot may commence persecutor, and better men be his victims." This was less a prediction than a barely disguised accusation of what he thought had recently happened in Staunton. Jefferson believed that Patrick Henry was the "zealot" who had launched a legislative inquiry into his performance in office. This assault on his character and honor was bad enough. But Jefferson was also convinced that his nemesis had been conspiring with fellow legislators to create a "dictator" with unlimited powers to meet the temporary emergency. Perhaps Henry himself aspired to this despotic role. Would he ever relinquish power once he seized it?[30]

This nightmare scenario enabled Jefferson to tell a self-exculpatory story in *Notes on Virginia* that projected responsibility for the debacle of his governorship onto nameless others. He could attribute the alleged dictatorship proposal in 1781 as well as an earlier effort in 1776 to constitutional failure: not only did the governor lack sufficient power under Virginia's defective constitution to meet existential threats from foreign enemies, but there was no "legal obstacle to the assumption by the assembly of all the powers legislative, executive, and judiciary."[31] And in assuming the right to determine their own quorum during the recent crisis, delegates had risked everything that a proper constitution, duly authorized and ratified by the people, would have secured. "From forty" the quorum might have been "reduced to four, and from four to one: from a house to a committee, from a committee to a chairman or speaker, and thus an oligarchy or monarchy be substituted under forms supposed to be regular."[32] Other states in the union had averted such threats because their governments were "unalterable by ordinary acts of assembly."[33]

Jefferson did not name names. "In enumerating the defects of the constitution," he insisted, "it would be wrong to count among them what is only the error of particular persons." The problem was instead structural. In the absence of well-defined constitutional limits, "zealots" would find the temptation to assume and abuse power irresistible. Needless to say, Jefferson was one of the "better men" who had resisted temptation, and his scruples had earned him the legislature's opprobrium. Referring to himself in the third person, Jefferson underscored his own central role in the constitutional debacle:

> One who entered into this contest from a pure love of liberty, and a sense of injured rights, who determined to make every sacrifice, and to meet every danger, for the re-establishment of those rights on a firm basis, who did not mean to expend his blood and substance for the wretched purpose of changing this master for that, but to place the powers of governing him in a plurality of hands of his own choice, so that the corrupt will of no one man might in future oppress him, must stand confounded and dismayed when he is told, that a considerable portion of that plurality had meditated the surrender of them into a single hand, and, in lieu of a limited monarch, to deliver him over to a despotic one![34]

The hypersensitive former governor cast himself as the embattled and misunderstood patriot, unfairly subjected to popular scorn and disapproval. The intensely private and self-effacing Jefferson was made into a public spectacle.

Jefferson struck a traditional antidemocratic chord when he blamed Virginia's defective constitution for his own recent political humiliation. When the people forgot what they had been fighting and dying for, he warned, the sacred fire of liberty would be extinguished. In its panicked response to the British invasion, the legislature had acted like a mindless mob, ready—even eager—to barter away its liberties in vain hopes of safety. Yet Jefferson could not turn against the "people" without repudiating his own fundamental commitment to the republican creed. Because the people lacked a proper constitution, he told himself, they could not see their way forward. The Spirit of 1776 had cast a bright light into the future, enabling Americans to recognize themselves as a people with a providential destiny; when the darkness descended in 1781, a united people became a disorganized mob, groping for safety and turning against their better selves. This was the classic moment for demagoguery. And Patrick Henry, a bruised and bitter Jefferson convinced himself, was the demagogue who had led the movement to censure him.

Henry evidently did *not* play a leading role in proposing a review of Jefferson's administration.[35] Governor Henry had experienced similar difficulties in mobilizing Virginia's defenses in an earlier emergency, and he and his colleagues had good reason to agree with Jefferson that the governor's powers must be significantly enhanced. What they could not know was the personal anguish Jefferson suffered as Virginia's defenses collapsed and the extent to which he correctly anticipated criticism—even from his friends—of the executive's performance. Righteously certain that he was not responsible for the government's near collapse, Jefferson had been "arraigned for treasons of the heart and not mere weaknesses of the head," as he wrote James Monroe in May 1782—shortly before the assembly decided *not* to proceed with its deliberations on the matter, instead unanimously resolving to thank him for his services. By then it was too late. Jefferson had declined election to the assembly and the opportunity to explain and exonerate himself, instead announcing his permanent withdrawal from public life. He could have "comforted myself under the disapprobation of the well-meaning but uninformed people," but the censure of colleagues who should have known better could not be borne. The "wound on my spirit" would "only be cured by the all-healing grave."[36]

Of course, Jefferson soon did return to public life. Reconciling himself with the "well-meaning" people, he resumed reform efforts that would guarantee their progressive enlightenment. His great goal was to persuade the legislature to complete the unfinished business of 1776 by authorizing a convention to draft a constitution that the people would ratify and make their own. At a time when his countrymen could see victory over the British as a vindication of republican government, Jefferson was convinced by bitter personal experience that the Commonwealth's constitution was fundamentally flawed. The tension between Jefferson's enduring faith in the people and their "uninformed" resistance to legal and constitutional reforms that would secure the liberty and well-being of future generations became acute in these dark days. That tension only could be resolved by identifying and neutralizing its proximate source. The great lesson of Jefferson's failed governorship was that his newfound enemy Patrick Henry was personally responsible for his disgrace and that Henry's "popularity" was the leading obstacle to constitutional reform.

Jefferson was wrong about Henry's enmity. Biographer William Wirt could not discover that his subject had ever made a single "invidious remark" about his supposed rival. Henry instead "spoke of him in the strongest and warmest terms, not only of admiration but of affection—styling him 'our illustrious fellow-citizen,'—'our enlightened and worthy country man,'—'our common friend.'"[37] But Jefferson was prophetic, perhaps in self-fulfilling ways, in anticipating that Henry would rally his popular following against constitutional changes that Jefferson considered urgent. "While Mr. Henry lives," Jefferson wrote his ally and fellow reformer Madison in late 1784, "another bad constitution would be formed, and saddled for ever on us." An ocean away, at his new diplomatic post in Paris, Jefferson counseled patience. "What we have to do I think is devoutly to pray for his death, in the mean time to keep alive the idea that the present is but an ordinance and to prepare the minds of the young men."[38]

III. DEMOCRATIC LEADERSHIP

Jefferson's hostility to Henry seems exaggerated and gratuitous, reflecting envy of his rival's political skills and a need to find a scapegoat for his own failures. Throughout his career, Jefferson cherished his privacy, juxtaposing the joys of domesticity to the miseries of public life.[39] His obsession with constitutional reform reflected his aversion to the rough and tumble of politics and his need to preserve his personal autonomy by keeping his distance from others. A properly constructed constitution would limit and contain political conflict, diminishing the scope of "popularity" and personal ambition, and so enable citizens and their representatives to better recognize their true, long-term interests. Jefferson thus imagined that the mechanisms of constitutional government would refine and improve the people, making them into enlightened, self-governing citizens. This would be a world to which the bruised and battered ex-governor could comfortably return, one that recognized the superior merits of a "natural aristocrat."

Jefferson's conception of human nature was abstract, filtered through the universalizing lens of moral philosophy. Its genius was to look beyond the historically constructed and contingent particularities of status, class, and ethnicity. If "all men were created equal," as Americans declared when they created their new republics, equality would also be the animating principle and ultimate goal of well-designed republican constitutions. Looking back and looking forward, Jefferson was prone to overlook the profound and abiding distinctions of his own, highly stratified and unequal world. They would all disappear in the fullness of time.

Patrick Henry's conception of human nature and his extraordinary success as a democratic leader were grounded in the world as he found it. In 1784, when Madison called on fellow legislators to initiate the process of drafting a state constitution to replace the 1776 "ordinance," Henry impatiently dismissed the project. Henry thought it would be, as his recent biographer Jon Kukla puts it, a "pointless, expensive, and empty exercise," "more theoretical than practical" and "rooted in an obsession with ideological purity [rather] than in concerns with the actual operation of government."[40] Unlike in 1776, when patriotic Virginians pressed their leaders to institute a new "plan of government" and declare independence, in 1784 there was no popular demand for constitutional reform. Henry did not question Madison's motives—as he would when Virginians convened to ratify the federal constitution four years later. But he did think that Madison's untimely initiative would be counterproductive. Whatever the theoretical defects of the state's constitution, its legitimacy only grew with the passage of time. If anyone could accurately gauge public opinion in Virginia, it was Henry. And Henry knew that his war-weary countrymen had little interest in risking everything by returning to the reformers' theoretical state of nature. Why would they repudiate the constitutional legacy of their own Spirit of 1776?

Henry knew what the people wanted because he identified and engaged with them. His lifelong friend Samuel Meredith testified that Henry's "invariable habit of close and attentive observation" enabled him to become an extraordinarily effective public speaker.[41] Honing his skills in the courtroom, Henry was "beyond doubt," Wirt reckoned, "the ablest defender of criminals in Virginia, and will probably never be equalled again." The great advocate was in his "natural element" before a jury. Because he "understood the human character so perfectly" in "all its strength and all its weaknesses, together with every path and by-way which winds around to the citadel of the best-fortified heart and mind," Henry never failed to sway a juror, "either by stratagem or storm."[42] His ability to move his auditors seemed uncanny. Hardin Burnley, a witness to Henry's pleading in litigation over

Virginians' debts to British creditors in 1791, was "astonished" by his performance. Henry "was perfect master of the passions of his auditory," Burnley told Wirt, "whether in the tragic or comic line. The tones of his voice, to say nothing of his matter and gesture, were insinuated into the feelings of his hearers, in a manner that baffles all description."[43]

The "people" were not an abstraction for Henry. He knew his countrymen as particular individuals with distinctive interests, aptitudes, and predilections, not as interchangeable parts in an enlightened lawgiver's constitutional design. As a good Christian, Henry recognized "the depraved nature of man" when freed from the constraints of civilized society: "he has a natural biass towards his own interest, which will prevail over every consideration, unless it be checked."[44] When Virginians declared independence in 1776, they sought to preserve a constitutional regime and social order that had secured liberty, not to engage in dangerous experiments with their rights. Henry had been no "demagogue" or "designing man" when he raised the alarm in the run-up to the Revolution, he told his fellow delegates at the Virginia ratifying convention in June 1788, for the people had immediately grasped what was at stake. As the "servant of the people of this Commonwealth" and "advocate" for "their rights, liberty, and happiness," Henry's identity was indistinguishable from theirs.[45] The good lawyer drew his authority from the righteousness of his clients' cause, making himself their instrument and so transcending his own depraved, self-interested nature. Far from rising above his countrymen and showing them the way forward, Henry drew closer to them. He offered Virginians a rhetorical mirror, enabling them to recognize themselves as a people.

Henry's success as a criminal lawyer suggested the limits to his ambition. Gaining a favorable verdict for his client might earn a handsome fee, but it would not make him a powerful man. A jury trial instead epitomized democracy in action: every man or woman, rich or poor, deserved his or her day in court; a jury of peers—citizen-neighbors who claimed equal rights—would weigh evidence and arguments and render impartial judgments on behalf of the people. It is hardly surprising that Henry and other criminal lawyers should rise to prominence in the new American republics, despite, or perhaps because of, traditional hostility to the mysteries and mystifications of professional lawyers and magistrates.[46] The people needed good advocates to argue their cases. They needed to preserve a legal system historically dominated by unprofessional lay people and responsive to community sentiment. The people needed to preserve jury trials, as Henry argued at the ratifying convention, in order to secure their liberties—and therefore their attachment to the Commonwealth.

Unlike Henry, Jefferson turned against the legal profession when he embarked on his political career. Never acknowledging that politics was itself a profession, Jefferson saw himself instead as a self-sacrificing public servant, reluctantly responding to the call of the people. Convinced of his own high-mindedness, he set out to inform and enlighten the people by establishing a new republican regime that would promote their progressive improvement. Why would Henry, the great patriot of 1776, oppose these efforts? Why did he obstruct Jefferson's efforts at every turn? Licking his wounds after his traumatic experience as governor, Jefferson briefly flirted with the idea that the demagogic Henry was a would-be despot. But Jefferson knew better. The real problem with Henry was that his ambitions were so contemptibly modest. "He was avaritious & rotten hearted," Jefferson recalled. "His two great passions were the love of money & of fame: but when these came into competition the former predominated."[47] Feeding his "insatiable" appetite for money with "great fees," the great orator selfishly turned away from public service.[48] This mean-spirited assessment was consistent with Jefferson's charge that the poorly educated Henry was too lazy to improve on and make good use of his natural gifts as an orator. But Jefferson's assessment also backhandedly acknowledged that Henry was not a demagogue who threatened the people's liberty. To the contrary, Henry was in perfect accord with his fellow Virginians, who all forgot themselves "in the sole faculty of making money."[49] Henry's enormous and enviable popular influence was a wasted asset, Jefferson concluded. It was an obstacle to progressive reform.

IV. PRESERVE THE POOR COMMONWEALTH

Patrick Henry "smelt a rat" when he heard about the proposed federal constitution.[50] What crisis called forth this "proposal to change our government"? Unlike the patriotic upsurge of 1776, when Virginians came together in the defense of their liberties, the movement to jettison the Articles of

Confederation was the "project" of Madison and a small cohort of fellow reformers. Federalist proponents of the new constitution claimed that the imminent collapse of the Confederation pointed toward an anarchic war of all against all among the disunited American states. Henry wondered if reformers were confusing causes with effects. The "perilous innovation" they proposed fostered bitter divisions within Virginia and jeopardized the union.[51] "If Gentlemen dread disunion," Henry warned, "the very thing they advocate will inevitably produce it."[52]

Henry dominated the debate in Richmond in June 1788 over whether to ratify the Constitution. Though the Federalists ultimately prevailed by a narrow vote, Henry's campaign for substantive amendments to the Constitution shaped the Commonwealth's agenda in the new national political arena over the next decade. By all accounts, his extemporaneous speeches were dazzling performances, earning praise from opponents as well as allies. They also offer an extraordinarily rich account of his political philosophy at a critical and confusing moment in the new nation's history. When Henry famously asked, "Who authorized" the authors of the constitution "to speak the language of, *We, the People,* instead of *We, the States?,*" he was not denying the existence of an American people.[53] He was instead challenging the presumption that the people were in any meaningful sense present, or adequately represented, in Philadelphia. Perhaps, Henry speculated, the convention meant to "recommend" their plan "to the people at large, to those citizens who are to be levelled and degraded to the lowest degree," a people who were, in Governor Edmund Randolph's infelicitous turn of phrase, "likened to a herd." Randolph betrayed the reformers' antidemocratic bias, to "degrade" the people, not to enlighten or improve them. "By the operation of this *blessed* system," Henry tendentiously concluded, liberty-loving Americans "are to be transformed from respectable independent citizens, to abject, dependent subjects or slaves."[54]

Jefferson would certainly resent and reject such a characterization of his own campaign for constitutional reform in Virginia. But the charge made much more sense in the case of Madison and fellow Federalists, who could barely conceal their hostility to state governments that seemed too responsive to popular sentiment and who sought to create a strong national government distant from, and therefore less responsive to, the people. Henry did not know that Jefferson prayed for his death and instead had good reason to believe that his erstwhile antagonist shared his misgivings about the proposed new regime: that "illustrious citizen's" support for amendments that would secure the people's liberties—and curb the new government's powers—was well known before delegates convened in Richmond.[55] But there was no mistaking *Madison's* personal animosity to Henry, given their recent history of political combat and the leading role Madison had played in drafting and in now defending the federal constitution.[56]

Henry framed the question before the Virginia Convention in zero-sum terms. Federalists were asking their countrymen to authorize a massive redistribution of power that would enable a new national ruling class to promote collective security and an ambiguously defined "general welfare." Under the Confederation, Henry asserted, "the people of Virginia" could choose to revise their own constitution, but their hands would be tied if they ratified the proposed plan. However "unanimous" they might be in wishing "to alter their Government," it would be too late: "they may be prevented therefrom by a despicable minority at the extremity of the United States."[57] "Is this tame relinquishment of rights worthy of freemen?" he asked the convention. "Is it worthy of that manly fortitude that ought to characterize republicans?"[58] Federalists parried such questions by evoking the prospective horrors of disunion. To say that citizens would be reduced to the condition of slaves might be absurdly exaggerated, but advocates of the new regime could not deny that they were calling on citizens to relinquish the authority they exercised through state governments in defense of their liberties. Henry thus anticipated Alexis de Tocqueville's fundamental insight, that the modern "passion for equality" was logically compatible with slavery.[59] Stripped of their liberties and reduced to impotent ("unmanly") subjection, members of the "herd" could still claim to be equal. But Henry's auditors knew that "liberty ought to be the direct end of your Government."[60] In 1776 "America viewed with indignation the idea of holding her rights of England." Then "you disdained to hold your innate indefeasible rights of any one." What sort of assurances could Federalists now offer?[61]

Henry's skepticism about the Federalists' reform agenda has led commentators to depict him as a localist "man of little faith" who could not look beyond the borders of his native state.[62] Yet as his frequent references to the Revolution and the "American spirit of liberty" suggest, his identity as a Virginian did not preclude a more inclusive, cosmopolitan identification with Americans everywhere—not to mention "mankind" generally. What he meant by "country" or "people" in any particular instance can only be inferred from his context. Of course, his audience in Richmond was made up of Virginians, but their attachments were equally ambiguous and ambivalent. When he described himself as a "democrat," he appealed to universal "maxims" of republican government that Jefferson articulated in the Declaration of Independence. Virginians were good republicans and therefore Americans; their union would endure as long as republican governments—and the Spirit of 1776—endured in the states. "Republican maxims were then esteemed," Henry told the convention. "Those maxims, and the genius of Virginia, landed you safe on the shore of freedom."[63]

Young reformers might look forward to the emergence of the United States as a great and powerful nation with "a grand seat of Government for thirteen States, and perhaps for 100 States hereafter." But Henry and his fellow skeptics "have no such projects."[64] They instead looked backward, still cherishing "an invincible attachment to the dearest rights of man." That might make him look "old fashioned" in "these refined enlightened days," Henry sarcastically noted, but it did enable him to see clearly where the proposed experiment would lead.[65] The new metropolis, like the old imperial capital London, would rule Virginia and its other provinces from a great distance and beyond their control; "there is to be a great and mighty President" who—despite his innocuous title—would exercise "very extensive powers; the powers of a King," and he would "be supported in extravagant magnificence" at a new imperial court. In short, Henry famously concluded, the proposed system "squints towards monarchy."[66] The patriots of 1776 were clear-sighted. It was the "enlightened" reformers of 1787 who were blinded by their own dazzling prospects under the new dispensation. But this would "be an empire of men and not of laws," and if these men should "prove ambitious, and designing, may they not flourish and triumph upon the ruins of their country?"[67]

In questioning Federalist motives Henry did not hesitate to exploit anti-aristocratic sentiments as he defended the "yeomanry of this country," or the "middling and lower class of people."[68] But this was not the vulgar demagoguery of a rabble-rousing populist, nor could his rapt audience in Richmond be characterized as a "mobbish suspected herd."[69] Henry instead meant to evoke and revive the patriotic Spirit of 1776. White Virginians of all ranks and conditions then saw one another as fellow citizens, equally capable of recognizing and defending their rights. Henry thus sought to bring Virginians back together in June 1788. His eloquence would enable them to transcend class and status distinctions—and the party divisions that the proposed constitution provoked. Snide references to the "illumined," the "enlightened," the "refined," and the "chosen few" were not designed to ostracize, but rather to embarrass his opponents and bring them back into the fold. (Governor Randolph *did* apologize for his reference to the "herd.") Only by disclaiming any intention "to convert this country [in]to a powerful and mighty empire" like Britain's and by securing the liberties American Revolutionaries had fought for by amending the Constitution and adopting a bill of rights could Federalists affirm their loyalty to Virginia and their identity as Virginians.

Henry's conception of democracy was predicated on overcoming, not expressing and exacerbating, class distinctions. For him, as for Jefferson, the "people" was a transcendent and inclusive corporate entity, not a random, disaggregated congeries of diverse and conflicting interests. Both took their bearings from that moment in 1776 when patriots became conscious of their identity as both Virginians and Americans. The critical choice at Richmond—one the absent Jefferson did not immediately face—was *not* between two conflicting identities. Henry instead framed the question as a kind of thought experiment that would assess the future prospects of *American* liberty and *American* union by considering the implications of the proposed plan for republican self-government *in Virginia.* Jefferson thought along similar lines. He and Henry agreed that the Confederation government needed to be strengthened, but not at the expense of liberty: "the relinquishment of our rights," Henry proclaimed, was too high a price to pay for the "aggrandisement of the Government."[70] And they both agreed that the government's strength depended on the people's patriotism, not on blind submission to superior authority. When Henry enjoined his fellow delegates to "be extremely cautious, watchful, jealous of your liberty," he struck chords that would resonate in Jefferson's subsequent career as a party leader. The people were the best judges of what affected them most directly. "Instead of securing your rights you may lose them forever," Henry warned. "If a wrong step be now made, the Republic may be lost forever."[71]

Yet if 1788 was an unwelcome reprise of 1776 for Henry, an ambivalent

Jefferson was not quite so sure. Madison constantly reminded him of the obstructive role Henry continued to play in Virginia politics. Perhaps constitutional reform in Virginia required a recalibration of the federal balance and the creation of a genuinely republican government for the union? Madison may have flirted with "unrepublican" solutions to the crisis of republican government in the barely united states—including a congressional veto of state laws and the still more radical idea of remaking states into subordinate administrative units, like counties within the states—but the ongoing process of ratification itself implemented the great desideratum of Jeffersonian constitutionalism on a continental scale.[72] If ratified by the requisite number of states, including Virginia, then the federal constitution could claim legitimacy in Virginia in a way that the Virginia constitution—thanks to Henry's pernicious influence—could not. Needless to say, Henry would have considered this comparison absurd. Virginia had a perfectly good constitution that had stood the test of time; as of yet, the new federal constitution was an untested "project" or "experiment." The people—in Virginia and the other states—remained to be convinced. It was in this critical spirit that Henry pledged to abide by his colleagues' ultimate decision to ratify.[73] That spirit would prove contagious in subsequent years, as Jefferson and Madison—the "father" of the Constitution—mobilized national opposition to "consolidationist" tendencies emanating from Hamilton's Treasury. Indeed, Jefferson would celebrate his ultimate ascension to office as the triumph of the spirit that Henry epitomized in 1776 and sought to revive in 1788.

It is tempting to see Henry and Jefferson as mismatched democrats, lovers of liberty sadly separated by Jefferson's misunderstanding of Henry's role in his gubernatorial humiliation and by differences of temperament and character and partisan political rivalries that neither man could fully explain or justify. But the debates in Richmond suggest another, more fundamental philosophical divergence. When the two former friends looked back to 1776 and beyond, they saw different "Virginias." Those visions of their country's past pointed toward different democratic futures: Henry sought to keep the Spirit of 1776 alive in order to preserve the Revolutionary achievement; Jefferson sought to build on that achievement, envisioning Virginia as a progressively more perfect republic. Henry's great accomplishment was to revolutionize provincial politics, displacing an entrenched, self-dealing elite with the cohort of young patriots—including Jefferson—who declared independence. Jefferson's frustrating career as a reform-minded politician showed that important work remained to be done.

The distinctive character of Henry's democratic vision was most conspicuous at Richmond in his extraordinary celebration of the *British* constitution. The proposed federal constitution, a mere "paper" project, was inferior in all its features. Henry would "infinitely" prefer having "a King, Lords, and Commons" to "a Government so replete with such insupportable evils."[74] He was "struck" with the "beauty" of the British government in comparison with the "deformity" of the proposed system.[75] "In the British Government there are real balances and checks—In this system, there are only ideal balances." The unchecked power of the American president made him a potential despot, much more dangerous to the liberties of the people than Britain's constitutional monarch. "The President and Senators have nothing to lose," he charged. "They have not that interest in the preservation of the Government, that the King and Lords have in England."[76] Virginia, which was "as large as England," would only have ten representatives in the lower house of the federal legislature; "in England they have 530." Would those few representatives be worthier than their English counterparts? "Will they be incorruptible?"[77]

Of course, Henry's dire warnings were all highly speculative, a lawyer's hyperbolic "parade of horribles." But the questions he raised were compelling, and would remain so for future generations of Virginia patriots. Despite the Constitution's federal features, the framers clearly intended to create a single great continental republic for the American people. But if the beautiful British constitution had failed to secure the liberties of distant American subjects, how could its deformed American replica possibly do so? Before independence Henry and his fellow Whig Patriots had struggled to secure the constitutional protections that the English people had gained through the Glorious Revolution and the Bill of Rights. "Our glorious forefathers of Great-Britain, made liberty the foundation of every thing," he told the Richmond convention. But corrupt ministries and a misguided king had driven Americans from the empire, making them a separate people. "We drew the spirit of liberty from our British ancestors," and "by that spirit we have triumphed over every difficulty."[78]

Some delegates were taken aback by Henry's apotheosis of, and seeming identification with, "British liberty," wondering whether he "loved the British Government better than our own."[79] But nobody could impugn Henry's patriotism. Nor was it surprising that Henry embraced a history of liberty that linked present-day patriots with "our British"—and provincial American—ancestors. The framers drew liberally on that same tradition when they drafted the Constitution, but from a distinctively top-down, metropolitan perspective. They failed to recognize the critical role that provincial governments had played—and that the states should play—in checking and balancing the central government's power. Throughout his career, Henry insisted that Virginian liberties depended on maintaining a constitutional balance of power. In 1758, when he sought to vindicate the Virginia's exclusive right to legislate on matters of strictly local, provincial concern, Henry thus invoked "the original compact between king and people."[80] His conception of constitutional government did not change with the Declaration of Independence and the end of royal rule in America. Government, he still insisted, "is an express or implied compact between the rulers and ruled, stipulating reciprocal protection and obedience."[81]

Under the new federal regime, the "rulers" had changed, but it was still necessary to secure the liberties of the "ruled"—the American people in their respective states. Henry's commitment to upholding the rights of the people made him a popular hero and a democratic icon. That commitment was deeply conservative. "By harnessing the transformative drive for private redemption to the reform and perfection of an existing but threatened civic republican status quo," Jon Kukla writes, Henry embodied "the perplexing amalgam of radical ideals supporting conservative ends" that characterized the American Revolution.[82] Henry did not seek to turn the world upside down by setting common folk above their superiors or by redistributing property. His inclusive conception of the "people" instead obliterated social distinctions: the Spirit of 1776 enabled patriots to recognize one another as equal citizens and therefore to define and defend the rights they shared. The great challenge was to forge a new, postimperial compact that would secure the liberties of Americans in their state-republics.

Henry and fellow Antifederalists across the continent testified to their devotion to the union and to their identity as Americans. But they also insisted that the proposed federal system had to be true to the original intentions of patriots who sought to vindicate their rights—as Englishmen and then as men—within their provinces and against an overreaching metropolitan government. Many were reflexively suspicious of a "perilous cession of powers" proposed by self-styled lawgivers pretending to superior wisdom and enlightenment.[83] But critics who proposed thought experiments to assess the new regime's potential impact on states' rights and individual civil liberties were no less enlightened than their Federalist counterparts. Henry's sustained comparison between the federal and British constitutions was itself a classic exercise in what contemporaries had begun to call "political science." Would British liberty survive *in Britain* if the proposed American constitution were adopted there? Would an inferior, knock-off version of the British constitution work effectively in—or over—the American states? If the federal constitution, with its inadequately defined checks and balances, instead facilitated a potentially boundless and despotic concentration of authority, could the state governments even survive? What then would be the fate of the American people?

When Jefferson returned to America and joined the new federal government, he soon began to ask similar questions. But the way Jefferson framed those questions revealed how much his conception of democracy diverged from Henry's. In 1788 their positions on federal constitutional reform seemed very close. Before Jefferson's friends at the convention set him straight, Henry thought he was following a Jeffersonian script in urging delegates not to ratify the Constitution until the other states agreed to amendments that would better secure the people's liberties—and Virginia's vital geopolitical and economic interests. Nor was it clear that the political conflicts that had embittered their relations in the 1780s would now be salient: Jefferson was certainly committed to promoting the state's interests from within the Washington administration; and Henry, who venerated the former commander in chief, pledged to use his enormous political influence in Virginia to promote his reform agenda in a "constitutional" way.

Henry and Jefferson might have collaborated in Richmond, and they might have forged an alliance in the early years of the Washington administration. Jefferson probed, but the rapprochement never took place. For these principled patriots deeper disagreements could not be so easily and opportunistically dismissed. As Henry gradually moved toward support of the Federalist administrations of George Washington and John Adams, Jefferson and Madison launched a crusade against the "aristocrats" and "monocrats" that led the new nation into unholy alliance with Britain and war with France. While Jefferson the party leader became a "democrat," Henry recoiled from his partisanship, fearing for the nation's survival.

V. THE PARTISAN AND THE APOSTATE

Henry and Jefferson were both republican patriots who claimed to abhor political parties. In the increasingly polarized 1790s Henry remained true to his antipartisan convictions; as he took a leading role in the emerging Democratic-Republican opposition, Jefferson feigned reluctance and protested his innocence. He had no choice but to mobilize against a high-toned federal government that betrayed powerful aristocratic and monarchical tendencies: the future of republican government in America—and across the world—hung in the balance. The catastrophe Jeffersonians predicted would make Henry a prophet. In late 1793 one of Jefferson's correspondents reported that "most of the Inhabitants of this state are true Republicans" and were beginning "to fear the truth" of Henry's observation "that th[is?] Government has an awful squinting at Monarchy."[84] But where was this "great Patriot" in his country's hour of need? Perhaps he had been premature in seeking to rekindle the Spirit of 1776 at Richmond, but now and in the years ahead the people needed to rise up in defense of their liberties against a distant and unresponsive central government. Henry was conspicuously silent.

Jefferson could explain why Henry did not rise to the challenge. Selfishly accumulating a fortune from his legal practice, Henry hired out his eloquence. Jefferson saw his own public service in these years—as Washington's secretary of state and Adams's vice president—as a great personal sacrifice that jeopardized his family's prospects. What Jefferson could not appreciate was that Henry might retreat from the public stage for patriotic reasons. Once Virginia ratified the Constitution and the Bill of Rights was adopted (however inadequate its provisions), the battle was over: Henry and his fellow Virginians must abide by the outcome and turn to peaceful pursuits. Henry thus followed the lead of the great Roman patriot Cincinnatus, and Washington would follow the same script. Henry's oratorical brilliance was his "sword," and it would now be his "ploughshare": he would deploy it for productive private purposes in order to secure the well-being of his growing family. This was a perfectly honorable thing to do, and Jefferson knew it. In insisting on Henry's avarice Jefferson may have been acknowledging his own failures as the head of a plantation household.

For his part, Henry might well question Jefferson's motives. Why would the partisan leader risk the awful consequences of disunion? "Let us not split into factions which must destroy that union upon which our existence hangs," Henry exhorted a crowd at the Charlotte County Courthouse when he stood for election to the Virginia legislature in March 1799. "Let us preserve our strength" to repel our real enemies, "the French, the English, the Germans, or whoever else shall dare invade our territory, and not exhaust it in civil commotions and intestine wars."[85] In urging his countrymen to step back from the precipice in order to save the union, Henry was echoing the warnings of Madison and his Federalist colleagues at the ratifying convention of 1788. Now Madison and Jefferson were leading the charge against the very system they had created. In response, Henry rose from his sickbed to sound the alarm, putting his life on the line (he would die in June, before taking office), not as a self-interested partisan but as a patriot.

For Jefferson the struggles of the late 1790s reenacted the imperial crisis of the 1770s. There was no "nonpartisan" middle ground: every American had to choose between liberty and slavery, true republicanism and crypto-monarchical despotism, enlightenment and the new "reign of witches."[86] For good patriots the choice was obvious. Jefferson's Republican followers—or, rather, "friends"—transcended self-interested partisanship, and their Federalist foes were enemies of the people. Henry was worse than a partisan. In his Inaugural Address, the victorious Jefferson welcomed temporarily deluded opponents back into the fold: "we are all federalists, we are all republicans."[87] But the deceased Henry could not be posthumously rehabilitated, precisely because he had once so eloquently testified to his and America's republican faith. He was an apostate.

Jefferson told biographer William Wirt that "mr Henry's apostacy, sunk him to nothing, in the estimation of his country." Federalists had hoped to exploit his "influence" with the people, but instead the unholy alliance had destroyed Henry's reputation. The sad result, Jefferson recalled, was that "a man who, through a long & active life, had been the idol of his country, beyond any one that ever lived, descended to the grave with less than it's indifference, and verified the saying of the philosopher, that no man must be called happy till he is dead."[88] Why was Jefferson so vindictive? Perhaps he knew that Henry would have dismissed his inflated claims for the so-called Revolution of 1800 as partisan bombast. Perhaps Henry would have seen Jefferson's election as the repudiation of Washington's legacy, not as redemption of the American Revolution's promise. For Henry partisanship was the negation of patriotism.

Jefferson and his allies invoked the Spirit of 1776, insisting on their undying fealty to the principles of the Declaration of Independence. If they remained true to the American creed, it was axiomatic that their opponents had lost their way and renounced their faith. By refusing to align himself with the Republicans, Henry consigned himself to the wrong side of history. Henry could not take Jefferson's long view. Emphasizing the immediate and catastrophic consequences of party divisions, he instead remained true to the patriotic spirit that had brought Virginians together in 1776 and made American independence possible. As party battles heated up in 1796, Henry explained himself in a private letter to his daughter, Betsey Aylett. Reports "you have heard of my changing sides in politics were not true."[89] What had changed was the increasingly polarized political landscape. As Republicans began to embrace the positions Henry staked out at the Richmond convention, they expected him to join their ranks.

Party divisions hardened in the wake of the Senate's narrow ratification of the controversial Jay Treaty in 1795. Republicans saw the pact with Britain as a betrayal of the alliance with France that had secured American independence; the administration, they charged, had relegated the United States to a humiliating, subordinate role in the British-led coalition against republican France. Henry agreed that the treaty was "a very bad one indeed," though he broached the heretical possibility that it might be the only realistic option. "My first principle," he told Mrs. Aylett, "is, that from the British we have every thing to dread, when opportunities of oppressing us shall offer." In the meantime, he had no patience with Republican efforts to block the treaty in the House of Representatives by refusing to authorize necessary funds for its implementation. Madison and his colleagues had not listened when Henry warned them about potential abuses of the treaty power. Now they must live with the consequences. The survival of the union—and therefore of American independence—depended on fealty to the Constitution.

Geopolitical common sense demanded accommodation. This recognition did not mean that Henry was eager to align with Britain and thus sacrifice American independence. He instead agreed with President Washington that the United States must pursue a neutral course, avoiding entanglement in European wars. Henry was deeply distressed when "our old commander-in-chief" was "most abusively treated" by Republican critics of the Jay Treaty.[90] To question Washington's patriotism was a sacrilege. The party conflict in America was not, as Republicans assumed, yet another front in the world-wide war between the forces of "democratic" progress and "aristocratic" reaction.[91] The Jay Treaty, however unsatisfactory its terms, preserved American independence by keeping the United States out of harm's way.

Republicans preached that the democratic revolution that began in America and was now crossing the Atlantic would bring an end to war and initiate a new era of peace and prosperity. Defenders of the treaty responded that republican institutions were most vulnerable during wartime. Americans therefore should steer clear of the European conflict, an embittered Washington warned in his Farewell Address, regardless of their "inveterate antipathies" and "passionate attachments." Union was the great desideratum. "It is of infinite moment, that you should properly estimate the immense value of your national Union to your collective & individual happiness." Americans should recognize and avoid the "baneful effects" of faction. The "Spirit of Party" led deluded followers to substitute their own will for the "will of the Nation": it was the perversion and negation of the spirit of American patriotism.[92] Henry could not have said it better: this is what he meant to express when he withdrew from politics. "I no longer consider myself as an actor on the stage of public life," he wrote Mrs. Aylett, "and I shall never more appear in a public character, unless some unlooked-for circumstance shall demand from me a transient effort, not inconsistent with private life—in which I have determined to continue."[93] That "unlooked-for circumstance" would arise in 1799, when Washington called on Henry to resist the Republican juggernaut in Virginia.

Washington clearly had the Republicans in mind when he condemned parties. The partisan spirit "exists under different shapes in all Governments, more or less stifled, controuled, or repressed," he asserted; "but in those of the popular form it is seen in its greatest rankness and is truly their worst enemy."[94] To Jeffersonians, Washington's belligerent language signaled a profound hostility to all forms of popular political mobilization: if unruly citizens questioned the government's legitimate, "constitutional" authority, they should be "stifled, controuled, or repressed"—and all the more severely *because* it was their government. But muzzling the people in a supposedly popular government was nonsensical, as much a self-contradiction for Republicans as the proliferation of parties in a republic was for defenders of the Washington and Adams administrations. Jefferson's solution to this conceptual conundrum was to conflate "party" and "people"—thus denying his own partisanship and validating emerging, extraconstitutional forms of popular political mobilization. He and his allies identified this party formation with the patriot mobilization that had led to independence. They too were inspired by the Spirit of 1776.

Jefferson's conception of democracy—and his growing comfort with the term itself—was the ultimate product of his engagement in party politics. From his position as party leader, he could see the "people" emerging in all their majesty as a great national monolith. His relations with his countrymen were mediated through party institutions, most importantly a robust party press, and through public pronouncements that aligned party policies and principles with the enlightened reformer's inspiring vision of the nation's destiny, which transcended partisanship.[95] The genius of Jefferson's understanding of democracy was that it simultaneously connected him with voter-citizens, fostering their ongoing and uplifting engagement in politics, while lifting him above the fray, authorizing the philosopher-statesman to conduct the nation's business. This made no sense to Patrick Henry, the antipartisan democrat. Frustrated by Henry's influence and popular resistance in his efforts to reform Virginia, Jefferson now imagined a more inclusive national community that would be more responsive to his vision. Under the aegis of a political party to end all parties, even his most stubborn opponents in Virginia would see the light. Jefferson had hoped and prayed that republican government would be an engine for moral progress; that prayer might be answered by the whole American people, pursuing happiness and fulfilling their national destiny under the Republicans' enlightened and enlightening leadership.

Jefferson's vision for America was a crucial component of the Republican Party's appeal and electoral success. It inspired a new generation of patriots to look beyond themselves and to think in the future tense. For Madison and the Federalist reformers of 1787, the "Republican remedy for the diseases most incident to Republican Government" was to increase the distance between overheated popular politics and the cooler, more refined stewardship of an enlightened national ruling class.[96] Exulting in the "mighty wave of public opinion" that had swept him into the highest office in the land, Jefferson envisioned the distance the people would travel—through the generations and across the continent—as their destiny became manifest.[97] His Inaugural Address invited Americans to take possession of their "chosen country, with room enough for our descendants to the thousandth and thousandth generation." Possessed by their vision of the nation's manifest destiny, "enlightened by a benign religion" and "adoring an overruling Providence," enterprising Americans would achieve great things and so fulfill their God-given potential.[98]

Jefferson appropriated the democratic mantle from Henry, casting the apostate into historical oblivion. While partisan supporters made the soft-spoken author of the Declaration of Independence into a democratic icon and voice of the people, the great orator withdrew from public life. "I have long learned the little value which is to be placed on popularity," Henry told his daughter, if it is "acquired by any other way than virtue."[99] The popularity of party leaders was manufactured to serve party purposes. Republicans projected their own self-interested motives onto the administration, making its supporters into a counterrevolutionary "English party" infested by "monocrats" and "aristocrats." Henry rejected such hyperbolic and divisive claims. Republicans were a party, not the "people"; their ostentatious patriotism was cynical and opportunistic.

Republicans demonized the mother country. As revolutionary France's inveterate foe, Britain epitomized everything that was evil and corrupt about the Old World. With most other Americans, Henry at first welcomed the French Revolution. But its radical turn tarnished its republican image and polarized American opinion. Jefferson devoutly believed that the French Revolution—despite its excesses—pointed the way toward the ultimate triumph of republicanism and demise of the monarchical old regime throughout Europe, including Britain. Appalled by the French Revolution's assault on Christianity, Henry feared that the contagion of irreligion would cross the Atlantic. The enlightenment that Jefferson championed made America vulnerable. "The view which the rising greatness of our country presents to my eyes," Henry told Mrs. Aylett, "is greatly tarnished by the general prevalence of deism, which, with me, is but another name for vice and depravity." Deists even claim "that I am one of the number; and, indeed, that some good people think I am no Christian." For Henry, this charge was more painful than "the appellation of tory; because I think religion of infinitely higher importance than politics." Questioning his patriotism, piety, and virtue, Henry's critics sought to alienate him from the people and destroy his "popularity."[100]

Henry was happy to call himself an "old-fashioned" democrat and man of the people. As Jefferson and his followers redefined democracy in a new era of party political mobilization, they banished Henry to a mythic past. Enlightened public opinion now triumphed over personal influence. Democracy would not be the union of patriots, animated by the Spirit of 1776, as it was for Henry. With the old regime destroyed and the machinery of republican self-government operating smoothly, Jefferson was confident that the stage was finally set for the fulfillment of his progressive enlightenment vision. The "Revolution of 1800" created a great political arena within which competing interests—and ersatz partisan patriotisms—competed for votes and power. The enlightened philosopher was bound to be disappointed. In a pluralistic political environment, the democratic mechanisms that enlightened lawgivers constructed and Jeffersonian Republicans perfected enabled the people to define and pursue their own, often unenlightened ends. Hard-pressed to sustain his democratic vision of popular enlightenment and moral improvement, Jefferson looked back to 1776 for inspiration and consolation, cherishing the patriotic spirit he and Henry had once shared.

3

Constitutions

THOMAS JEFFERSON AND JAMES MADISON

It was axiomatic for Thomas Jefferson and James Madison that the people's participation in their own government was critical to the success of the new nation's republican experiment. Yet it was unclear who the "people" were or how exactly they would participate. Membership in the new Revolutionary republics could not be taken for granted. Peoples only came into existence when provincial Anglo-Americans abjured their allegiance to King George III, organized new governments, and recognized one another as fellow citizens. Rebels against royal authority could only establish their legitimacy by performing these constitutive acts in the most solemn and authoritative fashion. Jefferson and Madison were convinced that Virginians had fallen far short of that exalted standard by failing to draft and ratify a proper constitution to replace the charter hastily adopted by the Revolutionary Convention of 1776. The great popular leader Patrick Henry thwarted their repeated efforts to promote constitutional reform; he had no doubts that his countrymen constituted a patriotic, self-governing people, notwithstanding their constitution's supposed defects.

When Jefferson left for his diplomatic assignment in Paris in 1784, Madison continued to push for reform. Jefferson was particularly gratified by his younger colleague's success in persuading the legislature to pass his Bill for Religious Freedom.[1] But Madison fared less well in other legislative struggles with Henry and his followers. Frustrated by Henryite obstruction, Madison looked to a more energetic and powerful federal government for relief from majority tyranny in Virginia and the other states. Replacing the dysfunctional Articles of Confederation with a proper constitution—drafted by a duly authorized convention and ratified by the peoples of the respective states—would check the democratic excesses that threatened to subvert state governments and destroy the union.

Madison's campaign for a new federal constitution reflected what he saw as a broad crisis of republican government in the increasingly disunited states. His faith in republicanism was sorely tested by the "multiplicity," "mutability," and "injustice" of state laws, which led him to condemn legislative majorities and their all too easily duped constituents. "Public opinion" could not temper factious majorities, he insisted, for the "opinion of the majority" was simply the "standard . . . fixed by those whose conduct is to be measured by it."[2] Madison's celebrated effort to constitute an extended republic on a continental scale affirmed his fidelity to republican principles. But it also betrayed misgivings about the people's capacity for self-government.

Factiousness would be tempered in Madison's "extended republic" by the authority of a distant federal government insulated from selfish and unruly local majorities. The regime would be republican: the people would be represented, either directly or indirectly, and their liberties secured in separate branches of the federal government that checked and balanced one another; the will of the American people would be authoritatively expressed by ratifying a new federal constitution that made them into a single people and guaranteed their independence in a dangerous world.

Madison's project resonated with the American minister in France. Jefferson recognized the urgent need to reform or replace the Articles of Confederation. But he was much more impressed—and embarrassed—by the Confederation Congress's incapacity than by the endemic factiousness that Madison thought was subverting the state republics. The "anarchy" that troubled Jefferson was the geopolitical "state of nature," which threatened to demolish the union.[3] Jefferson was no less a "nationalist" than Madison. By virtue of his position, he was more immediately concerned with the ability of the United States to function as a "treaty-worthy" nation than Madison, for whom foreign relations were a secondary concern.[4] From his distant perch in Paris, Jefferson could also view Shays' Rebellion and other agrarian disturbances with equanimity, even enthusiasm. Where Madison saw a rising tide of popular disorder, Jefferson celebrated a vigilant populace asserting its rights and exercising a vitally important censorial function over governments.

If Jefferson and Madison brought different perspectives to the critical period of the 1780s, the crisis led both of them to reaffirm their commitment to Revolutionary republican principles. Their disagreements were always cautiously expressed—or generously overlooked—and their ongoing political alliance and friendship were never in doubt. The two Virginians did not experience the "Madison problem," which has so preoccupied scholars. Their divergent perspectives generated a constructive conversation that laid the groundwork for their great collaboration in the 1790s and beyond.[5]

Madison's advocacy of a strong central government was a function of his efforts to conceptualize constitutional government on a continental scale. The failures of republican governments in the states he catalogued in his "Vices of the Political System of the United States" persuaded him that a comprehensive, top-down reform of American politics was imperative. Further efforts to amend the Articles were pointless: only by transforming the Confederation itself into a republic could the central government overcome debilitating legitimacy deficits; only when Americans constituted themselves as a single people would they be able to govern themselves.

Jefferson never doubted that patriotic Americans constituted a single people or nation.[6] The ambivalence of his initial response to the proposed constitution reflected his conviction that the republicanism of his countrymen was fixed and irreversible and that future constitutional reforms—in the states and in the union as a whole—should build on that solid foundation. His advocacy of a bill of rights and of a second convention to amend the Constitution was predicated on his faith in the durability of American republicanism. "I think our governments will remain virtuous for many centuries," Jefferson reassured a skeptical Madison in late 1787.[7] Jefferson never embraced Madison's characterization of American politics as irredeemably factious, but Madison did succeed in convincing him that ratification *without* prior amendments was urgent and imperative.[8]

Madison's and Jefferson's perspectives were complementary. The younger Virginian's great contribution was to recast their republican project on a grand, continental scale. In order to justify his radical reconstruction of American politics, Madison offered an uncharacteristically dire diagnosis of its pathological factiousness. To reverse the customary formulation, creating an "extended republic" of imperial dimensions was as much an end in itself as it was a "remedy for the diseases most incident to republican government."[9] Jefferson endorsed that expansive goal. The Constitution was "a good canvas," he told Madison, "on which some strokes only want retouching."[10] Madison got the big picture right. And with a few appropriate strokes—most notably the adoption of a bill of rights—the newly constituted American people would see themselves in that picture.

I. CONSTITUTIONAL COLLABORATORS

Jefferson's critics, in his own time and ever since, have accused him of being overly theoretical or "philosophical," prone to grand and often empty abstractions. The realistic, down-to-earth Madison is credited with exercising a calming influence over his friend, the "philosophical Legislator."[11] Jefferson's blithe comment about Shays' Rebellion—that "the tree of liberty must be refreshed from time to time with the blood of patriots and tyrants"—seems to confirm that judgment.[12] But if Jefferson's language was provocative, it also reflected a thoughtful comparative assessment of the political cultures of Old World and New. The intense engagement of Americans in their own government, occasionally leading them to challenge legitimate authority, was preferable to the oppression of the masses and much more frequent outbreak of violence in European monarchies. The "people" of the American republics were their own sovereigns: popular dissidence was predicated on the belief that their rights and vital interests were jeopardized by the abuse of power supposedly exercised in their name and for their benefit. For Jefferson, that sense of the people's active presence in and ownership of their governments was the genius of a truly republican constitution.

Madison's focus on factionalism in the critical period of constitutional reform authorized a pessimistic assessment of American political culture. The people had to be saved from themselves by being "refined" and improved by the elaborate constitutional machinery of a compound, extended republic. This was Madison's Enlightenment project: in a constitutional sense, the "people" would be produced by the regime. Americans were not an "exceptional" people animated by their virtuous commitment to the public good. What was exceptional about them was the extraordinary opportunity they had to transcend their factiousness and rise above themselves by ratifying the Constitution.

Madison leveled the people down to the lowest common denominator, asking voters to recognize that what made them equal was their irresistible natural impulse to form alliances—or factions—that would enable them to promote their own selfish interests. An evanescent majority might claim to speak for the "people," but it could never be more than a "party" or "faction"—terms that were then interchangeable. There was no such thing as "public opinion" distinct from the particular groups that sought to promote their own particular purposes; "national character" simply described the ways subjects or citizens adapted to the distribution of power in particular regimes. In Madison's reductive analysis of American politics, the "people" signified the total number of self-interested actors in the civic arena. The sum of individual parts constituted the whole.

Yet all was not lost. The success of Madison's constitutional project depended on the ability of his countrymen to recognize—and therefore rise above—their own factious tendencies. If they would only see beyond their parochial and immediate interests, they could avoid the otherwise inevitable descent into the anarchic abyss. Voters at the state ratifying conventions would now determine the fate of the union. Madison had no illusions about the self-abnegating, "classical" virtue of his fellow Americans: they were not "angels."[13] But he could help them see that their destinies were inextricably linked, and that they risked forfeiting everything the Revolutionaries had achieved at such great cost. Recognizing themselves in Madison's unflattering portrait, they would authorize a new regime that would channel and control their own factious tendencies, constructing a continental constitution from the recalcitrant and uncompromising building materials that came to hand. It was a "miracle" that the delegates who assembled at Philadelphia had been able to overcome their own diverse and conflicting interests. Their great compromises should be an inspiration to voters in the state conventions.

Jefferson saw things differently. Developments in France as well as in America led him to a much more positive assessment of the role of the "people" in the constitution of a durable republic. While the disenchanted Madison came to question the very existence of the "people," national differences became increasingly conspicuous to Jefferson. His efforts to shape public opinion in Europe by vindicating the American national character made him what we now call an "American exceptionalist."[14] Distance gave the enlightened reformer a fresh, more forgiving perspective on Virginia's defective constitution and the demoralizing "manners" of his fellow slaveholders. Comparing America with France, Jefferson looked beyond Virginia. The new nation enjoyed obvious advantages in everything from widespread literacy and political participation to wholesome gender relations and family forms: even American slavery seemed relatively benign in comparison with the misery and exploitation of the European masses.[15]

In the exciting days leading up to the French Revolution, Jefferson could imagine that the benighted peoples of France and other old regime monarchies might eventually—in the far distant future—fulfill their human potential and achieve the exalted condition of their American counterparts. But it was absurd to suggest that the French were in any meaningful sense "equal" to and interchangeable with the Americans. To do so would be to deny the world-historical significance of the American Revolution and of the uniquely fortunate circumstances of the American colonies before independence. Failure to reform the Articles and strengthen the union would jeopardize the new nation's prospects, but republicanism was firmly and irrevocably imbedded in the American national character. In 1787 Madison was so overwhelmed by the immediacy of a political and constitutional crisis that threatened to destroy everything he cherished that he lost sight of the role a spirited people had played in winning their own independence and constituting the new American republics.

In their conversation about constitutions in the critical years from 1787 to 1790, Jefferson was much better attuned than Madison to the sentiments of wary electorates fearful of radical change. Jefferson's was the voice of prudence, cautioning his younger colleague to avoid alienating skeptical voters who were determined to secure their liberties against an overly energetic, consolidated central government. For Jefferson, the republican character of a highly politicized people was the new regime's greatest asset, not a problem to be overcome by the ingenious design of complicated constitutional machinery. For Madison, the struggle to draft and ratify the Constitution was an often humbling "learning process," teaching him that there was no escape from politics and preparing him for his great collaboration with Jefferson in forging a popular opposition party in the 1790s.[16] Jefferson embraced Madison's Constitution and Madison embraced Jefferson's people as the two Virginians worked together to shape public opinion and overthrow the Federalists.

II. EXTENDING THE REPUBLIC

Madison's great contribution to American constitutionalism was to conceive of the federal union as an "extended republic." Commentators on the bookish framer's intellectual journey from commonwealth to continent generally emphasize the ways he built on—and broke with—the conventional wisdom on a republic's optimally small size. By scaling up, they argue, Madison assumed the leading role in an elite nationalist campaign against popular political forces in the states. Madison's constitutionalism thus diverged significantly—if only temporarily—from Jefferson's more consistent commitment to democracy and states' rights. There is considerable evidence for this characterization: during the campaign for a new federal constitution Madison called into question the role of the state governments, and his indictment of endemic factionalism revealed his misgivings about popular politics. But Madison's supposedly antidemocratic turn is largely a function of contingent political circumstances and a historical narrative originating in debates over the ratification of the Constitution that pitted "democracy" against "aristocracy." When Madison conceptualized the continental republic, he took his bearings from the British imperial past, not from the supposed class interests of an emerging national elite.

In the tenth number of *The Federalist,* Madison famously offered his conception of the "extended republic" as the solution to the endemic factionalism that threatened the new nation's republican experiment. According to the conventional wisdom, as articulated in Montesquieu's *Spirit of the Laws,* republican regimes were best suited to small states, in which "virtuous" peoples could sustain high levels of civic participation and govern themselves; it followed that authority was necessarily consolidated in larger states, culminating in the despotic rule of monarchs over subject populations in great empires. Madison turned Montesquieu's logic on its head. Drawing inspiration from David Hume's "Idea of a Perfect Commonwealth," Madison argued that "over-bearing," mobbish majorities inevitably subverted the "public good" in small republics. Only a "well constructed union" on an enlarged scale could "break and control the violence of faction."[17]

Hume helped Madison shift his focus from Virginia to the union as a whole and so imagine Americans collectively as a properly constituted people. Yet most Americans did not need Hume to convince them of the continental destiny of their rising republican empire. At a time when the legitimacy of state governments was eroding, liberty-loving Americans were prepared to embrace constitutional government on a continental scale. Popular devotion to the Revolutionary "common cause" transcended parochial attachments, and wartime mobilization and economic dislocation promoted extraordinary geographical and social mobility. Extending the republic was the Revolution's logical outcome—provided that the rights of ordinary Americans, including the right to participate in their own government, were adequately secured.

Convention delegates alarmed by popular tumults and "democratic despotism" in the states might be swayed by the Humean indictment of factiousness—though some, including Alexander Hamilton, were not persuaded.[18] They might also be flattered by the juxtaposition of factious local interests to their own, presumably disinterested continental patriotism. But there is scant evidence that Madison's argument for the extended republic in *The Federalist* persuaded very many wavering readers to support the Constitution.[19] Skeptics were more likely to find Madison's polemic on the volatility and instability of democratic politics countersuggestive, confirming the Antifederalist narrative of an "aristocratic" plot against the people's liberties. They might well question Madison's good faith in offering a "republican remedy" to the "mortal diseases" that supposedly had afflicted every republic, including the American states, throughout history. How republican would his extended republic actually be?

Doubts about Madison's republicanism would have been deepened had readers been privy to his original, aborted design for the Constitution. Madison was convinced, Alan Gibson persuasively argues, that the survival of the extended republic depended on the institution of a central government with the authority to "negative," or veto, state legislation.[20] Factiousness, Madison told his fellow delegates in Philadelphia, was symptomatic of the "centrifugal tendency" of a plurality of sovereign states unconstrained by a strong central government.[21] The "prerogative of the General Govt. . . . must control" the states, lest they "continually fly out of their proper orbits and destroy the order & harmony of the political System." Madison's analogy of the American political "System" to the solar system reflected his Enlightenment cast of mind—and his stunning failure to grasp political realities. Yet Madison's failed vision also testified to his enduring republican faith.

Madison first broached his proposal "to arm the federal head with a negative *in all cases whatsoever* on the local Legislatures" in letters to fellow Virginians in the weeks before the convention met.[22] This would be the same sort of authority "the K[ing] of G[reat] B[ritain] heretofore had" to review colonial laws before independence, he told Edmund Randolph.[23] As subjects of King George III, colonists had recognized the need for this royal prerogative: their allegiance was predicated on the protection he afforded them. The king was obliged to guarantee Americans' rights as Englishmen as well as their collective security; as long as this "protection covenant"—or imperial constitution—was honored and upheld, provincial Americans could think of themselves, as Jefferson put it in his draft of the Declaration of Independence, as part of "a free and a great [British] people."[24] But George III betrayed his trust and made war against his loyal subjects. Cast into a state of nature, Americans were forced to declare themselves an independent people. Before 1787, however, they failed to secure their union and collective identity as a people, leaving them vulnerable to the centrifugal tendencies Madison decried.

As a constitutional theorist, Madison reasoned impeccably; as a practical politician, he fell far short.[25] His proposed federal veto invoked the old empire as a template for constitutional reform in the new nation. Most remarkably, he seemed to endorse the *British* case for reforming the empire along consolidated lines when he invoked the language of Parliament's 1766 Declaratory Act, asserting its sovereign authority over the legislatures of the American provinces "in all cases whatsoever."[26] The difference, of course, was that Madison rejected Parliament's "unconstitutional" claims to rule the colonies as subject provinces, instead investing veto authority in the Crown. Madison's new "federal head," drawing its authority from the people's suffrage, would succeed to the sovereign authority George III had forfeited. His proposed constitution would create a republican government for the American people as a whole that fulfilled Revolutionary patriots' exalted conceptions of monarchical authority.[27] In their sovereign capacity, the people would rise above self-interested factiousness and exercise their authority impartially, securing their cherished liberties under the rule of law.

Madison's version of popular sovereignty stands in apparent contrast to Jefferson's conception of the people's continuous, active participation in their own government. A sovereign people would ascend toward "one paramount Empire of reason, benevolence and brotherly affection," as Madison later wrote in his *National Gazette* essay "Consolidation."[28] Jefferson was more intent on sustaining the vitality and legitimacy of republican government by bringing it down to the level of the sovereign people. But these differences should not be exaggerated. Popular sovereignty is an inherently ambiguous and protean construct, justifying both the concentration and diffusion of authority.[29] In their protracted conversation about constitutional government, Madison and Jefferson pushed the idea of popular sovereignty to its conceptual limits. Their democratic constitutionalism exalted the "majesty" of the people's will and the mandate it conferred on its true representatives, even as it authorized popular political mobilization—or "factiousness"—on an unprecedented scale.

Madison's most urgent imperative in the period leading up to the Constitutional Convention was to conceptualize Americans as a single people. As he did so, he focused his intellectual energy on cataloguing the "Vices of the Political System" and demonstrating, to his own satisfaction at least, that the state governments were the chief obstacles to creating a more perfect union.[30] His great theoretical breakthrough—and near breakdown—came when he embraced the "modern," unitary idea of sovereignty: the stability and ultimate survival of *any* political community depended on establishing the ultimate locus of authority. Embracing the idea did not make Madison an absolutist, for the Anglo-American constitutional tradition demonstrated that sovereign authority could be constitutionally limited. Liberty and power coexisted in his idealized vision of the old empire and could coexist again in a continental republic. But Antifederalist opponents of ratification were not inclined to make such fine distinctions; the legal supremacy of Congress—or federal judiciary—epitomized what they called "consolidation."[31]

Madison's campaign to create a constitution for the American people authorized his sustained and ultimately frustrated campaign against the state governments.[32] But his focus on factionalism in the states did not express a judgment on human nature, nor should it be seen as an indictment of popular politics. He was instead underscoring "the evil of imperia in imperio," the multiplicity of sovereign authorities in a particular state or of peoples within the bounds of a great empire.[33] Endemic factiousness was a function of the "American system" of politics, not a reflection of the people's character. The distinction was not always clear, for Madison was in fact deeply troubled by democratic excesses in the states. But his intention was reconstructive, to overcome the anarchic, antirepublican "licentiousness" of competing sovereignties by constituting a true continental republic. Patriotic Anglo-Americans had been loyal subjects of the British king, and there was no reason to doubt their allegiance to a new republican regime that would secure their individual rights and collective interests.

Sovereignty was indivisible, Madison repeatedly insisted. It was therefore axiomatic, he told Washington, "that an individual independence of the States is utterly irreconcilable with their aggregate sovereignty." Recognizing that abolishing the states would be "inexpedient" and "unattainable," Madison "sought for some middle ground." After all, "local authorities" might be "subordinately useful" to the new central government. In order "to support a due supremacy of the national authority," however, it was necessary to preempt potentially divisive initiatives by the state legislatures.[34] Madison thus persuaded himself—and sought to persuade Washington and other correspondents—that his negative on state legislation was a significant concession, "the least possible abridgement of the State Soveriegnties."[35]

Madison's "middle ground" did not offer a viable framework for serious compromise at the Philadelphia Convention. His supposed concession only made sense if the states claimed to be or were in fact becoming independent "Soveriegnties." The plain implication of his proposed scheme was that states in the reconstituted union would be subordinate administrative units, like counties in the various states.[36] Madison's advocacy of proportional representation in both houses of the new federal congress was animated by the same logic. If citizens from different states were equally represented, Congress would speak for the American people as a whole. "A Citizen of Delaware was not more free than a Citizen of Virginia," Madison told the Convention, "nor would either be more free than a Citizen of America."[37]

Madison assumed the republican high ground when he argued that citizen equality was irreconcilable with state sovereignty. But if the state governments were subjected to the "aggregate sovereignty" of a federal government in which they had no voice, representatives of Delaware and other small states rejoined, they might just as well be abolished altogether. David Brearly, of New Jersey, provocatively suggested that "a map of the U S be spread out" and all existing state "boundaries be erased, and that a new partition of the whole be made into 13 equal parts."[38] The Virginia delegation, needless to say, was not prepared to sacrifice the state's vast land claims on the altar of citizen equality in a consolidated continental republic. For Madison, national sovereignty was nonnegotiable, the fundamental principle that could not be compromised; for wary delegates at Philadelphia, sovereignty—the actual distribution of authority in a reconstituted union—was precisely what *was* being negotiated. A "more perfect union" was the best possible compromise they could craft.

Madison was deeply disappointed with the final draft of the Constitution. In his contributions to *The Federalist* and in speeches at the Virginia ratifying convention he struggled to put the best possible face on the document's potentially fatal flaws. The framers had not constituted a republic, he complained in an extraordinary letter to Jefferson in October 1787. The Constitution "presents the aspect rather of a feudal system of republics" rather "than of a Confederacy of independent States." The Constitution failed to express the sovereign will of the American people. It instead threatened to exacerbate the destructive factional conflicts among rival power centers that had brought Madison to Philadelphia in the first place.[39]

Madison's federal negative evoked a republicanized conception of monarchical authority, exercised impartially on behalf of loyal subjects. Without the negative, disorder was sure to reign. "And what has been the progress and event of the feudal Constitutions?" Madison asked Jefferson. Of course, his friend must agree, "the head and the inferior members" were doomed to struggle "until a final victory has been gained in some instances by one, in others, by the other of them." There was "a remarkable variance," however, between the Americans' misbegotten "feudal system" and the feudalism of yesteryear. Though the early modern sovereign exercised only limited authority, he was nonetheless "independent." "Having no particular sympathy of interests with the great Barons," the king would ultimately triumph over them in their "mutual projects of usurpation." The *sovereign* thus would come to embody the principle of *sovereignty,* preparing the way for the "people" to declare *their* independence and govern themselves. But "the American Constitution" threatened to reverse this progress by disuniting the people and making it impossible for them to exercise their sovereign will. "The general authority will be derived entirely from the subordinate authorities," Madison gloomily concluded. Federalism and republicanism were ultimately irreconcilable.[40]

The contrast between Madison's misgivings and Jefferson's cautious endorsement of the Constitution is striking. Madison feared the game might have been lost when the Convention failed to establish the ultimate authority of the proposed federal government. For his part, Jefferson never would support a consolidated regime that deranged the federal balance and neutered the states. In June, while the Convention was still sitting, he dismissed Madison's sovereign remedy, the federal negative, as absurdly disproportionate to the problem it was supposed to resolve. "Not more than. 1. out of 100 state-acts concern the confederacy" and should be of any concern to Congress, he told Madison. But instead of giving the central government the "1. degree of power which they ought to have" over acts that affected the union as a whole, the federal veto "gives them 99. more which they ought not to have, upon a presumption that they will not exercise the 99." Perhaps, Jefferson suggested, federal judicial review of unconstitutional state legislation would "be as effectual a remedy, and exactly commensurate to the defect."[41]

For Madison the very existence of the state governments was problematic. The one bad law out of a hundred Jefferson stipulated (certainly a low estimate by Madison's accounting) was symptomatic of an underlying pathology. Jefferson could not disagree more. The challenge, as he saw it, was to delineate the proper sphere of the states' authority, not to destroy them. The bundle of interlocking compromises that the Constitution codified represented the delegates' best effort to recalibrate the federal balance. This was the constitution that Jefferson, with some reservations, was prepared to support. It was the same compromised constitution that Madison, writing as "Publius," had to defend in his contributions to *The Federalist.*

Jefferson recognized that the Constitution was a great improvement on the Articles. He had misgivings, however, about the presidency and the absence of a bill of rights. Both reflected his overarching concern with balancing the claims of a plurality of governments, autonomous within their respective spheres and all drawing their legitimacy from the sovereign people. An overly powerful executive authority threatened the people's liberties: the president's eligibility for reelection could make him "an officer for life" (Jefferson had Washington in mind) and so pave the way for a return to monarchy.[42] The best defense of the republic was a vigilant citizenry. "A bill of rights," Jefferson lectured Madison, "is what the people are entitled to against every government on earth, general or particular, and what no just government should refuse, or rest on inference."[43] Harking back to the imperial crisis, he conjured up the threat of unchecked despotic power—or sovereignty—to American liberties.

Sovereignty was a practical political problem for Jefferson. How, he wondered, could authority be distributed in ways that enabled the people to govern effectively without jeopardizing their rights? In thrall to his theory of the extended republic, Madison answered that sovereignty was the solution, not the problem. When they ratified the Constitution, Americans secured their rights by empowering the government that made them a people. The federal government would express and enforce the people's sovereign will, offering the only efficacious remedy for the pathologies that inevitably afflicted *all* forms of government. The logic of sovereignty thus persuaded Madison that the relationship between the people and their government must be direct and unmediated. State governments with some degree of independent or autonomous authority compromised the purity of his republican design. Popular political activity within an inherently unstable system of governments was "factious," by Madison's definition, for an imperfect union of "peoples" with conflicting interests and identities could never articulate a transcendent and inclusive conception of the public good, or *res publica.*

Jefferson did not question his friend's fundamental commitment to republicanism. He recognized that Madison's sustained polemic against factiousness did not represent a counterrevolutionary rejection of popular government but instead reflected his vision of a single, self-governing people within an extended, continental republic. Jefferson embraced Madison's conception of a constitutional people, and both shared the contemporary aversion to divisive and self-interested partisanship. Yet Jefferson could only breathe a sigh of relief when the Convention rebuffed Madison's efforts to radically diminish the role of the state governments in the proposed federal system. Patriotism was not a zero-sum game: the attachment of the people to their respective states—and to the constitutions that made them into "peoples"—was the crucial predicate of more inclusive, national attachments.[44]

Madison deployed the Humean argument against factionalism to evoke the specter of unrestrained state sovereignty and clear the way for constituting the extended republic. With the failure of his negative, however, his vision of a single great continental republic was compromised. He instead had to argue that the misbegotten "feudal system" that had emerged from the Convention's compromises would sustain the balance between state and federal authority that he had originally sought to transcend. "The federal constitution," he assured readers of *Federalist* number 10, "forms a happy combination in this respect; the great and aggregate interests being referred to the national, the local and particular to the state legislatures."[45] In number 39, he asserted that the Constitution was "neither a national nor a federal constitution but a composition of both. In its foundation it is federal, not national; in the sources from which the ordinary powers of the government are drawn, it is partly federal, and partly national; in the operation of these powers, it is national, not federal; in the extent of them again, it is federal, not national; and finally, in the authoritative mode of introducing amendments, it is neither wholly federal, nor wholly national."[46] Madison's famous formulation may have been the best possible description of the Constitution, but it was conceptually incoherent. It represented the return of the confusing world of conflicting, factious interests and interpretative ambiguity that Madison the theorist had sought to escape.[47]

Madison's theory of the extended republic loomed behind his *Federalist* essays, erupting in his recurrent outbursts against factiousness. But when he was reluctantly forced to abandon the principle of federal sovereignty that animated his theory, Madison refashioned himself as a more interesting and consequential advocate of what Jeremy Bailey calls "constitutional imperfection."[48] Thrown back on the fundamental commitment to majority rule that he and Jefferson shared, Madison reconceptualized the role of the people in his constitutional design. When he celebrated the "judicious modification and mixture of the *federal* principle" into its structure, Madison begrudgingly acknowledged the independence, or "sovereignty," of the states.[49] The authority of the people did not descend from on high, but moved upward by the people's active consent, through ascending levels of government. The people were present, in all their factiousness, at all these levels.

As Publius, Madison brought the people back into his constitutional design, beginning the process of adapting the theory of the extended republic to the political realities of an expanding federal union that culminated in his polemics for the Jeffersonian-Republican opposition in the *National Gazette* in 1791–92. He sought to assuage Antifederalists' anxieties about the ways in which a consolidated, neomonarchical federal government might jeopardize their liberties—and immobilize them politically. "A dependence on the people is no doubt the primary control on the government," he acknowledged in *Federalist* number 51. Of course, the people were the ultimate source of authority, and they had the right to overthrow a despotic regime that violated their fundamental rights. But revolutions would not be necessary in a well-constituted republic, because citizens participated and therefore were present in their own government. By ratifying the Constitution, Americans would constitute themselves a people: the Constitution would be their own handiwork and therefore subject to their ongoing supervision and future amendment.[50]

The people's presence emerged only gradually over the course of Madison's contributions to *The Federalist.* Beginning with his dire diagnosis of epidemic factiousness, Madison emphasized the dangerous tendencies of misdirected popular political energy. But if at first the creation of a continental republic seemed like the obvious "remedy," the threat of concentrated power in a distant, all-powerful central government became increasingly conspicuous to liberty-loving Americans. Of course, Americans needed to be protected from one another—and from themselves. But the greatest threat would come from a remote and unresponsive governing class, or what Revolutionary republicans reflexively called "aristocracy." In his later essays, Madison argued that no such class could ever exist in a "partly federal, partly national" government with its elaborate "auxiliary precautions."[51] Divisions *within* the federal government (and the federal system as a whole) channeled factiousness in ways that secured American liberties.

In *Federalist* number 10, Madison demolished the idea that a small republic could survive without "giving to every citizen the same opinions, the same passions, and the same interests."[52] As he told Jefferson shortly before drafting that essay, "No Society ever did or can consist of so homogeneous a mass of Citizens."[53] Yet by the end of the series, Madison had conjured up an American people, "a mass of Citizens" who overcame conflicting opinions, passions, and interests in a shared commitment to the republican principles animating the Constitution. In the process, Madison had begun to overcome his contempt for state governments and small republics.[54] The genius of the new system, he argued, was that it was republican at all levels and in all its branches, either directly or indirectly. Madison thus gradually came to terms with a compromised and complicated federal system that he at first reluctantly defended. Initially, he promoted ratification out of desperation: the new constitution was a stopgap measure, better than nothing. But he ultimately came to see that the Constitution's virtues transcended its defective parts. Madison's resistance to the addition of a bill of rights reflected this much more positive assessment. Such amendments would be redundant, mere "parchment barriers." By creating a federal government of limited and delegated powers, the Constitution offered Americans ample security for their rights; it was therefore the equivalent—and superior—to bills of rights in state constitutions.[55]

Madison was by no means in perfect agreement with his senior colleague when Jefferson returned to America in late 1789, but their paths were converging.[56] Jefferson overcame misgivings about the Constitution and urged its unconditional ratification. And though Madison remained wary of democratic excesses, questioning his friend's enthusiasm for frequent elections and tactfully ignoring his rosy view of popular dissidence, he adapted his theory of the extended republic to the realities of popular politics. Madison's contribution to their future collaboration was to conceptualize constitutional government within a continental framework. Casting Americans as authors and agents of their own government, he prepared the way for Jefferson's more dynamic, democratic conception of popular political participation. Together they would transform selfish factiousness into high-minded partisanship, dedicated to upholding the new constitutional order.

III. THE PEOPLE'S CONSTITUTION

An important part of Jefferson's mission in France, as he saw it, was to defend the political character of his countrymen against the slurs of the anti-American press. The "London newspapers," he complained, were filled with reports of "mobs and riots," fabricated by hacks in the pay of the British government "to deter strangers from going to America."[57] British polemicists projected familiar images of lower-class disorder and dissidence onto the former colonies, warning of dire threats to person and property. They used the term "democracy" in a conventionally derogatory sense, as a synonym of the "anarchy" that signified the absence of government. This was not simply propaganda. Hostile observers in high government circles were convinced that the Revolution would still fail. Unruly Americans were bound to suffer the consequences of their rebellion against legitimate authority: the postwar Confederation was disintegrating, and the states would soon follow.[58]

Jefferson's determination to vindicate the American character was reinforced by troubling reports from home. The democratization of state legislatures, increasingly dominated by new men with modest backgrounds and responsive to popular constituencies, generated an antidemocratic backlash. Displaced elites yearned for some sort of restoration, perhaps even a return to monarchy.[59] "Without some alteration in our political creed," General Washington warned Madison, the "superstructure" of the Confederation, "raised at the expence of much blood and treasure, must fall. We are fast verging to anarchy & confusion!"[60] Constitutional reformers exploited such sentiments as they mobilized support across the continent for a "more perfect union." At the same time, of course, they had to persuade skeptical voters of their fidelity to Revolutionary republican principles. This was the fine line, or "tightrope," Madison sought to negotiate as Publius.[61] By diagnosing factiousness, he could distinguish the disease from the body politic; his heroic remedies would restore the republic to good health.

Jefferson did not respond in writing to Madison's polemical assault on faction. It seems likely, however, that he avoided using the term because of its association with key words in the ministerial arsenal of anti-American abuse. To say Americans were "factious" was to characterize them as unruly and riot prone; to argue that their factiousness was a function of defective constitutions was to call into question the American contribution to the progress of political civilization. "With all the defects of our constitutions, whether general or particular," Jefferson exclaimed to a Virginia correspondent, "the comparison of our governments with those of Europe are [*sic*] like a comparison of heaven and hell."[62] As Madison's coadjutor in a long-term campaign to reform Virginia's constitution, Jefferson was certainly eager to rectify these "defects." But advocates of the federal constitution seemed all too determined to wipe the slate clean and erect the "superstructure" of a more powerful central government on an entirely new foundation. Most disturbingly, their assault on the supposed excesses of popular politics in the states echoed—and seemed to justify—anti-American polemics in the British press.[63]

Jefferson's ambivalence about the value of foreign travel reflected anxiety about antirepublican, aristocratic tendencies at home and the seductive appeal of the aristocratic way of life for visitors to Europe. Impressionable young Americans, male and female, should stay at home; once their republican characters were fully formed, mature Americans would come to share Jefferson's horror at the exploitation, misery, and degradation of old regime society. They could be edified and enlightened by the glories of European civilization without risking their republican souls. Jefferson thus urged Madison and James Monroe to take the trip: their fresh perception and appreciation of their heavenly homeland would strengthen their commitment to its republican creed.[64] They would recognize the moral superiority of American family life, grounded in consensual and affectionate marital ties and cultivating successive generations of good citizens. They would agree with Jefferson that that the exalted character of the American people was the foundation of republican constitutions that drew the admiration of enlightened Europe and called into question the legitimacy and survival of its despotic governments.[65]

Jefferson is famous for his stark, binary oppositions. The distinction he drew between New World and Old, "heaven and hell," is exemplary. Yet if this Manichean cast of mind could blind him to complexity and nuance, it also helped him to see through and beyond the conventional wisdom of friend and foe alike. His campaign to vindicate the character of the American people is a classic case in point. While Madison focused obsessively on factious behavior, Jefferson's wide-angle view enabled him to generalize from more comprehensive data and reach far different conclusions: by his account, Americans were much *less* prone to rioting and mob action than their European counterparts. Shays' "rebellion in Massachusets"—an armed insurgency of distressed taxpayers in the western part of the Commonwealth—"has given more alarm than I think it should have done," Jefferson wrote Madison and other correspondents in late 1787. "Calculate that one rebellion in 13 states in the course of 11 years, is but one for each state in a century and a half." The comparison with France was striking. "With all it's despotism, and two or three hundred thousand men always in arms," Jefferson wrote, France "has had three insurrections in the three years I have been here in every one of which greater numbers were engaged than in Massachusets and a great deal more blood was spilt."[66]

The American advantage, Jefferson plausibly inferred, reflected the closer and more harmonious relation between the people and their governments under their republican constitutions. The low incidence of popular political violence was obviously a good measure of the people's welfare, or "happiness." Jefferson further insisted on a qualitative as well as a quantitative difference between popular uprisings in Europe and America. Turning Madison's dire diagnosis on its head, he argued that Shays' Rebellion signified civic good health: engaged citizens had a right to demand responsive government. "What country can preserve it's liberties," Jefferson asked John Adams's son-in-law, William Stephens Smith, "if their rulers are not warned from time to time that their people preserve the spirit of resistance?"[67] In Europe, riots reflected the desperation and misery of oppressed peoples. According to Voltaire's famous formulation, cited approvingly by Jefferson, they were like the "anvil," seeking relief from the "hammer" blows of rapacious and despotic rulers.[68]

Anti-American critics equated democracy with mob rule. Jefferson replied that "mobs," in the European sense, did not exist in the United States. Americans were law-abiding because they made their own laws. "There is not a country on earth where there is greater tranquillity, where the laws are milder, or better obeyed," Jefferson told his dear friend Maria Cosway. The explanation for this happy state of affairs was the independence and self-sufficiency of individual citizens. There was no place in the civilized world "where every one is more attentive to his own business, or meddles less with that of others: where strangers are better received, more hospitably treated, and with a more sacred respect."[69] As they cultivated their own properties, Americans developed a healthy regard for their own rights and a corresponding respect for the rights of their neighbors.

The broad distribution of property and a widely dispersed agricultural population fostered rights-consciousness and the rule of law in the new American republics. "The mobs of great cities" were conspicuously absent in America, Jefferson reassured readers of his *Notes on the State of Virginia:* those cities and their mobs "add just so much to the support of pure government, as sores do to the body politic."[70] Far from being diseased, as Madison suggested, the American body politic was fundamentally healthy. When citizens or their elected representatives gathered, they did not lose themselves—and their minds—in factious mobs or crowds. Their political character was formed at home, in the "natural" attachments of family relations and the business of household management. Jefferson believed that naturally sociable individuals were endowed with a moral sense that flourished in republican America. Political participation enabled vigilant citizens to secure their autonomy and promote their collective interests.[71]

Jefferson's celebration of popular politics stood in stark contrast to Madison's indictment of demagoguery and factiousness. For Jefferson, a "spirit of resistance" to abuses of authority brought liberty-loving citizens together, giving them a clearer sense of their rights. The Revolution marked the original, character-forming moment for Americans as a people. Had patriots been rational, self-interested calculators, they would have balked at independence: they had too much to lose, including their lives. But "hearts" triumphed over "heads," enabling Americans to transcend profound divisions in their dedication to the common cause. Jefferson's revolutionary people was not a *mob:* it was the mirror image of Madison's *faction.* "If our country, when pressed with wrongs at the point of the bayonet, had been governed by it's heads instead of it's hearts," Jefferson asked Cosway, "where should we have been now? hanging on a gallows as high as Haman's."[72] By overcoming the "lethargy" and ignorance that sustained despotic regimes, Revolutionary patriots provided inspiring examples of good citizenship for future generations.

Jefferson acknowledged that the people might sometimes be misinformed and their resistance unjustified. "The people can not be all, and always, well informed," he told William Stephens Smith. "The part which is wrong will be discontented in proportion to the importance of the facts they misconceive. If they remain quiet under such misconceptions it is a lethargy, the forerunner of death to the public liberty." Shaysites thus were following a patriotic script when they mobilized against the Commonwealth's tax gatherers in defense of their farms and families. Their resistance communicated crucially important information about the impact of apparently misguided policies. Authorities should explain and justify those policies, while mitigating the damage they inflicted. “The remedy” he prescribed to Smith was “to set them right as to facts, pardon and pacify them.”[73]

Jefferson elaborated the medical metaphor when he assured Madison that “a little rebellion now and then is a good thing, and as necessary in the political world as storms in the physical.” The survival of despotic regimes depended on brutally suppressing popular dissidence and convincing the people that they had no rights. But it was incumbent on “honest republican governors” to be “so mild in their punishment of rebellions, as not to discourage them too much. It is a medecine necessary for the sound health of government.”[74]

For Jefferson, the pathologies of republican government proceeded from natural causes and, if properly diagnosed, would be self-correcting. Republican government should be transparent, legible to the people and responsive to their concerns; as they scrutinized the conduct of public servants, vigilant citizens would guarantee good government.[75] “Cherish therefore the spirit of our people,” he enjoined Edward Carrington, “and keep alive their attention,” for they “are the only censors of their government.” The greatest threat to republicanism was that complacent and preoccupied citizens would become depoliticized and withdraw from public life.

Shays’ Rebellion reaffirmed Jefferson’s faith in the American people. The rebels displayed a love of liberty and a willingness to die that had formed the character of “our people” in the crucible of the Revolution. The contrast with European regimes was stark: “under pretence of governing they have divided their nations into two classes, wolves and sheep.” The Shaysites were not sheep, and their grievances demanded a respectful hearing. The appropriate remedy was education and enlightenment, not the heavy hand of despotic power. Not coincidentally, Jefferson famously opted for newspapers over government in his letter to Carrington: “Were it left to me to decide whether we should have a government without newspapers, or newspapers without a government, I should not hesitate a moment to prefer the latter.”

Properly constituted republican governments depended on the circulation of political information. A well-informed, self-governing people would not be driven to the desperate measures taken by the rebels in Massachusetts. But before the “tree of liberty” was firmly rooted in American soil, patriot blood would nurture, or “manure,” its growth, as Jefferson so provocatively put it to Smith. Bloodshed was not the inevitable concomitant, or overhead cost, of popular politics. It instead marked the failure of *one* American republic to respond in a timely fashion to the people's legitimate concerns—as it soon would, in the rebellion's aftermath.[76] The republican "experiment" was unfolding in the thirteen states and in subordinate jurisdictions as well, testing an array of constitutional models and offering multiple sites for citizen engagement. Jefferson emphasized the national character that emerged from, depended on, and ultimately transcended this diversity. Madison reached the opposite conclusion: where Jefferson saw a single American people, Madison saw a multiplicity of conflicting factions. This was why he thought it so imperative to establish a strong central government.

Madison's campaign for a more energetic and effective national government prompted Jefferson—and Antifederalist critics of the proposed charter—to look back to 1776, to a time when a (supposedly) united people rose up in arms against a distant and despotic royal government. For Jefferson and like-minded patriots, there was no question that Americans then constituted a single people. Ministerial writers might call the Americans "rebels," juxtaposing the factiousness and licentiousness of the small minority of demagogic leaders and their deluded followers to the great majority of loyal and passive Anglo-American subjects. Outraged patriots rejected and reversed this characterization, silencing, ostracizing, and driving factious "enemies of the people" into exile. In declaring independence, Americans became conscious of their collective identity as a people. Oblivious critics of the Revolution did not recognize the ties that bound Americans to one another, enabling them to transcend their differences. For a moment, at least, they shared "the same opinions, the same passions, and the same interests."

The great question was whether that unity could be sustained. With the war won, Jefferson worriedly predicted in his *Notes on the State of Virginia,* "we shall be going down hill." Because political leaders would no longer need "to resort to the people for support," they would be "forgotten" and "their rights disregarded." For their part, the people "will forget themselves, but in the sole faculty of making money, and will never think of uniting to effect a due respect for their rights."[77] The alienation of the people from one another and from their governments jeopardized the republican experiment in America. But Shays' Rebellion was a hopeful portent: when provoked, Americans would still unite to defend their rights; they would not be forgotten. The moral Jefferson drew from disturbances in Massachusetts thus had broad significance for constitutional reform on a continental scale. Of course, reformers had to reassure voters that their rights would be secure under the proposed system. Jefferson also suggested, however, that the new regime's legitimacy and longevity depended on incorporating a spirited, politically active citizenry into the ordinary, ongoing business of government. A new continental constitution was certainly necessary: without one, the union would fall apart and the American people cease to exist. The new constitution could only survive and flourish if the people recognized it as *theirs,* and not a project designed to serve particular classes, interests, or factions.

Jefferson's democratic constitutionalism was shaped by developments in France as well as at home. The fiscal crisis of the French monarchy precipitated a broader constitutional crisis, in which the "people" emerged as a distinct, self-conscious force. For Jefferson, the great achievement of the American Revolution was to create a free and independent people who would show the world that they—and peoples everywhere—were capable of self-government. Viewed from afar, Shays' Rebellion vindicated his faith in the American people. As long as the spirit of liberty endured, Americans would preserve the precious legacy of their independence. Jefferson could justify "a few lives lost" because of his confidence in the republican character of the people and their genius for self-government.[78] Jefferson was not bloodthirsty. When tremors of change awakened the French people to their rights, there would, he predicted, be a peaceful, bloodless revolution—a "revolution in the public opinion"—that would produce a new constitution.[79] The French would follow the lead of constitutional reformers in America.

There could be no "public opinion," as it is now understood, until there was a more or less autonomous "people" capable of possessing it. Jefferson's first use of the term, in his January 1787 letter to Carrington, was "conjectural," celebrating the role of opinion among "those societies (as the Indians) which live without government" and who "enjoy in their general mass an infinitely greater degree of happiness than those who live under European governments." Among the Indians, "public opinion is in the place of law, and restrains morals as powerfully as laws ever did any where." European nations, by contrast, suffered from a surfeit of oppressive laws. Zealous in defense of their property rights, Americans could not emulate Indians and live without law. Self-governing Americans avoided these extremes, making laws that benefited them individually and collectively. "The basis of our governments being the opinion of the people," Jefferson concluded, "the very first object should be to keep that right."[80]

Over the subsequent years, Jefferson excitedly reported, the French began to follow the American example. Though his enthusiastic support for the French Revolution is usually seen as a mark—or the source—of his "radicalism," his response to ongoing events in Paris points in another, more complicated direction.[81] "In the course of three months," he wrote John Adams in August, "the royal authority has lost, and the rights of the nation gained, as much ground, by a revolution of public opinion only, as England gained in all her civil wars under the Stuarts."[82] Jefferson looked to Anglo-American history for the appropriate interpretative framework. Over the centuries, the English had successfully struggled to make monarchy serve the public interest. American patriots sought to participate in the benefits of constitutional monarchy, but George III foolishly refused to be king on American terms and ended up forfeiting a great empire. Surely the French king, Louis XVI, would want to serve the interests of loyal subjects and strengthen their attachment to him. The happy outcome Jefferson thus envisioned for France was a British-style monarchy, governing in tandem with the people's representatives in a national legislature.[83]

Jefferson had no illusions about the political capacity of the French masses: they were far from ready to govern themselves, or to mobilize on a national basis to overthrow the old regime. He took heart, however, from the enlightened views of the privileged and powerful people he knew best in France. For Jefferson the idea of "public opinion" invoked the sentiments of this increasingly influential class—the civil society of the old regime—and an inspiring vision of the emergent nation. He was convinced that the French fiscal crisis would climax in a constitution that would redefine the relationship between king and people. "The nation is pressing on fast to a fixed constitution," Jefferson wrote Washington in May 1788. "Such a revolution in the public opinion has taken place that the crown already feels it's powers bounded, and is obliged by it's measures to acknowlege limits."[84] In the process of this great struggle the fragments of old regime society coalesced and became conscious of their shared interests and identity. "At some epoch not distant," the Estates General would meet, and the French people would assert their claims against the Crown. The bloodless "revolution" would be complete.

Jefferson proved to be a notoriously poor prophet. As the French Revolution lurched violently through successive regime changes, "rivers of blood" flowed.[85] European devastation cast a disturbing light on his enthusiastic commentary on popular uprisings in America. Yet Jefferson remained convinced that the nation-making "revolution of public opinion" in both the United States and France was peaceful and progressive: self-governing peoples under republican constitutions would only make war in their own defense. The counterrevolutionary "Conspiracy of kings" brought on the European bloodbath.[86] In America, the successful conclusion of the campaign for constitutional reform secured peace in the disintegrating union. Both Jefferson and Madison recognized that such a "peace plan" for the American state system was absolutely imperative. Jefferson also recognized that republican government on a continental scale faced a fundamental and ongoing crisis of legitimacy. His answer was to mobilize the people and sustain their spirited engagement in their own government. Jefferson would thus exploit the factiousness—or spiritedness—that Madison originally had sought to suppress.

The articulation of public opinion enabled the people to be an ongoing force in government as well as its original source. A robust, ever-vigilant public opinion would sustain the vital connection between the people that the new constitution had brought into being and their government. It would help solve the fundamental problem of size and legitimacy in Madison's "extended republic." Rather than feeling "veneration" for a distant, all-powerful central authority, the people would see themselves in their own governments, at all levels.[87] At the same time, however, their presence and voice would be mediated, therefore cool and collected. The people were not a riotous mob, prone to spontaneous combustion. They would keep instead the "sacred fire of liberty" burning by upholding the rule of law. Their dedication to the Constitution would make democracy possible.

IV. GENERATIONS

Over the course of the campaign to draft and ratify the Constitution, Jefferson and Madison conceived of the character of the American people and their role in the expanding federal republic in contrasting ways. Overlooking the endemic factionalism that Madison feared would subvert state governments and destroy the union, Jefferson celebrated the spirit of the people. The coincidental "revolution in the public opinion" in France provided an optimistic framework for interpreting American developments that ratification of the Constitution ultimately vindicated. Madison and his allies were able to direct the current of public opinion in a progressive direction, thus overcoming "factious" opposition and widespread skepticism about their own good faith. Ratification logically led Madison to embrace Jefferson's narrative of democratic constitutional change. When the American people, acting through their state conventions, ratified the Constitution, they became its true authors. The people had made the Constitution, and they could revise it to suit their changing needs.

Jefferson explored the broad implications of his democratic constitutionalism in an extraordinary letter to Madison from Paris in September 1789. Jefferson famously told Madison that the "earth belongs in usufruct to the living" and then went on to elaborate his conception of generational sovereignty.[88] According to calculations he based on mortality tables, a new generation appeared roughly every nineteen years, and its coming of age should be marked by drafting a new constitution. This was not, of course, a description of demographic reality, but rather a provocative thought experiment designed to illuminate the fundamental principles of political society. Preoccupied with the practical business of organizing the new federal government, Madison had little inclination to indulge Jefferson's theoretical fancies. The two men did spend some time together after Jefferson's return from France in November, when Madison recruited his friend to serve in Washington's cabinet as the first secretary of state. Evidently the generation theme did not come up in conversation.[89] Madison only responded to Jefferson's letter in February, politely but dismissively.[90] It might be easy for Jefferson to theorize about writing a new constitution every nineteen years, but it was a prospect the "father" of the recently ratified federal constitution could not happily contemplate.

The exchange between Jefferson and Madison has inspired much excellent scholarship.[91] Focusing on the immediate context, most writers understandably highlight the contrasting perspectives of the "philosophical legislator" and the practical politician. By most accounts, Madison makes the most sense. Jefferson's call for a periodic return to first principles was a prescription for "anarchy" and "licentiousness," exacerbating endemic factiousness and "subverting the very foundation of Civil Society." Jefferson insisted on the right of each generation, "by the law of nature," to determine its own destiny, freed from the past's dead hand: "one generation is to another as one independant nation to another."[92] But generations only existed in Jefferson's mind, not in the real world. Starting all over again "at the end of a given term" risked the "consequences of an interregnum," Madison replied. In this period of no government, or state of nature, the "voice of the majority" could no longer bind the minority: majority rule was predicated on a "compact founded on utility," not on natural law.[93]

Jefferson's theory was based on his idiosyncratic conception of the "generation." In Madison's world of endless conflict among competing factions, no such thing as the generation could possibly exist. Pretending that it did would have disastrous consequences, dissolving all the attachments and obligations that enabled individuals to escape their brutal natural state. "No person born in Society, could on attaining ripe age, be bound by any Acts of the majority," Madison concluded, "and either a unanimous renewal of every law would be necessary, as often as a new member should be added to the Society, or the express consent of every new member be obtained to the rule by which the majority decides for the whole."[94]

Refusing to suspend disbelief, Madison could easily demolish Jefferson's theoretical edifice. Jefferson undoubtedly anticipated Madison's criticism. The point of his exercise was not to plan for another constitutional convention that would undo his friend's hard work and thus precipitate another, potentially violent regime change. To the contrary, Jefferson was charting an agenda for popular political engagement that would guarantee the new constitution's continuing legitimacy and efficacy. If the people's engagement was essential for the Constitution's enduring success, it was also true that the future of popular self-government depended on the Constitution. Jefferson's letter to Madison explored these reciprocal connections, sketching out the broad ideological framework for party political mobilization in the 1790s. Jefferson's ideas had practical implications that Madison recognized and developed in his *National Gazette* essays.

Jefferson's challenge was to make the idea of popular sovereignty practically meaningful. The compromises to his original design for the Constitution that Madison had been forced to accept represented the crucial first step in this direction. In the "partly national, partly federal" regime authorized by the Convention, the state governments would continue to be important sites of political activity, thus serving as mediating links in a chain of authority originating in the people. Madison originally intended to minimize these links, so insulating the new national government from the endemic factiousness that jeopardized property relations and social order in the states. His idea of the American people or nation was abstracted from—and in opposition to—popular politics. Following the maxim of "divide and rule," he hoped to suppress factions and immobilize the people.[95] Jefferson pushed back, calling for *more* popular political participation. The broad distribution of authority in a federal regime would bring the people closer to their government—and to one another. When the people divided the government, *they* would rule.

Jefferson's argument for generational sovereignty represented an important contribution to the development of his democratic constitutionalism. His idea of the "generation," like that of the "people," only made sense within a constitutional framework. Madison was quite right: there is no such thing in nature, and Jefferson certainly knew this. But this is equally true of a "people," whose collective identity is an artifact of their distinctive history or, as in the case of Americans, of their deliberate choice. "Sovereignty" was also a social construction, as we would say, not a naturally occurring phenomenon. American patriots recognized this when they declared their "independence," so invoking yet another term of art. Jefferson understood that all these terms were closely related: their ambiguous, apparently promiscuous deployment reflected efforts to stabilize and fix meanings in an era of rapid conceptual change.[96]

When Americans drafted and ratified constitutions, they were defining the terms they would live by. If the people made the Constitution, the Constitution made the people. And they could also constitute themselves into distinct "generations," each possessing the same authority that Americans exercised in 1776 and again in 1787–88. Successive generations seized the moment, and those moments constituted the nation's history. It could also be said, with equal plausibility, that the moment made the generation.

In Jefferson's assertion that "between society and society, or generation and generation, there is no municipal obligation, no umpire but the law of nature," the cascading analogies seem strained beyond common sense.[97] Yet

Jefferson moved logically from man in his most natural form of association, or "society," to the highly artificial and conventional "law of nature and nations" governing relations among supposedly civilized modern states. Imagining generations in a state of war illuminated the fundamental challenge to the success of the new nation's republican experiment. "Tacit assent" to the outmoded, antiquated constitutions and laws of previous generations was incompatible with the living generation's self-government. "The dead have neither powers nor rights" over the living. Submitting to the hereditary claims of monarchical and aristocratic regimes enabled their dead founders to rule living subjects from their graves. The foundational principle of equal rights should be applied through time, between generations, as well as across space, among citizens within the living generation.

The idea of generations came naturally to Americans. In a society in which landowning farmers and planters enjoyed an extraordinary degree of autonomy, each household could be seen as a patriarchal republic, with property and authority passing from father to son. Political and military mobilization promoted solidarity among "sons of liberty," linking family to family and emphasizing the ties of brothers-in-arms in the Revolutionary struggle against King George III, the despotic father figure. Radical republicans distinguished between "society"—grounded in the natural, spontaneous attachments that created families and drew them together—and "government"—the arbitrary, unnatural rule of a few privileged families over all the rest.[98] When the living generation threw off the dead hand of the past and declared independence, the distinction between society and government disappeared. Under well-designed republican constitutions, successive generations would secure their own independence by reaffirming their patriotic ties to one another and their obligations to future generations. If it was natural for one father to provide for the future independence of his sons, it was equally natural for all fathers acting collectively—as a *constitutional* generation—to provide for their sons, the rising generation.

The crucial point for Jefferson was that the living generation would be continuously active in politics, whether as voters, officeholders, or "censors" assessing the government's performance. The generational cycle of constitution writing would renew and sustain political engagement, preempting dangerous concentrations of power. Madison worried about an anarchic "interregnum" as one constitutional regime gave way to another; Jefferson insisted that continuous popular political activity would guarantee peaceful transfers of power. Standing outside government, the "people" provided the stabilizing force in a constitutional republic: they could initiate a "revolution" in government by constitutional means, without recourse to violence. Despite the absence of constitutional forms of collective action in France, Jefferson witnessed a peaceful "revolution in public opinion" there that promised to transform its constitution. Jefferson's French friends faced formidable obstacles to reform, for they would have to dismantle a "whole catalogue" of privileged interests and "hereditary orders" in church and state that were incompatible with his principle of generational sovereignty. The contrast with America, where there was no deeply entrenched old regime to overthrow, was striking. Jefferson predicted that the "public opinion" of an enlightened vanguard in France would work wonders; he feared that the complacency of an ill-informed, disengaged public in America would jeopardize everything the American Revolution had achieved.

Applying the principle of generational sovereignty in America therefore would not entail radical changes. This was instead Jefferson's prescription for keeping the "old spirit of 1776" alive and preserving the civic health of republics that depended on engaged and vigilant citizens.[99] The authority of the American people to write their own constitutions and their capacity for self-government were already well established: the success of Madison's campaign for a federal constitutional reform testified to the emergence and progressive enlightenment of a national political public. The challenge was to sustain political engagement on a continental scale. The solution Jefferson proposed to Madison was to mobilize Americans on a regular basis to renew their fundamental attachments to one another. Each successive generation would reenact the Revolution, modeling itself on the first revolutionary generation. Conscious of its own mortality, the "living" generation would be spurred to action on behalf of its successors.

V. FACTION TO PARTY

Jefferson's conception of the generation was a template for party political mobilization. The patriots of 1776 were a "party" in this exalted sense, a generation that forged its identity in the struggle against monarchical despotism. Their dedication to constitutional government and the rights of man lifted them above the sordid machinations of the self-interested "factions" that Madison railed against. In practice, the distinction between party and faction hinged on the plausibility of high-minded professions: one man's party was another's faction. In a June 1792 letter to Madison, Jefferson thus excoriated his nemesis Hamilton for "daring to call the republican party *a faction*" in newspaper essays defending the proposed national bank.[100] Jefferson and Madison had no doubts about their own disinterested motives. The "republican" designation signified devotion to the pure principles of disinterested patriotism. Theirs was a party devoted to the public good.[101]

As party divisions threatened to rip the country apart later in the decade, Republicans insisted that they spoke for the whole people.[102] Jefferson's old friend John Page contrasted the "infernal Spirit" of the Federalists—"that Spirit which in all Countries & in all Ages has been found inflating agitating & infatuating Factions against the Liberty & true Interests of the People"—and "the celestial Spirit which influences [the] pure patriotic Party" of the Jeffersonian-Republicans. "The truely virtuous," Page exhorted, "should firmly unite & form a Party capable at all Times of frustrating the wicked Designs of the Enemies of the Doctrine of Equallity & the Rights of Man."[103] Of course, credulous citizens were easily led astray. But factiousness, Jefferson insisted, was not the "natural" condition of the people under republican governments. It was instead symptomatic of corrupt, self-dealing, antirepublican tendencies within governing elites that brought on yet another "long train of abuses" under Federalist rule. As Republicans mobilized in the 1790s, they sought to revive "the celestial Spirit" of their Revolutionary predecessors. They thought of themselves in generational terms.

When Jefferson elaborated his generational-sovereignty theme to Madison in 1789, he could have no idea that he would play a leading role in forming a "Party of the People" in opposition to the administration he soon joined.[104] Jefferson had every intention of supporting the new federal constitution, as ratified and amended. Yet when he proclaimed that the "earth belonged *in usufruct* to the living," he articulated the fundamental justification for partisan mobilization. Defining the "people" in relation to *their* constitution in generational terms, he cast ordinary citizens as the authors and active agents of their own government.

The Constitution enabled citizens to monitor the new administration's performance according to strict construction of its delegated powers and of their own rights. The crucial conceptual distinction between "people" and "government" thus was mediated by the Constitution. Through the ongoing operation and periodic renewal of their Constitution, the people became more than an abstraction or legitimating fiction. The living generation became conscious of itself in the sequence of generations, past and future, and therefore of its urgent and momentous responsibilities. Most momentous of all was the obligation to preserve the constitutional republic itself.

Jefferson's ultimate goal was to sustain republican government through future constitutional revision and regime change. The ratified Constitution provided the original framework within which a constitutional people emerged on a national, continental scale. Identifying with that people, Republicans justified constitutional mobilization against the new federal government: Jefferson's generation became Madison's party. The essays Madison contributed to the *National Gazette* from late December 1791 through the following year offered a compelling ideological rationale for forming a great, nationwide political party.[105] Elaborating on themes Jefferson first developed in letters from France, Madison launched a campaign to enlighten and energize the American political public.

The origins of party conflict in the first Washington administration have been exhaustively chronicled. Treasury secretary Hamilton's controversial fiscal policies, loose construction of the Constitution, and conspicuous solicitude for creditors raised troubling questions for cabinet colleague Jefferson and congressman Madison about the character of the new regime. Hamilton's successes belied Madison's efforts to assuage Antifederalist anxieties by adding the Bill of Rights to the Constitution, and Congress proved alarmingly ineffectual in resisting administration initiatives. The only hope for the embattled Virginians was to mobilize the people at large, or "out-of-doors." By shaping and directing public opinion, self-styled "republicans" could counteract consolidationist tendencies within the federal government. If the national character were sufficiently republican, the regime would be republican. But Madison recognized that the American character was not yet fixed. There was work to be done.

Public opinion was both the subject and the object of the *National Gazette* essays.[106] By writing *about* public opinion Madison sought to make readers fully aware of—and capable of expressing—their own sentiments.

"The Republican party," he wrote, was "conscious that the mass of people in every part of the union, in every state, and of every occupation must at bottom be with them, both in interest and sentiment."[107] With the progress of political enlightenment, the republican part would become the American whole: eventually, the people would come to know itself. "How devoutly is it to be wished, then, that the public opinion of the United States should be enlightened; that it should attach itself to their governments as delineated in the *great charters,* derived not from the usurped power of kings, but from the legitimate authority of the people." American constitutions were "political scriptures" that must be secured against any augmentation or diminution with "holy zeal."[108] Strictly construed, the Constitution would sustain the balance between the people and their government.

Enlightened public opinion would empower the people. When Madison wrote that "public opinion sets bounds to every government," he was expressing the conventional wisdom. But when he added that it "is the *real* sovereign in every free one," he was throwing down the partisan gauntlet, exhorting republicans to challenge the authority of the Washington administration.[109] Jefferson anticipated that public opinion would transform the French constitution; Madison now claimed that it was "the force of public opinion" that upheld "the boasted equilibrium" of the British constitution. The problem was that—as of yet—the boastful British were too enamored of their partly republican, partly monarchical regime. "If a republican form of government were preferred," he asked, "how could the monarch resist the national will?"[110] A parallel question was implied: was it the will of the American people to uphold their republican constitution, or would they regress to some sort of British-style mixed regime? What, then, was the point of the American Revolution?

When patriots rallied to the common cause, as they did in the Revolution, they exercised irresistible force. "Philosophy has been searching, and humanity . . . sighing" for a government that derived its "energy from the will of the society."[111] The people's presence in the government was the genius of republicanism. Echoing Jefferson, Madison put the framers' (and therefore his own) contribution in perspective: "the partitions and internal checks of power" in the Constitution certainly merited "eulogies," but "they are neither the sole nor the chief palladium of constitutional liberty. The people who are the authors of this blessing, must also be its guardians."[112] As patriots stepped forward, they would simultaneously affirm their identity with fellow patriots, honor the memory of the Revolutionary fathers, and secure the liberty of succeeding generations. Mobilizing in defense of the Constitution, they would see that the distinction between "enemies and friends to republican government" was the only one that mattered. Working to promote "a general harmony among the latter, wherever residing, or however employed," they would transcend "circumstantial and artificial distinctions" and become a great, self-governing people.[113]

Madison situated the emergence of the Republican Party in the context of Revolutionary history. There were two prior moments when patriots had mobilized in defense of their liberties and formed a party, not a faction. The first had pitted "those who espoused the cause of independence" against "those who adhered to the British claims"; the drafting of the federal constitution "gave birth to a second and most interesting division of the people" that "was terminated by the regular and effectual establishment of the federal government in 1788." In both cases, Americans had faced a profound, existential crisis. Would the people be able to vindicate the independence they had declared in 1776? Would they ratify the Constitution and so preserve and perfect the union that had made them a people? Now, Madison announced, a "third division . . . has arisen" out of controversy over the "administration" of the new federal government.

Yet again, the very existence of a self-governing people was at stake. Whether out of self-interest or from an impulse to dominate, Federalists in the administration and their supporters had "debauched themselves into a persuasion that mankind are incapable of governing themselves." They were convinced that "government can be carried on only by the pageantry of rank, the influence of money and emoluments, and the terror of military force." Federalists constituted the most dangerous sort of faction. Under the plausible cover of the Constitution, this small and insidious minority captured the machinery of the people's government and turned it against them. The Republicans, like earlier generations of patriots, sounded the alarm. "Believing in the doctrine that mankind are capable of governing themselves, and hating hereditary power as an insult to the reason and an outrage to the rights of man," Madison and like-minded "friends" rallied the people in constitutional resistance to the antirepublican "aristocrats" and "monocrats" who infested the administration. A "revolution in public opinion" would redeem the people's Constitution, preempting recourse to violent means in defense of the liberties it was meant to secure.

Madison's *National Gazette* essays constituted a precocious prospectus for party building. Early divisions within the new national governing class did not yet resonate with fragmented, state-based political publics. But Madison anticipated the shape of things to come, as public opinion coalesced in a great partisan conflict over the new nation's place in a world turned upside down by the French Revolution. Republicans who identified with the French "sister republic" could turn back to Madison's essays for a road map into the future. It was uncertain then "whether the republican or the rival party will ultimately establish its ascendance," and that uncertainty deepened in subsequent years. "On one hand experience shews that in politics as in war, stratagem is often an overmatch for numbers," and the looming prospect of war itself strengthened the hand of government.[114]

Throughout the 1790s, Federalists exploited the reflexive—Republicans would say, unthinking—patriotism of the American people. At the same time, however, military mobilization and the burdens it imposed energized the Republicans' countermobilization. Even in the darkest hours of what Jefferson called the Federalist "reign of witches," Republicans kept the faith.[115] The American people would come to their senses and see the light. If they failed to do so, there was no hope for republican self-government anywhere on earth. Madison's *National Gazette* essay "State of Parties" in 1792 struck characteristically anxious and urgent notes in looking to the future. "The superiority of numbers is so great, their sentiments are so decided, and the practice of making a common cause, where there is a common sentiment and common interest, in spight of circumstancial and artificial distinctions, is so well understood," he wrote, "that no temperate observer of human affairs will be surprised if the issue in the present instance should be reversed, and the government be administered in the spirit and form approved by the great body of the people." The Republicans were the party of the American people—or would be, when the people became conscious of the identity the Revolutionary fathers had first forged in 1776.

Madison's history of the parties adapted Jefferson's abstract, idealized schema of generational sovereignty and succession to the particular circumstances of the American Revolutionary experience. Jefferson proposed to constitutionalize time, to establish a recurrent cycle of regime change that would enable each "living generation" to reconstitute and so perpetuate the republic.[116] He did not imagine that political conflict would be banished. Quite to the contrary, the point of his constitutional conjectures was to imagine conditions in which majority rule would be most legitimate in the eyes of the whole people, including minorities. His solution was to make the Constitution the mirror of the people, a higher law in which they saw themselves—not some long-gone generation of lawgiving founders—as its authors. Only then, he suggested, would the people willingly submit to their own authority.

At first Madison balked at the practical implications of Jefferson's ideas. But his constitutionalism was animated by similar intentions: to establish a stable and legitimate regime, based on the ultimate authority of the people, that would secure liberty, property, and the rule of law. As he came to see the threat of a minority faction capturing and corrupting the new federal government, Madison took Jefferson's teaching about the ongoing presence of the people in their own government to heart. The formation of a great political party that would mobilize the people to secure their liberties in the name of the Constitution and through constitutional means would bring the body politic to life and thus serve Jefferson's larger purposes.

Madison explicitly discussed the generation theme only once in his *National Gazette* essays. In "Universal Peace," he anticipated the deepening partisan divisions over foreign policy that the threat of American entanglement in European wars would provoke. Madison now invoked Jefferson, "our republican philosopher," who "might have proposed as a model to lawgivers, that war should not only be declared by the authority of the people, whose toils and treasures are to support its burdens, instead of the government which is to reap its fruits: but that each generation should be made to bear the burden of its own wars, instead of carrying them on, at the expence of other generations."[117] Of course, this was precisely what Jefferson *had* "proposed" to an impatient Madison in September 1789. When Americans faced the prospect of war, they would become conscious of themselves as a people. In these clarifying moments, the living generation would hold the government to the Constitution's high standard.

Republicans would not resort to force. Were they to do so, Jefferson told his old friend Edmund Pendleton in February 1799, they would "check the progress of the public opinion" and rally the people "round the errors of the government." The genius of republicanism was peaceful. Eschewing violence, the patriotic opposition would "bear down the evil propensities of the government by the constitutional means of election & petition."[118] In the "Revolution of 1800" a "mighty wave of public opinion" swept across the land and vindicated the people's Constitution. Desperate Federalists could have blocked Jefferson's ascension to the presidency, but the people would have risen to the occasion. "The federal government would have been in the situation of a clock or watch run down," Jefferson wrote Joseph Priestley. "There was no idea of force, nor of any occasion for it. a Convention, invited by the republican members of Congress with the virtual President & Vice President, would have been on the ground in 8. weeks, would have repaired the constitution where it was defective & wound it up again." This was the "peaceable & legitimate resource" of a constitutional people, "superseding all appeal to force, and being always within our reach, [which] shews a precious principle of self-preservation in our composition."[119]

With Jefferson's election, a new generation redeemed the Constitution and looked forward to a glorious future. "Possessing a chosen country, with room enough for our descendants to the thousandth and thousandth generation," the new president promised, Americans would fulfill the imperial ambitions of American Revolutionary patriots.[120] Madison and his fellow framers had made a constitution for an "extended republic," reversing powerful centrifugal tendencies that had threatened to destroy the union. When Madison and Jefferson mobilized opposition to the Federalist regime and ultimately triumphed at the polls, they democratized the Constitution. Size was no longer a problem. An expanding union of republican states would spread across a boundless hinterland. "Who can limit the extent to which the federative principle may operate effectively?" Jefferson asked in his Second Inaugural Address in March 1805. He exulted in "the union of sentiment now manifested so generally, as auguring harmony and happiness to our future course."[121]

4

Empire

THOMAS JEFFERSON AND GEORGE WASHINGTON

George Washington devoted his career to securing the independence and the glorious future prospects of the "empire of liberty" Thomas Jefferson envisioned in his First Inaugural Address. The great general Washington was the "father" and "saviour" of his country, commanding the loyalty and love of Americans across the continent. Jefferson, the author of the Declaration of Independence, identified with future generations of grateful children. In this "chosen country," he promised, there would be "room enough for our descendants to the thousandth and thousandth generation." As he took his oath of office, the new president spoke *for* a newly united people coming into its continental inheritance. We are "brethren of the same principle," he proclaimed: "we are all republicans, we are all federalists." Who could doubt "that this government, the world's best hope" would "want energy to preserve itself?" Who could set limits to this "rising nation" as it "spread over a wide and fruitful land"?[1]

Washington had shown the way. He had been "our first and greatest revolutionary character," Jefferson told his Inaugural audience. His "preeminent services . . . entitled him to the first place in his country's love, and destined for him the fairest page in the volume of faithful history." The new president acknowledged Washington's providential role in securing the new nation's independence, linking him in death with "that infinite power, which rules the destinies of the universe." The "Spirit of 1776," which had animated Jefferson and his "democratic" followers in their struggle against "aristocratic" Federalists, was now manifest in the unifying love of "a "happy and prosperous people" for Washington, their departed father. In contrast, Jefferson portrayed himself in modest, self-effacing terms. Relying "on the patronage of your good will," the people's humble servant pledged to do "all the good in my power" to "conciliate" partisan foes and promote the "happiness and freedom of all." Jefferson did not expect to reap great rewards from high office: "it will rarely fall to the lot of imperfect man to retire from this station with the reputation, and the favor, which bring him into it." But he was confident that successive generations of Americans, "acknowledging and adoring an overruling providence" and gratefully remembering the sacrifices of Washington and the Revolutionary generation, would advance "rapidly to destinies beyond the reach of mortal eye."

Jefferson's First Inaugural Address offered an inspiring, expansive vision of the new nation's future, deflecting attention away from the partisan warfare of the preceding decade. Geography played a crucial role in Jeffersonian revisionism. The great ideological divisions that had transformed the Atlantic world in the Revolutionary age mapped neatly onto the distinction between Old World and New that he elaborated during his years in Paris.[2] From this comparative perspective, the "contest of opinion" that marked—and marred—partisan combat in the 1790s took on a more benign, much less threatening cast. The contrast between the blood-soaked "throes and convulsions of the ancient world, during the agonizing spasms of infuriated man" and sometimes heated debates about the most prudent "measures of safety" to secure the New World from collateral damage could not be more striking.

For Jefferson, the amount of blood spilled and the number of lives lost was the critical measure, as it had been in the case of agrarian disturbances in the 1780s. And yet again, the violence that did occur in America was a result of governmental overreach, not of the popular dissidence that supposedly justified the heavy hand of power. Europeans killed one another; enlightened Americans changed their opinions. As they unleashed murderous rhetorical barrages against their partisan enemies, Federalists and Republicans might imagine that they were fighting the same great fight as their European counterparts.[3] But as the new day dawned, republican Americans saw the light and redeemed their national character. Jefferson was swept into office by a "mighty wave of public opinion," he told Joseph Priestley. This peaceful revolution, like the "great extent of our republic," was "something new under the sun."[4]

The story Jefferson told about the rise and sudden collapse of the first American party system cauterized deep wounds in the young body politic. With a brief era of peace dawning in Europe and party conflict subsiding in America, the new president imagined a posthumous reconciliation with Washington and a glorious, imperial future for the new nation. Consigning the vicious partisanship of the 1790s to a rapidly receding past, Jefferson looked westward. United "with one heart and one mind," future generations of settlers would come together—as Americans—in the peaceful conquest of the continent. The Spirit of 1776, which had inspired Jefferson's followers to drive Federalist apostates from the republican temple, would lead them to restore the revered father—now extricated from earthbound, partisan entanglements—to his exalted place in the hearts and minds of his countrymen.

The immortal Washington played a crucial role in the empire of peace and plenty Jefferson envisioned for his fellow Americans. The author of the Declaration of Independence certainly hoped that his own contributions to the providential cause would be remembered.[5] But these were the contributions of a faithful servant who had given voice to the American people in 1776 and who pledged, in 1801, to do the people's business. Jefferson promised that he and his Republican successors would preside over a more perfect union that would enable future generations to extend the "empire of liberty" across the continent, to its natural limits. Jefferson offered his enterprising countrymen an inspiring national narrative, enlisting Providence and the immortal Washington in his "Revolution of 1800." Partisan differences might not yet be fully submerged in a "mighty wave" of patriotic sentiment: wary Federalists did not abandon their party, and factious Republicans soon fell to squabbling. But the sense of existential crisis shared by both parties in the late 1790s had begun to subside well before Jefferson's inauguration. Weary veterans of party warfare were receptive to the new president's optimistic overtures. Jefferson's vision of the new nation's boundless future transcended seemingly intractable ideological differences: partisanship would diminish and patriotism would flourish in an expanding union of self-governing republics.

I. WASHINGTON'S IMPERIAL VISION

Empire loomed large in the geographical imagination of enterprising Anglo-Americans.[6] Washington, the father figure, and Jefferson, speaking for the rising generation, both embraced an expansive vision of the new nation's imperial destiny. Yet these two great Virginians conceived of their country's future in strikingly different ways. Emphasizing continuity across regime change, Washington did not hesitate to call the United States an "empire"; Jefferson, the apostle of American exceptionalism, rarely used the term, emphasizing instead the fundamental break between royal and republican governments.[7]

Washington's perspective was shaped by his career as a surveyor and land speculator in provincial Virginia. An avid exponent of internal improvements, Washington sought to exploit "the extensive & valuable Trade of a rising Empire" to the west.[8] After independence, Washington continued to promote and exploit his own western claims (with little success), while emphasizing the larger public purposes westward settlement and economic development would serve.[9] The promise of American empire could only be fulfilled under the aegis of a government with the capacity to protect and promote settlement. If Americans did not rise to the occasion, their empire would be lost. Washington's empire was a legacy of the British imperial past, to be secured by victorious arms; unlike Jefferson's, it was not "something new under the sun."

Washington's imperial vision expressed the aspirations of Revolutionary imperial patriots with enlightened and cosmopolitan sensibilities. It also spoke to—and for—the "middling" and "common" sorts whose lives had been transformed by the war. Wartime mobilization democratized patriotism, enabling ordinary Americans to join Washington in speculating about future prospects in distant places: the "people's war" gave rise to a people's empire.[10] Throughout the war, Washington struggled to contain and transcend local interests and attachments; when the victorious commander in chief resigned his commission, he admonished state governors to preserve "an indissoluble Union of the States under one federal Head." They must overcome "local prejudices and policies" and make "mutual concessions," he told them in his circular letter to the governors, recognizing that "it is only in our United Character, as an Empire, that our Independance is acknowledged."[11]

For Washington, empire was the predicate of republican government, not its antithesis. "The foundation of our Empire was not laid in the gloomy Age of ignorance and superstition," Washington assured the governors, "but at an Epocha when the rights of Mankind were better understood and more clearly defined, than at any former period." In a private letter to the marquis de Lafayette in August 1786 Washington expressed his vaulting hopes for the new nation in uncharacteristically enthusiastic language. Describing himself as "the member of an infant-empire, as a Philanthropist by character, and . . . as a Citizen of the great republic of humanity at large," Washington eagerly anticipated an enlightened commercial age when "mankind may be connected like one great family in fraternal ties." For this glorious vision to be fulfilled, however, the "infant-empire" would have to reach maturity. "This country" would have to carry sufficient "weight in the scale of Empires."[12]

Yet even as Washington's hopes soared, his anxieties deepened. Madison exploited these concerns when he helped persuade Washington to preside over the Philadelphia Convention in the summer of 1787.[13] The formidable obstacles to a more perfect union were all too familiar to the former commander in chief. Yet again, shortsighted partisans mobilized in defense of local interests, insisting on the "sovereignty" of the separate states. Washington's contempt for the exaggerated pretensions of these "insignificant & wretched fragments of Empire" was boundless.[14] Without a more energetic central government, he insisted, the union would collapse, and the "sacred fire of liberty" would be extinguished.[15]

Some of Washington's closest friends in Virginia failed to grasp the imminent danger. George Mason refused to sign the Constitution; Patrick Henry "smelt a rat," accusing reformers of plotting to establish a "powerful and mighty empire" on the wreckage of American liberties.[16] A thin-skinned Washington took opposition to the Constitution personally, identifying its Antifederalist critics as a dangerous faction. His presence at Philadelphia represented a great personal investment in the new government's ultimate success, and his endorsement reassured ambivalent voters who shared his capacious and inclusive conception of America's "rising empire." Citizen-soldiers risked everything to secure American independence, not to defend the petty interests of entrenched local elites. Patriots were not partisans; the continent was their country.

In Washington's lexicon, the terms "empire," "union," "power," and "nation" were inextricably linked. American empire would have to be built on a foundation of citizen sacrifice. To be recognized "among the powers of the earth," the United States would have to *become* a recognizable, "treaty-worthy" power.[17] The success of the new nation's republican experiment depended on its ability to survive in a world dominated by empires. The nation-making imperative therefore was to secure an "equal standing" relative to other sovereignties; the first law of nature, jurists agreed, was self-preservation.[18] This top-down, geopolitical perspective stood in uneasy tension with the antistatist precepts of radical republicans who sought to overturn the British imperial old regime. Reliance on a professional "standing army" was anathema to advocates of the bottom-up mobilization in citizen militias.[19] But the "rage militaire" of 1775–76 proved short-lived. The Revolution would have collapsed if Congress had not exercised its tenuous authority to create the Continental Army, which could engage British armies on American battlefields while Congress negotiated alliances with foreign powers.[20]

Wherever sovereignty ultimately lay, the United States collectively had to act like a single sovereign power. Straddling the rift between republican ideology and state-building imperatives, Washington quickly emerged as the central figure in the American Revolutionary imagination, the symbolic embodiment—and resolution—of the tension between civilian ends and military means. Even before independence was declared, the Massachusetts patriot Josiah Quincy predicted that Washington's "Name" would be "handed down to Posterity, with the illustrious Character of being the Saviour of your Country."[21] Thirteen years later, a job-seeking supplicant called President Washington "the best of Men. and under God, the Saviour of our Country."[22] It was not the great general's battlefield successes that prompted such effusive, almost sacrilegious encomiums. It was instead the extraordinary self-restraint and self-sacrifice he displayed in *not* seizing power that made him seem almost God-like.[23]

Most extraordinarily, Washington deferred to civilian authority—even when a cash-strapped, dysfunctional Congress failed to provide his troops with adequate support.[24] The punctilious general recognized that his fate was inextricably linked to Congress's and that one could not survive without the other. The specter of despotic authority loomed large for anxious patriots who mobilized to overthrow King George III. Washington knew that the people would turn against him, and his Christ-like aura soon dissipate, if he turned against his civilian superiors. Shortsighted, factious, and incompetent politicians might fail to articulate and implement the public will, but the long-suffering, self-sacrificing commander sustained his faith in the American people, and they in him. The "people" were not an abstraction for Washington: they were immediately present in the troops who served with and for him, his fellow "Citizens in Arms."[25]

Washington's career in the provincial ranks of the British army shaped the persona he so carefully cultivated as commander in chief of the Continental Army. Acutely conscious of the prerogatives and responsibilities of rank, he commanded the respect of civilian authorities as well as of his troops. Extensive service in the Seven Years' War had made him the obvious choice to take charge of the ragtag patriot army that materialized so rapidly around Boston at the outset of the war.[26] The new general's greatest challenge was to impose order and discipline on enthusiastic and unruly troops, largely from New England. Washington brought the self-assured presence of an experienced officer, planter, and gentleman to his post in Massachusetts. His success depended on winning the loyalty of (and overcoming his own antipathy to) Yankee troops, who had a distinctive military culture of their own. A long history of conflict with French and Indians on the northern imperial frontier gave New Englanders more military experience and a better sense of their rights as soldiers than their counterparts anywhere else on the continent.[27]

Yankee soldiers represented the prototypical citizen-soldiers Jefferson celebrated in his Inaugural Address. General Washington's success in establishing his authority over them enabled Americans to reconcile a professional, standing army with the nation-making "common cause." A successful military career promised to fulfill the young Washington's social ambitions; high rank and social status remained linked in the Continental Army—though problematically, given the dearth of qualified gentlemen.[28] Washington and his fellow officers now vindicated their social aspirations by dedicating their lives and fortunes to the defense of a new republican regime predicated on the fundamental premise of citizen equality. The chain of command in a professional army justified hierarchy in instrumental terms, as the necessary means toward an end—victory on the battlefield—that officers and soldiers shared; by the same logic, authority was justified in meritocratic terms, according to its more or less successful exercise. Command over others depended on self-command in service of a higher cause. For the self-sacrificing patriot, honor was an asset.[29]

Washington did not win many battles. He recognized that the war would be won by avoiding potentially disastrous engagements and keeping his army in the field to fight on another, more promising day. The war made Washington and the men he commanded "Americans," for the country's fate depended on their survival. Drawn from diverse places across the continent and diverse backgrounds, the Continental Army constituted a precociously heterogeneous and inclusive microcosm of the nation as a whole. Though many of his countrymen remained wary of the ways a professional army might jeopardize their liberties, Washington's paternalistic devotion to his troops—and theirs to him—came to epitomize republican patriotism. The army's hierarchy transcended the distinctions it enforced by serving a larger, ultimately egalitarian purpose; during the national emergency, the sentimental analogy of family to society—a great family of families—made the temporarily unequal distribution of authority in the army seem natural. Washington referred to his immediate circle of aides as "my family."[30] Not surprisingly, his paternal role resonated through the ranks and among the people at large.

Washington's highly developed sensitivity about the prerogatives of his rank reflected the aristocratic sensibility of the provincial old regime in Virginia. That punctiliousness also constituted a formidable defense against the temptations of power. Washington's virtuous self-restraint and deference to superior constitutional authority made him a culture hero in republican America. As a loyal British subject he had deferred to the king; after independence he deferred to Congress and the state governments; as president he deferred to the will of the sovereign people as it was expressed under the Constitution. The distinction between man and office was absolute. When he resigned his commission or retired from the presidency, he resumed the life he cherished most, as a citizen. In his official capacity, however, Washington demanded the respect that he accorded his own superiors. There could be no higher honor than to serve as the chief executive of a free people.

In showing due respect to their president, Americans honored themselves. By sustaining the union of hearts and minds that won the war, they would fulfill the imperial vision that had inspired Washington and the generation of liberty-loving patriots who sacrificed so much to secure the new nation's independence.

II. PARTISAN DIVISIONS

Washington worried about his legacy. As long as Americans preserved their independence, his immortal reputation would be secure. Yet his experiences in war and peace had taught him that his presence at the head of his troops or of his administration was indispensable to the new empire's survival. His dilemma was acute. Washington earned the love of his countrymen by resisting the temptations of power and retiring from office. But quarreling partisans threatened to forfeit the empire Washington and his army had won for their countrymen at such great cost in the Revolutionary War.

Partisan conflict jeopardized the union. As commander in chief of the Continental Army, Washington complained that "party disputes & personal quarrels" deflected attention away from "the momentous concerns of an empire."[31] If "party matters were at an end," he wrote Governor Joseph Reed of Pennsylvania in 1778, "we should be soon left to the enjoyment of that Peace and happiness which every good Man must wish for."[32] Too often Americans failed to recognize the need to sacrifice partial, short-term advantage for the greater good of the nation as a whole. "We who are Citizens in arms," General Washington told the troops at Valley Forge, willingly risked everything "in the glorious task of laying the foundation of an Empire."[33] Patriotism and partisanship were irreconcilable.

If the new nation failed, Washington's fame would prove short-lived. He expressed his anxieties in addresses he delivered to the American people on his retirement from the Continental Army and then from the presidency. Exiting the stage of public life, the father of his country asked patriotic citizens to honor his memory by cherishing their union. Honor-bound to preserve the new nation from internal and external threats, he implored his countrymen to sustain the solidarity he had inspired as their wartime commander by pledging allegiance to their own, duly elected governments. Washington's identification with the new American empire was profoundly personal yet self-consciously—even ostentatiously—disinterested. By relinquishing power, he sought everlasting fame, resisting the monarchical temptation and returning to private life like the Roman hero Cincinnatus.[34] Yet his retirements, whether from command of the Continental Army in 1783 or from the presidency in 1796, were shadowed by anxious forebodings. Perhaps, he feared, his continuing service was the only guarantee against the descent into anarchy that partisan conflict portended.

Washington took the nation-building project personally. He interpreted the emergence of a continentwide opposition party under Jefferson's leadership as an assault on his honor.[35] Secretary of State Jefferson first fomented opposition to administration policy from within the cabinet, and he continued to do so when he "retired" to Monticello. Always careful to keep his distance from the partisan fray, the duplicitous Jefferson worked through Madison and other proxies while maintaining ostensibly cordial, but increasingly strained relations with the president. By the time Washington retired from office in March 1797, the two Virginians had come to represent irreconcilable conceptions of the character and constitution of the federal republic and its place in the world. When the Adams administration subsequently mobilized against France in the "Quasi-War" and Washington agreed to serve as commander in chief of the Provisional Army, Francophile Republicans mobilized *against* the American war effort.[36]

In a period of extraordinary geopolitical instability, preserving independence depended on perpetuating and perfecting the union. An anxious Washington feared that deepening party divisions would demolish America's rising empire in its infancy. In his Farewell Address, published in a Philadelphia newspaper on September 19, 1796, he aimed his sharpest barbs and rebukes at the Jeffersonian Republicans, accusing them of setting party above country.[37] He condemned the Republicans' corrosive assault on constitutional government. "The very idea of the power and the right of the People to establish Government," he insisted, "presupposes the duty of every Individual to obey the established Government." The citizen's duty to submit to government was a necessary corollary of consenting to the delegation of authority through free elections under the Constitution.

Disobedient citizens neglected their duties when they participated in angry protests against the Jay Treaty, a controversial trade pact with Britain negotiated by John Jay in 1794 and narrowly adopted by the Senate in June 1795.[38] Following James Madison's lead, Republicans in the House of Representatives sought to block the treaty's implementation, accusing Federalists of compromising the new nation's independence by capitulating to the mother country's onerous terms and betraying France, the "sister republic." For their part, Federalists feared the spreading contagion of French Revolutionary radicalism. Prudence dictated accommodation with Britain, and patriotic Americans should rally once again behind their commander in chief.

Washington prayed that "Union & brotherly affection may be perpetual" among Americans, "that the free constitution, which is the work of your hands, may be sacredly maintained." "All obstructions to the execution of the Laws," he proclaimed, "all combinations and Associations, under whatever plausible character, with the real design to direct, controul counteract, or awe the regular deliberation and action of the Constituted authorities are distructive of this fundamental principle and of fatal tendency." Echoing the Madisonian indictment of factions in *The Federalist,* Washington now condemned Madison and his fellow Republicans for putting "the will of a party . . . in the place of the delegated will of the Nation."

A united people owed their allegiance to a chief magistrate who, by virtue of his office, stood above parties.[39] Washington modeled this exalted role in his highly formal and self-conscious performance as president. Maintaining an appropriate social distance from subordinate officers, he avoided undignified familiarities. Yet if Washington was not a king, the new nation's official society was something like a court—though on the diminutive, somewhat awkward scale of the "courts" surrounding royal governors before independence.[40] And if the new president knew how to carry himself, those who danced—or bowed stiffly—in attendance were easily confused with the sycophantic, self-seeking courtiers who figured so prominently in the American Revolutionary imagination. There was no questioning Washington's republican credentials, and this made him the safe, presumptive choice to be the new empire's chief magistrate. But vigilant Republican oppositionists feared that the structure of the new regime and the more ambiguous intentions of its advocates set the stage for a return to monarchy, or something even worse. Court life incubated factionalism, and factionalism spread "out-of-doors" through the formation of a corrupt and corrupting court party bent on destroying American liberty. By the end of his second term, Washington himself had become the target of escalating abuse: he was either the dupe of his advisors or complicit in their designs.[41]

Washington's rhetorical assault on partisanship in his Farewell Address would be remembered as a crucially important part of his legacy, a gift to future generations of patriotic Americans. In its immediate context, however, the address eloquently testified to pervasive partisanship. Mobilizing in defense of the administration, Federalists condemned their Jeffersonian critics as unpatriotic partisans. Republican oppositionists reversed the charges. They justified opposition to the administration party by invoking the glorious precedent of the American Revolution, the first great, nation-making mobilization of patriots. The union would only survive and prosper when the federal government was thoroughly purged of counterrevolutionary and antirepublican tendencies. Republicans thus rallied under the banner of a strictly construed Constitution, insisting that the "people" were the document's true authors and that their continuous political presence was critical to its legitimacy.[42] Their rights should always be construed generously, while the authority of government officials was strictly limited. "Partisanship" in support of the Constitution therefore epitomized high-minded patriotism, not the betrayal of the union.

The American Revolution was itself a great party conflict, pitting Whig patriots against Tory defenders of the Crown. It set the stage for subsequent divisions over ratifying the Constitution and over controversial administration policies in the 1790s. The challenge was to channel partisan energies within a federal constitutional structure in ways that strengthened attachments and avoided civil war. In retrospect, acceptance of the idea of a loyal opposition and normalization of partisan conflict in successive party "systems" was the obvious solution.[43] Looking forward, however, Americans framed the problem in less institutional, functional terms. The future of the new American empire depended on synthesizing Washington's self-sacrificing patriotism with the robust political—that is, partisan—participation of the sovereign people.

In death, Washington could achieve the everlasting fame he craved, the fame that, during his lifetime, partisan divisions threatened to subvert. He became the nation's symbolic embodiment, "first in war—first in peace—first in the hearts of his countrymen."[44] Identifying with the father figure, Jefferson could direct Washington's antipartisan admonitions against his former supporters, the vanquished Federalists. Washington then could be seen in a new light, ascending to an exalted, semidivine status above the party conflict he so abhorred. The "living generation" could then take the reins of power into its own hands.

Jefferson eased his succession to power by getting right with Washington. That meant coming to terms with the legacy of Federalist state-building. Jefferson put a new, expansive gloss on the rising empire Washington and his troops had created, constitutional reformers made more perfect, and Federalist administrations consolidated. The history of American empire, Jefferson suggested, was continuous across regime change. The distinctive ways he and Washington talked—and did not talk—about empire are nonetheless illuminating. The "empire of liberty" Jefferson imagined in his First Inaugural Address was unimaginable without General Washington as its presiding genius, or without the federal state President Washington and the Federalists had built.

III. SOVEREIGNTY

The two Virginians' conception of American empire grew out of divergent military and civilian perspectives. Those perspectives entailed distinctive Revolutionary chronologies. Washington's Revolution began with the outbreak of hostilities in April 1775, and its successful outcome depended on strict adherence to a chain of command, with the new commander taking orders from Congress. Washington's "country" was a series of battlefields, shifting from place to place across the continent. Jefferson focused instead on political mobilization and constitution writing in Virginia and the other states, culminating in the consummation of their union in July 1776. Washington's top-down perspective was unitary and comprehensive, or "nationalist." Jefferson's was bottom-up, moving from states to union, and therefore "democratic."

The United States constituted a new nation when the thirteen colony-states declared their independence. At the same time, however, Jefferson emphasized the histories and constitutions of the separate states dating back to their original settlement. Washington's time frame was foreshortened, focusing on the mobilization of American forces and the onset of hostilities in April 1775. The new commander in chief welcomed Congress's belated Declaration, ordering that it be read aloud to his troops.[45] But he and his men had already made their choices, acknowledging the Continental Congress's effectively sovereign authority and following its commands. If the Declaration clarified their status and boosted their morale, it changed nothing on the ground: independence was instead a "project," predicated on the army's ultimate success.[46] For Washington, the rising empire's coercive capacity came first, enabling Americans to transform the infrastructure of resistance into constitutional governments. Patriotic soldiers came first; self-governing citizens followed. Jefferson reversed the sequence, insisting that the Revolution was a people's war: mobilizing in defense of their rights, citizens became soldiers.

Washington had to deal with state governments that were predictably reluctant to provide desperately needed men and resources for the continental war effort. He understood that these governments, acting through Congress, were the source of his own authority. Yet the commander in chief's virtue and honor were often sorely tested by these "wretched fragments of empire." The North American Empire that the young Washington idolized and that Britain had so foolishly forfeited remained his frame of reference. For his part, Jefferson fervently believed that the collapse of the British Empire presented a historic opportunity for creating new republican governments grounded in the equal rights of sovereign citizens. Eager to be at home, where his countrymen were drafting a constitution for the new Commonwealth, Jefferson was a reluctant congressman in the spring and early summer of 1776.[47] He was convinced that the strength and survival of the union depended on laying a solid foundation in the respective states. The states were building blocks of the new regime, not radically defective fragments of the old. Focused on the constituent parts, Jefferson assumed that the whole—the government of the continent—would take care of itself.[48] From his position on the battlefield, Washington saw things much differently.

Washington and other centralizing nationalists did not hesitate to invoke the concept of sovereignty.[49] In contemporary usage the word itself constituted a compelling argument: common sense suggested that authority had to be located *somewhere* in every enduring association, from the patriarch in his household domain to the governors of great kingdoms—or extended republics.[50] When nationalists railed against the proliferation of sovereignty claims, or what contemporaries called *imperium in imperio,* they raised the awful specter of an anarchic war of all against all.[51] For them, sovereignty clearly meant the monopoly and exclusive exercise of coercive force. That authority, traditionally located in the Crown's prerogative powers to make war and preserve the peace, could only be exercised by a sufficiently energetic continental government. The American states would have to reconstruct the old imperial government on a republican foundation. As a nationalist committed to upholding America's claim to sovereignty and independence, Washington had no misgivings about calling the United States an "empire."[52]

Washington's campaign to reconstruct the old empire began on the battlefield, where the new commander in chief drew on his experience in the British military to shape a credible American fighting force.[53] He recognized that the United States would have to take the form of a recognizable state—that is, become more like the British enemy—in order to enforce its claims to independence. Attraction to the British model also reflected the original goals of the resistance movement, as frustrated imperial patriots sought to vindicate their rights as Englishmen and secure a more perfect constitutional union *within* the empire.[54] Provincial Anglo-Americans reluctantly assumed the sovereign powers the British imperial government had attempted to exercise over them. Independence was an unintended, irresistible consequence; the turn toward republican self-government was another. How else could patriot leaders mobilize this self-proclaimed "people" and justify themselves to the world?

Nation-making required the wholesale repudiation of the British connection. Americans had to think of themselves as a distinct people and their former British countrymen as foreigners.[55] State-building required replication of British state capacity. For Washington, any tension between the apparently conflicting imperatives of differentiation and emulation was definitively resolved in the war for independence. His choice was irrevocable, his patriotism beyond question. The continuities between old regime and new were clear to him: liberty-loving Anglo-Americans fought for their independence *because* they were more devoted to English rights than their corrupt and degenerate transatlantic cousins; the empire Americans rejected provided the territorial frame and fiscal-military model for the rising empire they sought to establish.

Washington was an orthodox republican who embraced the fundamental tenet of popular sovereignty. But he was also convinced that sovereignty could only be effectively exercised within a continental, postimperial framework. The commander in chief therefore pledged his allegiance to whatever passed for a national government, whatever its constitutional and institutional defects. His inclusive conception of the American people also reflected this continental perspective: anyone he could recruit qualified. Eventually the great Virginia planter even overcame his reflexive aversion to enlisting free blacks—including former slaves—in the Continental Army.[56]

If for Washington the new American nation was born on Revolutionary battlefields, Jefferson turned to the history of Virginia and the other colony-states for a legitimating pedigree. He was no less a patriotic American than his fellow Virginian, but his intellectual journey toward independence and nationhood ran through his home province toward union with other provinces across the continent.[57] The union that came into being on July 4, 1776, was not simply the British Empire by another name, but "something new under the sun." Because all the self-declared state-republics had distinctive histories and civic identities, the ability of their representatives in Congress to define and embrace a common cause and see one another as fellow Americans could hardly be taken for granted. For the deistic Jefferson there was something nearly miraculous—or rather, better than miraculous—in the American people's ability to grasp the "self-evident" principles of good government and declare their independence.[58]

The misguided policies of metropolitan reformers had led provincial patriots to recognize their common dilemma. They understood, as the long list of grievances catalogued in the Declaration of Independence made clear, that assaults on the rights of any province set dangerous precedents for them all. Yet Anglo-Americans could only act on that recognition because they possessed the civic capacity, developed under their respective provincial constitutions, to do so. At this critical, transformative moment of crisis, provincial Americans made themselves into a single, united people. The Declaration was the "fundamental act of union of these states," Jefferson later wrote.[59] Far from abolishing or transcending the states, Americans discovered their common nationality as citizens *of* those states. Mobilization in defense of their provincial constitutions made subjects into citizens capable of undertaking their bold experiments in republican and federal government. There could be no union without the simultaneous, seemingly spontaneous uprising of rights-conscious citizens across the continent.[60]

The independent states were drawn to one another because they were republics, Jefferson thought, not because they had been provinces in an empire with which they had so unequivocally broken. At the same time, however, his civilian perspective evoked a more distant, idealized imperial past—before 1763—when the rights of Anglo-Americans supposedly had been secure under their respective provincial constitutions. Jefferson resolved the apparent ambiguity by describing both the old empire and the new United States as "unions," emphasizing their consensual character. On the only occasions he did call the new nation an empire, his discomfort with the term was conspicuous. In late 1780, when he was governor of Virginia, Jefferson exhorted George Rogers Clark to capture the British fort at Detroit, thus establishing a defensive "barrier against the dangerous extension of the British Province of Canada" and adding "an extensive and fertile Country . . . to the Empire of liberty."[61] Almost three decades later, shortly after retiring from the presidency, Jefferson urged his successor James Madison to bargain with the French emperor Napoleon for Cuba and the Floridas in exchange for recognizing his claims to Mexico and the other former Spanish American provinces: "we should then have only to include the North in our confederacy, which would be of course in the first war, and we should have such an empire for liberty as she has never surveyed since the creation."[62] In both cases, Jefferson sought to secure the union from dangerous imperial rivals. Territorial expansion to the new nation's "natural" limits was a defensive measure, as it was in 1803, when American diplomats successfully negotiated for the Louisiana Purchase.[63] The United States would not be a conventional empire, extending its domain by force of arms. It was instead an empire "of" or "for liberty." "No constitution," he told Madison, "was ever before so well calculated as ours for extensive empire & self government."

Jefferson neutralized the negative connotations of "empire" by pairing it with "liberty." In his republican lexicon, the terms were logically opposed, as were "subject" and "citizen," "monarchy" and "republic." He deployed them to mark the fundamental break between the old, monarchical regime and its new republican successor. As long as Jefferson could envision a constitutional settlement short of independence, he could describe George III "as chief magistrate of the British empire"—not a lawless despot—and see himself as a loyal subject.[64] Jefferson could also insist to his distant cousin, the exiled Virginia loyalist John Randolph, that "there is not in the British empire a man who more cordially loves a Union with Gr. Britain than I do."[65] This was to say, of course, that remaining in the empire depended on sustaining a constitutional union Jefferson could love. But independence changed everything. The royal despot destroyed Britain's North American empire, making loyal subjects into self-governing citizens.

After the break with Britain, Jefferson jettisoned the servile, subservient language of the old regime. Profound hostility to the claims of the British sovereign made the very idea of sovereignty fundamentally problematic for Jefferson and like-minded patriots. The modern notion that the existence of a political society depends on the ultimate, absolute authority of its government—however it might be constituted—was antirepublican heresy. Jefferson could not extricate the concept of sovereignty from the personal authority of the sovereign. By the same logic, he conflated the terms "empire" and "emperor," a ruler who acknowledged no limits to his authority.[66] In Jefferson's geopolitical imagination, the United States modeled a new world order. Every other "power of the earth" was an empire, engaged in endless struggles for conquest and domination. Enlightened Americans were exceptional. Governing themselves under republican constitutions, they would only make war in self-defense in order to preserve their liberties.[67]

The goal of the Revolution, Jefferson wrote Benjamin Franklin in Paris, was to secure foreign recognition of "our absolute independance and sovereignty."[68] Sovereignty was located in the people as a whole, not in their various governments. When they drafted constitutions, rights-conscious American citizens delegated their authority to representatives—or public "servants"—under strictly defined conditions. For Jefferson, popular sovereignty was not a "fiction," a merely theoretical claim about the ultimate source of legitimate authority.[69] To the contrary, his goal as a democratic constitutionalist was to guarantee the presence of the people in their own government through the ongoing mobilization of public opinion as well as frequent elections and a generational return to founding principles. But turning the conventional, hierarchical understanding of government on its head made it difficult to define "sovereignty" for practical purposes. Except in the context of foreign relations, Jefferson therefore generally avoided using the term. Only when looking outward, to the rest of the world, could the Confederation or its federal successor speak for the people collectively; only in that limited sphere did the modern, unitary conception of sovereignty make sense to Jefferson. If Americans collectively constituted a nation in a world of nations, they also preserved their sovereign authority over their own governments at home. Sovereignty was ubiquitous, everywhere and nowhere.

Jefferson's radical republican commitments were eloquently expressed in his avoidance of terms such as "empire" and "sovereignty" and of the seemingly irresistible logic of their conventional meanings. He was careful to deploy these terms in verbal contexts that blunted or reversed that logic: sovereignty was something that *all* citizens possessed in their "empire of liberty." As Americans prepared to deliberate on the proposed federal constitution, Jefferson wrote George Wythe that "the states should severally preserve their sovereignty *in whatever concerns themselves alone.*"[70] He was not opposed to a stronger, more effective central government: it also would be sovereign within its appropriate sphere. Jefferson could say the same for each individual citizen when he considered the dangerous implications of a proposed federal bankruptcy act in 1792: would the power of commissioners to "enter houses, break open doors, chests, &c." be compatible with "that spirit of independance and sovereignty which a man feels in his own house"?[71]

Popular sovereignty was a protean concept for Jefferson. The identity of the people was contingent on the extent and purpose, or "sphere," of their freely formed unions, and at every level the people were sovereign. The motto *E pluribus unum,* "Out of many, one," which was inscribed in the new nation's Great Seal, captured the upward progress of inclusion. The vital presence of the "many"—of the people, governing themselves in their respective towns, counties, and states—thus sustained and empowered the "one."[72] Limited government, grounded in the sovereignty of the people, strengthened the federal union and enabled its limitless expansion. After the recently completed Louisiana Purchase doubled the nation's size, Jefferson posed the rhetorical question in his Second Inaugural Address, "Who can limit the extent to which the federative principle may operate effectively?"[73]

In Jefferson's mature conception of federalism, all levels of government, from the household to town, county, state, and nation, would exercise "sovereign" powers within their respective spheres. Sovereignty, according to this definition, was the security of individual and corporate rights at successive levels of republican self-governance. In effect, Jefferson challenged the conventional understanding of political authority: public servants were ultimately responsible to citizen-sovereigns. He thus construed sovereignty in negative, defensive terms, not as a license to exercise unlimited, despotic powers. Yet sovereignty also flowed upward from its source, as citizens sanctioned progressively higher levels of association and forged more inclusive corporate identities. The presence of the "people" became manifest at all these levels, animating governments and authorizing their claims to sovereignty.

Sovereignty flowed upward and outward, coalescing in Jefferson's ascension to the presidency. But the "Revolution of 1800" did not transform Jefferson into a conventional sovereign, or even a more modest replica of his great predecessor Washington. To the contrary, the self-effacing new president was the people's "servant," the instrument through which they acted in their collective capacity and became conscious of themselves as a people. The political mobilization that swept Republicans into office reinvigorated the vital connections among citizen-patriots across the vast spaces of the expanding republic, enabling them to identify with one another and to see themselves in their new president. Jefferson identified with the people, Jeremy Bailey persuasively argues, claiming a "mandate" to act on their behalf. He would exercise the Crown's prerogative powers according to that mandate, calibrating his actions to the will of a politically engaged public. If he misread the people, they could reject him at the polls. This "democratic prerogative," in Bailey's apt formulation, contained yet another Jeffersonian paradox, limiting the illimitable authority of the people's executive where he was empowered to act.[74]

There would be no emperor in Jefferson's empire, no imperial court or metropolis. The new president instead enjoined Americans to put their faith in "that infinite power, which rules the destinies of the universe." The hand of God was manifest in the heroic achievements of citizen-soldiers who followed the great commander in chief's self-sacrificing lead. The United States would have "the strongest government on earth," Jefferson concluded, as long as patriots kept Washington's "sacred fire of liberty" burning.

IV. MANIFEST DESTINIES

As Washington neared the end of his life on December 14, 1799, he had many good reasons to fear that the flame would flicker out and America's republican experiment finally fail. The violent upheavals unleashed by the French Revolution in Europe resonated with deepening party divisions in America and threatened to subvert public order. Insurgent Republicans jeopardized Federalist diplomatic successes in the West, culminating in 1795 with a major land cession from the Ohio Indians at Greenville and with Pinckney's Spanish Treaty giving Americans access to the navigation of the Mississippi through New Orleans.[75] If Jefferson and his allies captured the federal government, the empire was more likely to implode than to expand. Powerful imperial rivals on the northern (British) and southern and western (Spanish) frontiers could enlist Indian allies against a union tottering on the brink of collapse. To the east, Americans were unable to preserve a neutral stance in the escalating struggle between Britain and France for maritime hegemony, ultimately descending into an unpopular and undeclared Quasi-War with France. For Washington, Republican resistance to the administration's mobilization efforts underscored the connection between the ascendancy of partisanship and declining patriotism. The former commander in chief was yet again prepared to come out of retirement, assume command of American forces, and save the day. The father might be abandoned by some of his quarreling, ungrateful children, but he would sacrifice everything to prevent the "infant-empire" from disintegrating into its original, anarchic fragments.

When Jefferson ascended to the presidency in March 1801, the crisis had passed. John Adams, his defeated predecessor, negotiated an end to the Quasi-War, and the prospects for (what proved to be a very brief) peace in Europe were bright. Jefferson made it clear that he had no intention of dismantling the federal government and its fiscal-military apparatus during the succession crisis of 1801, when he and his running mate Aaron Burr were deadlocked in the Electoral College and the Federalist-controlled Sixth Congress (elected in 1798) was authorized to choose the next president.[76] Channeling Washington's anxieties, partisan Federalists had exaggerated the radical implications of Republican victory in the presidential canvas, offering Jefferson extraordinary political and rhetorical room to conciliate his partisan opponents and move toward the center.

Fearful Federalists defined Jefferson's prospective election as a radical "revolution," invoking images of violence, disorder, and despotism in France, while Republicans exulted in their nonviolent restoration of the original, uncorrupted republican order of 1776. Jefferson himself would only follow his enemies' lead and call his election "the revolution of 1800" many years later—late in his retirement—when he became convinced that the "sappers and miners" of the Marshall Court were subverting the democratic will of the people by consolidating power in an unelected, irresponsible judiciary.[77] But in 1801 the newly elected president minimized differences with his erstwhile opponents, insisting instead on continuity rather than revolutionary change. All good citizens were "brethren of the same principle," he told his fellow Americans in his Inaugural Address: "we are all republicans: we are all federalists," united in "our attachment to union and representative government."[78] Supporters of the discredited Adams administration did *not* constitute a popular political party, appearances to the contrary notwithstanding. Nor were victorious Republicans a party in the conventional, pejorative sense, for they were, according to Jefferson's generously inclusive definition, immanently—if not yet actually—the whole people.[79]

Jefferson envisioned a glorious future for the new nation in his First Inaugural Address. His tribute to "our first and greatest revolutionary character" helped secure Washington's iconic standing in the American pantheon, making him a touchstone for patriotic sentiment. In the recent era of bitter partisan division, Republicans had promoted the author of the Declaration of Independence as the people's alternative to Washington. But Jefferson now spoke for the people, as he had in the Declaration, when he paid homage to their recently departed father. The triumph of his partisan enemies thus gained Washington the love and respect that partisan rancor had threatened to deny him. In death he would preside over a reunited people, dedicated to upholding the union he cherished. "If there be any among us who would wish to dissolve this Union, or to change its republican form," Jefferson concluded, "let them stand undisturbed as monuments of the safety with which error of opinion may be tolerated, where reason is left free to combat it."[80] Washington would not stand with them.

Washington sought to preserve a rising empire from falling apart, diagnosing party conflict as pathological. In contrast, Jefferson told a dynamic, forward-looking story about popular political mobilization and the limitless expansion of Washington's empire. The American people swept Jefferson and his followers into office; now they would sweep westward to take possession of their "chosen country, with room enough for" their "descendants to the thousandth and thousandth generation." In both cases, the people provided the irresistible, animating force. Their successful pursuits of happiness depended on making government work for them, as enterprising settlers conquered space by improving a productive natural landscape. Free citizens governed themselves: they were not subject to the commands of any higher authority.

Sensitive to the significance of language, Jefferson was reluctant to call this expanding union an "empire": the term suggested the sort of powerful, consolidated government that the British (and their Federalist imitators) had failed to establish over the American states. Jefferson's union was predicated instead on bringing government home to the people, enabling them to exercise and therefore limit power through progressively more inclusive levels in a federal system. Far from lacking the "energy to preserve itself," the United States could claim "the strongest government on earth." The "more perfect union" was a more perfect empire, a new and improved republican version of its monarchical predecessor. Jefferson did not repudiate Washington's empire. To the contrary, the anti-imperial imperialist envisioned the progressive expansion of the federal union to its natural limits.[81]

Warning their countrymen of a neomonarchical plot against their liberties, Republicans resisted Federalist efforts to strengthen the central government at the expense of the states, so reinforcing the link between federalism and republicanism. But the Republican quarrel was with the aspirations of would-be "aristocrats" and "monocrats," not with the Federalists' administrative achievements or with the federal constitution that authorized them. Jefferson and Albert Gallatin, his treasury secretary, recognized the crucial importance of sustaining public credit under Hamilton's fiscal regime.[82] Jefferson's strict construction of the Constitution was designed to curb encroachments on the sovereign states, not to shackle the federal government's prerogative powers in promoting the states' collective interests and security in foreign relations, particularly in frontier regions. Fulfilling the promises

Jefferson made to the American people in his Inaugural Address depended on the capacity of the federal state to project power across the continent. Enterprising Americans could only exploit, or "improve," nature's bounty if they exercised their power collectively as a people, through their governments.

The fortuitous interval in the European wars meant that the Jefferson administration could direct its energies toward extending and consolidating American rule in the borderlands by pacifying and displacing Indian peoples, creating new jurisdictions in territories and new states, and privatizing public lands through federal land sales. Federalist state-makers pioneered the infrastructure of expansion, establishing precedents that Republicans subsequently built on.[83] Jefferson promised continuity, and to an extraordinary extent he delivered. His conciliatory overtures to former partisan foes extended to their institutional innovations; controversies in the early years of his administration focused more on how many Federalist officeholders would be purged than on the abolition of offices. With peace on the horizon, Jefferson could roll back taxes and begin paying down the national debt, so alleviating the threat of an increasingly intrusive federal state apparatus that had accompanied Federalist mobilization during the Quasi-War with France. But the federal state and the federal constitution remained intact.

Yet if the fundamental structure of the regime did not change, Jefferson insisted that his election transformed the relationship between the American people and their government. "This whole chapter in the history of man is new," he wrote Joseph Priestley, for governors and governed were no longer distinct classes, locked in eternal combat, nor would state governments ever again have to mobilize against the federal government's overreaching.[84] With the people governing themselves, the problem of *imperium in imperio* disappeared. Federalists had embraced Montesquieu's maxim that securing an extensive imperial domain depended on a proportionate concentration of coercive power in the central government, mimicking the misguided British ministers who had brought on the American Revolution.[85] Jefferson inverted Montesquieu's maxim. Under the new republican dispensation, the expanding union was a source of strength, not vulnerability, he told Priestley. "The great extent of our republic is new. it's sparse habitation is new. the mighty wave of public opinion which has rolled over it is new."

That voters successfully mobilized to preserve their liberties against High Federalist "aristocrats" and "monocrats" was a remarkable triumph. But the ascendant Republicans were not radical revolutionaries, bent on destroying their enemies. American patriots had always been profoundly conservative, vigilant in defense of their rights. In the Revolution, they had sought to vindicate the legacy of liberty left by the founders of their colonies; in the 1800 elections, they reclaimed their Constitution from Federalists' false constructions, reaffirming the principles of 1776. The point of departure for their historical narrative was an imagined moment, before the onset of the imperial crisis in 1763, when largely autonomous, self-governing colonies played a critically important role in extending and defending the British Empire's continental domain. If the "great extent" of the United States was something "new," it also harked back to the old, decentralized empire of colonizers and settlers. That empire had grown strong and prosperous despite, or rather because of, the absence of the powerful, centralized administrative superstructure that reformers sought to impose on the colonies, before and after independence. For impatient nationalists, federalism was the problem, effectively setting limits to the union's extent. For Jefferson and his allies, it was the solution that would enable a more perfect union to expand across the vast spaces of the continent.

Jefferson recognized the need for a strong federal state, just as provincial patriots before the Revolution looked to the Crown for protection. What was new under the republican dispensation was the relationship between a free people and the plurality of governments under which they governed themselves. The ascendancy of the Jeffersonian party—or, more accurately, a loose coalition of state-based parties—was critical to this transformation. If Jefferson could claim a popular mandate, it was because he listened to the people's voice, or what he heard as "public opinion," as it was channeled through the party press.[86] Continuous critical engagement made government seem legitimate, defusing the reflexive suspicions of rights-conscious citizens. The "mighty wave of public opinion" that swept Federalists from office did *not* demolish everything in its path. "Quickly subsiding," it left the Constitution and structure of the federal government intact, despite the desperate efforts of Federalists to hold on to power; it redeemed Washington from the antirepublican associations that had compromised his reputation. The people's determination to uphold the Constitution, Jefferson told Priestley, revealed "a strength of character in our nation which augurs well for the duration of our republic."[87]

The peaceful triumph of the people's party—a great, inclusive party to end parties—guaranteed the continuity of constitutional government in a fragile union that seemed destined to collapse. The challenge was not to abolish government but rather to make it accessible and responsive to self-governing citizens: the more the people identified with the regime, the less conspicuous and intrusive its presence would be. Federalists sought to simplify rule, empowering an all-powerful central government with the capacity to enforce order among citizen-subjects across the continent. Republicans were the true federalists, insisting that the multiplicity of jurisdictions in an expanding union made the United States strong. Jefferson's election guaranteed that the federal government would serve the people's purposes, exercising sovereign powers—the people's prerogative—within its constitutional sphere. Republicans promised to uphold the Constitution, recognizing that endemic conflict among independent, sovereign states threatened to subvert the union and unleash anarchic forces. Ratification brought tax relief to beleaguered taxpayers and dismantled emerging barriers to free trade within the United States; an energetic federal government guaranteed collective security, enabling the state-republics to coexist peacefully.[88] Most crucially, federal administration of the national domain preempted territorial controversies among the states and opened the way for enterprising speculators and settlers from all the states to colonize an expanding hinterland.

In his Inaugural Address, Jefferson invited his countrymen to take up the challenge of colonization. The people's frontier would promote the progress of civilization across the continent, guaranteeing the new nation's future prosperity and power. Under Article IV, Section 3, of the Constitution, Congress was authorized to privatize the national domain, establish temporary governments for frontier settlements, and admit new states to the union on an equal basis with the original states. Jefferson assured his countrymen that the constitutional promise would be fulfilled. In an expanding union of republican states, power would be broadly distributed in responsive local governments. Lightly populated new states would enjoy equal representation in the Senate, offsetting the dominance of populous eastern states in the House of Representatives. Rapid turnover in the House and the influx of new members mitigated against the concentration and consolidation of authority in an entrenched, "aristocratic" ruling elite.[89]

The dynamism of political mobilization in an expanding federal union animated the machinery of constitutional government. The people had triumphed in 1800, resuscitating a moribund Constitution. Looking to the future, Jefferson projected the irresistible energy of westward settlement, making a self-governing people's power manifest. The new president thus republicanized Washington's conventional conception of imperial government. The strong hand of the federal government was not needed to impose order on unruly, semibarbarous citizens on the nation's frontiers. To the contrary, settlers should be expeditiously enabled to follow the lead of citizens in the original states, drafting their own state constitutions and, by negotiating terms of admission to the union, ratifying the federal constitution. Just as Americans reaffirmed their commitment to the republican creed when they elevated the author of the Declaration of Independence to the presidency in 1800, frontier citizens reenacted the American Revolution in their progress toward statehood.[90]

Advocates of expansion anticipated the language of manifest destiny when they celebrated the westward tide of settlement. But if this great folk movement seemed like a spontaneous, natural force, Jefferson and his allies understood that it depended on what the legal historian Christopher Tomlins calls the "technology" of colonization.[91] The founders of new colonies depended on legal instruments—grants and charters from the Crown—to organize settlement. The replication of English legal regimes enabled colonizers to establish property rights in land and bound labor while expropriating and displacing indigenous peoples.[92] The common law was second nature to Anglo-American colonizers, the ground of provincial identities in Britain's far-flung empire. When metropolitan officials sought to rationalize imperial governance, law-minded patriots like Jefferson mobilized in defense of constitutions that codified the history of colonization in their respective provinces. Americans argued that the empire was the product of colonization, sanctioned by and implemented through law. This was the empire patriots had struggled to defend against unconstitutional innovations and encroachments. For Jefferson, it was also the template for the new federal republic. Deeply rooted in the provincial past, the expanding union would link the living generation to its predecessors while fulfilling the Revolution's democratic promise to future generations.

British imperial reformers threatened to transform the empire by subverting the autonomy of established provincial governments, attempting to curb land speculation and settlement in Indian country, and blocking the creation of new governments.[93] Far from revolting *against* government, patriots had mobilized in favor of their provincial governments and of a prosperous and expansive empire in which they saw themselves playing crucial roles. From the metropolitan perspective, American constitutional claims seemed dangerously archaic, as they seemed to subvert the Glorious Revolution settlement and the sovereignty of king-in-parliament. But Jefferson and other provincial expansionists saw the future unfolding in the West: they saw nothing archaic in the legal and civic institutions that enabled expansion. And the "technology" of colonization was reformed and improved in the new territorial system that Jefferson and his congressional colleagues established and the new federal government administered. The formation and admission of new states in the Northwest Territory, beginning with Ohio in 1803, and the completion of the Louisiana Purchase in the same year seemed to vindicate Jefferson's vision, setting the stage for popular affirmation of his "mandate" in his landslide reelection in 1804.[94]

Jefferson insisted that the American Revolution had changed everything by overthrowing the monarchical old regime and establishing a new republican regime based on the sovereignty of the people. In his First Inaugural Address he depicted the West as a blank slate awaiting the arrival of successive generations of enterprising settlers. In this visionary mode, the new president overlooked formidable obstacles to expansion: the absence of transportation and communications infrastructure; the presence of powerful Indian nations and European empires; the uncertain loyalties of frontier settlers. Jefferson imaginatively erased these obstacles, anticipating the successful implementation of a colonization regime that depended on the authority of a strong central government. When the process was complete, new states would govern themselves, thus internalizing and naturalizing—and making "invisible"—the technology of colonization.[95] Jefferson's blank slate was located in the distant future, and it would be inscribed with an inspiring myth of self-creation. Each successive generation, moving through time and across space, would be endowed with the civic capacity to determine its own destiny.

Jefferson's democratic constitutionalism closed the gap between the people and their government, pointing back toward an organic conception of the body politic and its "constitution" and forward to a fantasy of harmony and homogeneity in which an enlightened, self-governing people would feel, think, and speak with a single voice. He would not call the federal republic an "empire," for this would acknowledge the new nation's indebtedness to history and its ongoing entanglement in a world of competing empires. In contrast, Washington struck a more realistic note. The United States was of course an empire. Following a script he had written for himself as an ambitious military man in the imperial old regime, he focused anxiously on the present, perilous moment. Yet precisely because he was so firmly located in that moment and played such crucially important roles in the great crises that marked the new nation's birth, Washington was an iconic, indispensable figure in Jefferson's "empire for liberty."

V. THE SPIRIT OF 1776

Washington invoked and inspired the spirit of the American people, united in their dedication to securing and preserving the independence of their rising empire. The commander of American forces was a nationalist who preached against partisan divisions and local attachments. Authority flowed from the top down in the hierarchical structure of the Continental Army, a professional, or "standing," army of the kind liberty-loving Britons and Americans traditionally feared and despised. Yet if Washington expected unquestioning obedience from his men, he also considered them "fellow citizens," willing to sacrifice everything in the common cause. Military service leveled up. Ordinary soldiers could display the same virtue in voluntarily accepting the risks of war that officers and gentlemen customarily considered their exclusive prerogative. Following Washington's lead, they modeled a people's patriotism—a vernacular cosmopolitanism—that was detached from the land and from attachments to particular places.

Jefferson's conception of the patriotic citizen focused on political rather than military mobilization, cultivating the citizen on his home ground. Emphasizing landed independence and love of country in a familiar provincial, rather than national, sense, Jefferson's patriotism was more conventional than Washington's. Jefferson and fellow patriot leaders sought to build on the civic capacity that Virginia and the other colonies had developed under the old empire and demonstrated in the Revolution. Authority moved upward from local communities through the infrastructure of resistance and revolution. Mobilization demanded democratization, giving ordinary folk of modest means a significant personal stake in the movement.[96] Jefferson's concern with land reform reflected this imperative. Offering land bounties to soldiers, making land available to free citizens on generous terms, and abolishing primogeniture and entail in order to preempt the formation of great estates would all serve to raise the mass of the people up to the level of civic competence that republicanism required.[97] In Jefferson's agrarian world, freeholders were "the chosen people of God, if ever he had a chosen people, whose breasts he has made his peculiar deposit for substantial and genuine virtue."[98]

Jefferson and Washington were equally committed to the success of the republican revolution. They both cultivated citizen virtue, raising farmers and soldiers up to a new level of dignity and self-respect. The patriotic spirit they sought to inspire, inculcate, and exploit would transform subjects into citizens prepared to sacrifice everything for their continental homeland. Recognizing one another as civic equals, brothers-in-arms would look to the future and beyond themselves. Family values would reign supreme as Revolutionary fathers opened the way westward for future generations to fulfill the imperial promise the false father, King George III, had betrayed. Jefferson conjured up a new, antimonarchical image of empire in his Inaugural Address. The boundless hinterland he evoked was a screen on which to project the aspirations of future generations. In grateful remembrance of the fathers' sacrifices, sons and daughters would extend the frontiers of liberty's empire and so provide for the happiness of future generations.

The iconic figure of Washington, the good father, would preside over this glorious, unfolding spectacle. Jefferson's short-term political motives for celebrating "our first and greatest revolutionary character" in his Inaugural were transparent: he hoped to recruit, or at least conciliate, his Federalist foes by embracing their hero. Yet in death as in life, Washington proved indispensable. Jefferson now asked his fellow Virginian to play the key role in his narrative of the new nation's mythic origins and manifest destiny. In the party battles of the 1790s, Republicans had sought to counter Washington's outsized influence by exalting the Declaration of Independence and its author, Jefferson.[99] But the match was unequal: Jefferson recoiled from any suggestion of a cult of personality. The self-effacing penman transcribed the sentiments of the American people in the Declaration; he did not impose his own will on them.[100]

The patriotic sentiments and republican principles that Congress expressed on behalf of the people and that American communities across the continent expressed for themselves constituted a resource to be mobilized and directed toward victory on the battlefield.[101] Jefferson acknowledged this imperative when he invoked the figure of the citizen-soldier in his Inaugural Address. When liberty was threatened, every man would be a Cincinnatus. But Washington's presence in the Inaugural Address was equally important, for the people's patriotic energies had to be subject to the commander's control and discipline. The Spirit of 1776 flourished in the relationship between Washington and his men. It could only be sustained through the generations if patriotic Americans willingly submitted to their own authority, made manifest to them in the person—and living memory—of Washington, the Revolutionary father who would *not* be king. With their servant Jefferson, the people would look forward, upholding the Constitution, which ascendant Republicans had redeemed from High Federalist enemies of republicanism. They would preserve and expand the federal union, thus fulfilling the vision of a rising empire, an "empire for liberty," that Jefferson, speaking for the living generation he now served, shared with Washington, the father of his country, as he lived on in the loving memory of his countrymen.

The expanding union, Jefferson assured his countrymen, would redeem the promise of Washington's "infant empire." In his Inaugural Address, the new president emphasized continuity, not radical change. The framers of the Constitution had designed a "more perfect union," which could add new member states, guarantee public credit, and keep the peace at home and abroad; Federalist administrations had implemented the design, constructing the machinery of a functioning federal state. The new president promised that his administration would uphold the Constitution and govern through the institutions his predecessors had established. The union would not fall apart, as Washington had feared in recurring moments of crisis. Instead, a united people would extend its domain across the continent, fulfilling Washington's most cherished hopes for his children.

Jefferson was no revolutionary. His election constituted a course correction, preempting a dangerous concentration of power in the federal government that threatened to destroy, rather than strengthen the union. But his reluctance to use the term "empire" reflected a significant ideological divergence from Washington and the Federalists. For Washington, the empire as a whole came before its constituent parts, and the loyalty of American patriots superseded local attachments. The "more perfect union" was indissoluble. Americans constituted a single people, and the United States and its territories collectively constituted a single great country. The British Empire was a failed project and therefore not really an empire at all. As they successfully extended the new nation's sovereignty across the continent, Washington and his "fellow citizens" could exult in the prospects of their own, much more perfect empire. But if "sovereignty" and "empire" were inextricably linked terms for Washington, they were problematic for Jefferson. The idea of union offered the two Virginians a semantic common ground that the conciliatory Jefferson exploited in his Inaugural Address. But Jefferson defined union in ways that Washington would never have accepted.

Jefferson's conception of union was premised on the consent of citizens, who were the source of legitimate authority. According to the democratic constitutionalism he and Madison had developed in the party battles of the 1790s, that consent had to be continuously reaffirmed and renegotiated: the people never alienated their sovereignty or their rights as citizens to any supposedly higher authority. The ongoing presence of the people enabled their governments to act in their name. Continuous consent produced a constantly changing, ever more perfect union. This union was not Washington's empire, amassing force to contain powerful centrifugal forces and avoid fragmentation. With its boundaries extending to its natural, continental limits, the union was protean and progressive, something "new under the sun." Patriotic Americans rejected any higher earthly authority, instead invoking providential design in the progress of future generations; they envisioned better, more enlightened versions of themselves. The immortal Washington, "saviour" of his country, presided over this progress, his illustrious career proof of the divine favor vouchsafed to this "chosen people." But Americans would depend on themselves, one people "under God."

If Jefferson's union was dynamic, it was necessarily contingent, subject to the vagaries of changing times and to the problematic progress of democratic enlightenment.[102] It was also grounded in the capacity of vigilant citizens to discern and act on their own interests, rightly understood. Jefferson's lifelong obsession with education reveals persisting anxieties about the civic capacity of his countrymen.[103] God might have deposited "substantial and genuine virtue" in the yeomanry, but that virtue—which presumably had always been there—had to be cultivated, like the farmer's field. Enlightenment, as this analogy suggests, began at home. Jefferson therefore was a great advocate of family values, urging enlightened parents to raise children who could promote the progress of civilization, from the ground up.[104] Where Federalists promoted the iconic image of the living Washington as the country's father, Jefferson looked to the fathers of the country to cultivate patriotism. After all, it was the farmers in their direct, unmediated relation with the land who stood most firmly on patriotic ground. Standing closer to nature, the unsophisticated countryman displayed human nature in a less corrupted, more naturally virtuous form than did his overly civilized urban counterpart.[105]

For Jefferson, the relation between the farmer and his land was the original and originary ground of patriotic attachment, and his household domain was a microcosm of the Commonwealth. The core idea bore a strong resemblance to the great philosopher John Locke's labor theory of value: the mixture of man's labor in the soil of the earth was the ultimate source of property rights.[106] American patriots mobilized in defense of their property rights, and the rights these common-law constitutionalists claimed were ultimately derived from their God-given capacity to make and accumulate property under the legal regimes of their respective provincial constitutions. With an extraordinary abundance of land available for improvement, that capacity remained largely unfettered in British America before the imperial crisis. Hypersensitive about metropolitan threats to autonomous provincial institutions, patriot leaders sounded the alarm to their humble neighbors.

British tax and regulatory policies, they argued, represented the opening wedge of a broader assault on the liberty and property and therefore on the free status of King George III's American subjects. Patriotism and property rights were thus inextricably linked, even indistinguishable, for Revolutionary Americans.

This was a volatile combination, as fearful conservatives recognized. Jefferson pursued the rhetoric and logic of mobilization to their limits, banking on the capacity of humble folk to take a longer, enlightened view of their true interests as they risked their precious lives and modest fortunes in behalf of the common cause. Ordinary citizens, he insisted, were as capable of that long-term perspective as the so-called "better sort." Perhaps they were even more capable, for ordinary folk naturally sought to secure the welfare of their children and future generations. Privileged elites, with an unequal stake in the status quo, were more likely to harbor dynastic ambitions for their own families at the expense of other families; they would be less likely to identify with their neighbors in generational terms, as fellow citizens dedicated to the republic's welfare and happiness. Paeans to their virtue were flattering to the people, and spirited appeals—such as those Jefferson heard in Patrick Henry's speeches—might galvanize them into action. But where would such appeals lead? What sort of union, or unions, would emerge from the logic of self-interest, however enlightened? "For they [who] have sown the wind," readers of the King James Bible were well warned, "shall reap the whirlwind."[107]

Which way would the wind blow for American revolutionaries? Of course, Jefferson could not know. The young deist devoutly hoped that his understanding of human nature would be vindicated in the all too predictable tumults of revolution and regime change. Conformity to the will of Nature's God, dimly discerned in the light of moral philosophy, could lead Americans out of the wilderness and into their promised land. The enlightened self-interest Americans displayed in their Revolution was a great resource that Jefferson sought to cultivate throughout his career, whether as patriotic partisan in the 1790s, or as the people's president, or as theorist of constitutional democracy in his retirement. Yet the identification of enlightened self-interest and love of country on which Jefferson's hopes for the union's future rested would always be problematic, and therefore always subject to calculation.

Union and disunion, the historian James E. Lewis Jr. shows, were two side of the same coin.[108] The logic of free and voluntary association was the same logic that justified breaking old unions and forming new ones. By definition, interest was contingent and circumstantial; nor was the arc of history necessarily progressive, leading to ever more perfect unions. Revolutionary Americans destroyed one union when they broke with Britain (for good, enlightened, self-interested reasons), and succeeding generations of liberty-loving Americans—in all parts of the country—would conspire and threaten to break up the new federal union (also for good, enlightened, self-interested reasons). They could do so, as Confederates claimed in 1861, *because* they honored the Revolutionary fathers and loved the union as it had been or should be, freed from the incubus of metropolitan corruption and sectional domination. Virginians testified to their filiopiety in 1858 when they erected a grand equestrian statue of George Washington in Richmond, eventually surrounding him with a cast of distinguished Virginian Revolutionary patriots.[109]

Had Washington lived to see Virginians secede from the union, he would have been profoundly disappointed, but not surprised. The whole point of his career had been to save a union that encompassed *all* Americans; a prosperous and powerful empire would be the only appropriate monument to his legacy. While he lived, Americans seemed impervious to his warnings about partisan polarization and conflicting sectional loyalties. When he died, they cherished the memory of the man but neglected his stern admonitions. That the union endured so long, through so many crises, was remarkable, even providential. Perhaps Washington's words did resonate, after all, when American statesmen displayed their genius for union-saving compromise.[110] Yet that reservoir of patriotic feeling—and that willingness to compromise—ran dry in the 1850s, when Americans readied themselves, with unseemly eagerness, for a fratricidal civil war.[111]

Before the cataclysmic deluge, the cult of Washington and the founding fathers served as a national adhesive, helping to attach quarreling countrymen to a dynamic, expanding union. As Americans became increasingly aware of their intractably divergent interests, however, it became increasingly difficult to define the content and character of that union or to explain how exactly it served those interests. When southerners began to juxtapose "liberty" *to* "union," they raised their own interests—and a distinctive sectional vision of the future—to an exalted level, while demystifying and devaluing the bonds that tied (or bound) them to other Americans. In doing so, they reversed the open-ended historical sequence Jefferson envisioned in his Inaugural Address. If they betrayed Washington by destroying the union, they also turned against Jefferson as they calculated the union's value and discounted its worth.

Jefferson proclaimed the value of the union to be incalculable: it would only be revealed in the fullness of time. The dynamic process of expansion and the inevitable, providential convergence of interests animated Jefferson's "empire for liberty." Where Washington looked backward, anxiously seeking to preserve the union against centrifugal tendencies, a forward-looking Jefferson sought to unleash and exploit the energies of an enterprising people. As they pursued happiness in various, ultimately complementary ways, Americans would identify with one another in their shared concern for the welfare of future generations. The true interests of citizens, rightly understood, would draw them together, not drive them apart; the diffusion of authority in a well-constituted federal system would strengthen the union. Liberty was not a zero-sum game, with the favored few benefiting at everyone else's expense. "Every man" would have a stake in society and government, Jefferson wrote Joseph C. Cabell in 1816, and would sooner "let the heart be torn out of its body" than to let "his power be wrested from him by a Caesar or a Bonaparte."[112]

The expanding union over which Jefferson and his successors presided implemented his democratic constitutionalism on a continental scale. Waves of enterprising settlers provided the energy that moved the legal and political machinery of colonization, facilitating the "peaceful" conquest of the continent—and disguising its brutal force. The pursuit of self-interest seemed naturally to accord with, indeed to make possible, the prosperity and power of the union as a whole. Jefferson's idealization of the yeomanry offered an ideological gloss on the happy convergence of private and public interests, of a rapidly growing capitalist economy and an expanding union of free republican states. Enlightened self-interest animated the expansion of settlement, projecting his conception of generational sovereignty across the vast spaces of the continent. There were natural, practical limits to that expansion, and the loyalties of far-flung settlements had to be tested, as they were in the Burr conspiracy of 1806–7 and in the War of 1812. But the union's very survival and expansion eased anxieties about the future and apparently vindicated Jefferson's faith in the stability and durability of republican institutions.

Jefferson's faith was severely tested in the Missouri crisis of 1819–21. His response to the effort to restrict slavery in the new state reflected a sudden, shocking slippage between idealized expectations and political realities. The former president was in no mood to compromise. Congress's interference in "the exclusive right of every state" to manage its own business, including the "domestic" institution of slavery, was an assault on the very foundations of the union. Restrictionists, Jefferson told former congressman John Holmes of Massachusetts (Maine District), meant to draw "a geographical line, coinciding with a marked principle, moral and political," that would "never be obliterated." They would make Americans from different parts of the country foreigners to one another.[113]

What was remarkable about Jefferson's outburst was the angry passion he betrayed. Conceiving of union in familial terms, he sought to give it a more solid, less contingent and instrumental grounding: it was, he supposed, more like a marriage than a business partnership. But the more he invested in the bond, the more devastating the rupture. The misguided attempt to restrict slavery in Missouri filled him with terror: it was a "fire bell in the night" that tolled "the knell of the Union." While other statesmen struggled to find a compromise that preserved the fathers' glorious inheritance, Jefferson regretted that he would "now die in the belief, that the useless sacrifice of themselves, by the generation of '76. to acquire self government and happiness to their country, is to be thrown away by the unwise and unworthy passions of their sons." The optimism of his Inaugural Address gave way to a nightmare of regression. The younger generation had turned against Jefferson and the Revolutionary generation, so committing "treason against the hopes of the world."[114]

Jefferson characteristically projected blame onto others, particularly northerners who feigned solicitude for southern slaves. When he pointed the finger at the younger generation, however, his indictment hit much closer to home. The patriot's journey, as he once imagined it, followed a progressive route from home to the union and the world beyond. Jefferson was now moving in the opposite direction, fortifying his home and homeland against insidious foreign threats. He was a Virginian first, then—contingently, perhaps temporarily—an American.

Washington told his fellow citizens that the union was their highest good. If his empire failed, it was because erring children would not heed their father's wise counsel. Jefferson was no Washington. He did not set himself above the people, for he was merely their servant and spokesman. The "empire for liberty" that expanded westward under his aegis was their empire, not his. If and when that empire endangered liberty and thus revealed its despotic character, it was theirs—and his—to destroy.

Notes

INTRODUCTION

1. Dumas Malone, *Jefferson and His Time,* 6 vols. (Boston: Little, Brown, 1948–81).

2. On the stories associated with Monticello, see Rhys Isaac, "The First Monticello," in *Jeffersonian Legacies,* ed. Peter S. Onuf (Charlottesville: University of Virginia Press, 1993), 77–108. On Jefferson's attachment to home and family, see Annette Gordon-Reed and Peter S. Onuf, *"Most Blessed of the Patriarchs": Thomas Jefferson and the Empire of the Imagination* (New York: Liveright, 2016). Hereafter Jefferson is referred to as TJ.

3. On the centrality of federalism in TJ's career, see Kevin R. C. Gutzman, *Thomas Jefferson Revolutionary: A Radical's Struggle to Remake America* (New York: St. Martin's, 2017), 9–96.

4. I am indebted to the late Lance Banning for *Jefferson and Madison: Three Conversations on the Founding* (Madison, WI: Madison House, 1995) and much else.

5. TJ, The Declaration of Independence as Adopted by Congress, July 4, 1776, in *The Papers of Thomas Jefferson Digital Edition* (hereafter *PTJDE*), ed. James P. McClure and J. Jefferson Looney (University of Virginia Press, Rotunda, 2008–17), Canonic URL: http://rotunda.upress.virginia.edu.proxy01.its.virginia.edu/founders/TSJN-01-01-02-00176-0006.

6. On parts and wholes, I am indebted to my brother Nicholas's contributions to our *Federal Union, Modern World: The Law of Nations in an Age of Revolution, 1776–1814* (Madison, WI: Madison House, 1993), 53–58.

7. For a good introduction to the problem of defining Virginia and its vital interests in the Revolutionary era, see Kevin R. C. Gutzman, *Virginia's American Revolution: From Dominion to Republic, 1776–1840* (Lanham, MD: Lexington Books, 2007).

8. Peter S. Onuf, *The Origins of the Federal Republic: Jurisdictional Controversies in the United States, 1775–1787* (Philadelphia: University of Pennsylvania Press, 1983), 75–102.

9. See the excellent discussion of "American Union" in Brian Steele, *Thomas Jefferson and American Nationhood* (New York: Cambridge University Press, 2012), 237–90.

10. TJ to William Stephens Smith, Nov. 13, 1787, and TJ to William Short, Jan. 3, 1793, *PTJDE,* Canonic URLs: http://rotunda.upress.virginia.edu.proxy01.its.virginia.edu/founders/

TSJN-01-12-02-0348 and http://rotunda.upress.virginia.edu.proxy01.its.virginia.edu/founders/TSJN-01-25-02-0016.

11. TJ to John Holmes, Apr. 22, 1820, in *Thomas Jefferson Writings,* ed. Merrill D. Peterson (New York: Library of America, 1984), 1435.

12. TJ to Joseph C. Cabell, Feb. 2, 1816, *PTJDE,* Canonic URL: http://rotunda.upress.virginia.edu.proxy01.its.virginia.edu/founders/TSJN-03-09-02-0286.

13. Richard Price, *A Discourse on the Love of our Country, delivered on Nov. 4, 1789, at the Meeting-House in the Old Jewry, to the Society for Commemorating the Revolution in Great Britain* (Boston, 1790), 6, identifying "country" as "community of which we are members" or people, not the land we inhabit.

14. TJ to Cabell, Feb. 2, 1816.

15. Minutes of the Board of Visitors, University of Virginia, Mar. 4, 1825, in *Thomas Jefferson Writings,* 479.

16. Jack P. Greene, *Peripheries and Center: Constitutional Development in the Extended Polities of the British Empire and the United States, 1607–1788* (Athens: University of Georgia Press, 1986); Greene, *The Constitutional Origins of the American Revolution* (New York: Cambridge University Press, 2011).

17. Benedict Anderson, *Imagined Communities: Reflections on the Origin and Spread of Nationalism,* 2nd rev. ed. (London: Verso, 1991).

18. Matthew Crow, *Thomas Jefferson, Legal History, and the Art of Recollection* (New York: Cambridge University Press, 2017), 62, 73.

19. The Declaration of Independence as Adopted by Congress, July 4, 1776. In his rough draft, in a passage excised by congressional editors, TJ renounced "for ever these unfeeling brethren" and urged his fellow Americans "to forget our former love for them." TJ, "original Rough draught" of the Declaration, [June 11–July 4, 1776], *PTJDE,* Canonic URL: http://rotunda.upress.virginia.edu.proxy01.its.virginia.edu/founders/TSJN-01-01-02-0176-0004.

20. TJ, First Inaugural Address, Mar. 4, 1801, *PTJDE,* Canonic URL: http://rotunda.upress.virginia.edu.proxy01.its.virginia.edu/founders/TSJN-01-33-02-0116-0004.

21. Gerald Stourzh, "*Constitution:* Changing Meanings of the Term from the Early Seventeenth to the Late Eighteenth Century," in *Conceptual Change and the Constitution,* ed. Terence Ball and J. G. A. Pocock (Lawrence: University Press of Kansas, 1988), 35–54. For a compelling interpretation of the development of American constitutionalism in the Revolutionary era, see Jonathan Gienapp, *Fixing the Constitution: Constitutional Imagination at the American Founding* (Cambridge, MA: Harvard University Press, forthcoming).

22. I am indebted to R. R. Palmer, *The Age of the Democratic Revolution: A Political History of Europe and America, 1760–1800,* vol. 1, *The Challenge* (Princeton, NJ: Princeton University Press, 1959), 185–235.

23. Patrick Henry speech, Mar. 23, 1775, quoted in *Patrick Henry: Champion of Liberty,* by Jon Kukla (New York: Simon & Schuster, 2017), 170; see also the discussion on 165–72.

24. Bernard Bailyn, *The Ideological Origins of the American Revolution* (Cambridge, MA: Harvard University Press, 1967).

25. Ralph Lerner, "The Constitution of the Thinking Revolutionary," in *Beyond Confederation: Origins of the Constitution and American National Identity,* ed. Richard Beeman, Stephen Botein, and Edward C. Carter II (Chapel Hill: University of North Carolina Press for the Omohundro Institute of Early American History and Culture, 1987), 38–68.

26. Rhys Isaac, *The Transformation of Virginia, 1740–1790* (Chapel Hill: University of North Carolina Press for the Omohundro Institute of Early American History and Culture, 1982).

27. Michal Jan Rozbicki, *The Complete Colonial Gentleman: Cultural Legitimacy in Plantation America* (Charlottesville: University of Virginia Press, 1998). For a provocative general study of this theme, see Rozbicki, *Culture and Liberty in the Age of the American Revolution* (Charlottesville: University of Virginia Press, 2011).

28. For a devastating portrait of Revolutionary and early national Virginia that starkly contrasts with the exalted image of the Old Dominion that emerged in the antebellum decades, see Charles Royster, *The Fabulous History of the Dismal Swamp Company: A Story of George Washington's Times* (New York: Knopf, 1999).

29. Carl Lotus Becker, *The History of Political Parties in the Province of New York, 1760–1776* (Madison: University of Wisconsin, 1909), 22.

30. Hannah Spahn, *Thomas Jefferson, Time and History* (Charlottesville: University of Virginia Press, 2011).

31. TJ to Philip Mazzei, Apr. 24, 1796, *PTJDE,* Canonic URL: http://rotunda.upress.virginia.edu.proxy01.its.virginia.edu/founders/TSJN-01-29-02-0054-0002.

32. On the democratization of slaveholding in the Revolutionary era, see Alan Taylor, *The Internal Enemy: Slavery and War in Virginia, 1772–1832* (New York: Norton, 2013).

33. TJ, *Notes on the State of Virginia,* ed. William Peden (Chapel Hill: University of North Carolina Press for the Omohundro Institute of Early American History and Culture, 1954), query 14 ("Laws"), 138.

34. Ibid., query 18 ("Manners"), 163.

35. See the excellent dual biography by Andrew Burstein and Nancy Isenberg, *Madison and Jefferson* (New York: Random House, 2010).

36. Patrick Henry speech, Sept. 6, 1774, quoted in Kukla, *Patrick Henry,* 148: "The Distinctions between Virginians, Pennsylvanians, New Yorkers and New Englanders, are no more. I am not a Virginian, but an American."

37. George Washington to Henry Lee Jr., Sept. 22, 1788, in *The Papers of George Washington Digital Edition* (Charlottesville: University of Virginia Press, Rotunda, 2008), Canonic URL: http://rotunda.upress.virginia.edu.proxy01.its.virginia.edu/founders/GEWN-04-06-02-0469.

38. TJ, First Inaugural Address, Mar. 4, 1801.

CHAPTER ONE

1. Thomas Jefferson (hereafter TJ), First Inaugural Address, Mar. 4, 1801, in *The Papers of Thomas Jefferson Digital Edition* (hereafter *PTJDE*), ed. James P. McClure and J. Jefferson Loo-

ney (University of Virginia Press, Rotunda, 2008–17), Canonic URL: http://rotunda.upress.virginia.edu.proxy01.its.virginia.edu/founders/TSJN-01-33-02-0116-0004, as published that day in Samuel H. Smith's *National Intelligencer* (Washington, DC). For quotations here and below from Smith's wife, Margaret Bayard Smith, and authoritative discussion of the address's composition and publication history, see editorial note, *PTJDE,* Canonic URL: http://rotunda.upress.virginia.edu.proxy01.its.virginia.edu/founders/TSJN-01-33-02-0116-0001.

2. See chapter 2 below.

3. Draft of Instructions to the Virginia Delegates in the Continental Congress (MS Text of *A Summary View, &c*), [July 1774], *PTJDE,* Canonic URL: http://rotunda.upress.virginia.edu.proxy01.its.virginia.edu/founders/TSJN-01-01-02-0090.

4. On Americans' ambivalence about executive authority, see Kathleen Bartoloni-Tuazon, *For Fear of an Elective King: George Washington and the Presidential Title Controversy of 1789* (Ithaca, NY: Cornell University Press, 2014).

5. TJ to Spencer Roane, Sept. 6, 1819, Founders Online, https://founders.archives.gov/?q=%20Recipient%3A%22Roane%2C%20Spencer%22&s=1111311111&sa=&r=3&sr=Roa; Peter S. Onuf, *Jefferson's Empire: The Language of American Nationhood* (Charlottesville: University of Virginia Press, 2000), chap. 3.

6. TJ to Henry Lee, May 8, 1825, in *Thomas Jefferson Writings,* ed. Merrill D. Peterson (New York: Library of America, 1984), 1501.

7. R. R. Palmer, *The Age of the Democratic Revolution: A Political History of Europe and America, 1760–1800,* 2 vols. (Princeton, NJ: Princeton University Press, 1959–64); Armin Mattes, "Paine, Jefferson, and the Modern Ideas of Democracy and the Nation," in *Paine and Jefferson in the Age of Revolutions,* ed. Simon P. Newman and Peter S. Onuf (Charlottesville: University of Virginia Press, 2013), 95–117; Mattes, *Citizens of a Common Intellectual Homeland: The Transatlantic Origins of American Democracy and Nationhood, 1775–1840* (Charlottesville: University of Virginia Press, 2015).

8. TJ thus distanced himself from the great democratizing rupture of the mid-1790s that he helped precipitate. See Matthew Rainbow Hale's brilliant essay "Regenerating the World: The French Revolution, Civic Festivals, and the Forging of Modern American Democracy, 1793–1795," *Journal of American History* 103 (2017), 891–920. See also Seth Cotlar, *Tom Paine's America: The Rise and Fall of Transatlantic Radicalism in the Early Republic* (Charlottesville: University of Virginia Press, 2011).

9. On how partisan controversy over the status of the Constitution as an "interpretive object" made it into a "sacred text," see Jonathan Gienapp's superb study *Fixing the Constitution: Constitutional Imagination at the American Founding* (Cambridge, MA: Harvard University Press, forthcoming).

10. See chapter 3 below.

11. TJ to Joseph Priestley, Mar. 21, 1801, *PTJDE,* Canonic URL: http://rotunda.upress.virginia.edu.proxy01.its.virginia.edu/founders/ TSJN-01-33-02-0336.

12. TJ to John Taylor of Caroline, June 4, 1798, *PTJDE,* Canonic URL: http://rotunda.upress.virginia.edu.proxy01.its.virginia.edu/founders/TSJN-01-30-02-0280.

13. TJ, First Inaugural Address, Mar. 4, 1801.

14. TJ to John Adams, Apr. 11, 1823, Founders Online, http://founders.archives.gov/documents/Jefferson/98-01-02-3446.

15. Paul K. Conkin, "The Religious Pilgrimage of Thomas Jefferson," in *Jeffersonian Legacies,* ed. Peter S. Onuf (Charlottesville: University of Virginia Press, 1993), 19–49; Eugene R. Sheridan, *Jefferson and Religion* (Charlottesville: Thomas Jefferson Foundation, 1998); Andrew Burstein, *Jefferson's Secrets: Death and Desire at Monticello* (New York: Basic Books, 2005), 237–63; Peter S. Onuf, "Jefferson's Religion: Priestcraft, Enlightenment, and the Republican Revolution," in *The Mind of Thomas Jefferson* (Charlottesville: University of Virginia Press, 2007), 139–68; Matthew Stewart, *Nature's God: The Heretical Origins of the American Republic* (New York: Norton, 2014); Annette Gordon-Reed and Peter S. Onuf, *"Most Blessed of the Patriarchs": Thomas Jefferson and the Empire of the Imagination* (New York: Liveright, 2016), 273–82. For an authoritative analysis of the ongoing controversy surrounding TJ's religious faith, see Burstein, *Democracy's Muse: How Thomas Jefferson Became an FDR Liberal, a Reagan Republican, and a Tea Party Fanatic, All the While being Dead* (Charlottesville: University of Virginia Press, 2015), 162–92.

16. I am indebted to Ari Helo, *Thomas Jefferson's Ethics and the Politics of Human Progress: The Morality of a Slaveholder* (New York: Cambridge University Press, 2014).

17. TJ to Benjamin Waterhouse, July 19, 1822, Founders Online, http://founders.archives.gov/documents/Jefferson/98-01-02-2965.

18. TJ to Edward Dowse, Apr. 19, 1803, *PTJDE,* Canonic URL: http://rotunda.upress.virginia.edu.proxy01.its.virginia.edu/founders/TSJN-01-40-02-0168; TJ, *The Jefferson Bible: The Life and Morals of Jesus of Nazareth Extracted Textually from the Gospels in Greek, Latin, French & English* (Washington, DC: Smithsonian Books, 2011).

19. TJ to George Wythe, Aug. 13, 1786, *PTJDE,* Canonic URL: http://rotunda.upress.virginia.edu.proxy01.its.virginia.edu/founders/TSJN-01-10-02-0162.

20. Hannah Spahn, *Thomas Jefferson, Time, and History* (Charlottesville: University of Virginia Press, 2011).

21. TJ to Le Comte Diodati, Mar. 29, 1807, Founders Online, http://founders.archives.gov/documents/Jefferson/99-01-02-5381.

22. TJ, Second Inaugural Address, Mar. 4, 1805, in *Thomas Jefferson Writings,* 522–23.

23. Declaration of Independence as Adopted by Congress, July 4, 1776, *PTJDE,* Canonic URL: http://rotunda.upress.virginia.edu.proxy01.its.virginia.edu/founders/TSJN-01-01-02-0176-0006.

24. Thomas Hobbes, *The English Works of Thomas Hobbes of Malmesbury; Now First Collected and Edited by Sir William Molesworth, Bart.,* 11 vols. (London: Bohn, 1839–45), vol. 3, Online Library of Liberty, http://oll.libertyfund.org/titles/585.

25. On TJ's "anthropology," see Maurizio Valsania, *Nature's Man: Thomas Jefferson's Philosophical Anthropology* (Charlottesville: University of Virginia Press, 2013). TJ's engagement with moral philosophy has generated a rich and controversial literature. See, e.g., Helo, *Thomas Jefferson's Ethics;* and Jean M. Yarbrough, *American Virtues: Thomas Jefferson on the Character of a Free People* (Lawrence: University Press of Kansas, 1998).

26. TJ to Henry Lee, May 8, 1825, in *Thomas Jefferson Writings,* 1501.

27. Peter S. Onuf, "Thomas Jefferson and American Democracy," in *A Companion to Thomas Jefferson,* ed. Francis D. Cogliano (Malden, MA: Wiley-Blackwell, 2012), 397–418; Onuf, "Epilogue," in *Between Sovereignty and Anarchy: The Politics of Violence in the American Revolutionary Era,* ed. Patrick Griffin, Robert G. Ingram, Peter S. Onuf, and Brian Schoen (Charlottesville: University of Virginia Press, 2015), 285–301.

28. Montesquieu (Charles Secondat), *The Spirit of the Laws,* trans. and ed. Anne M. Cohler, Basia Carolyn Miller, and Harold Samuel Stone (Cambridge: Cambridge University Press, 1989). For further discussion, see Nicholas Onuf and Peter S. Onuf, *Nations, Markets, and War: Modern History and the American Civil War* (Charlottesville: University of Virginia Press, 2006), 42–48; and Gordon-Reed and Onuf, *"Most Blessed of the Patriarchs,"* 83–84, 90–94.

29. TJ, First Inaugural Address, Mar. 4, 1801.

30. TJ to James Madison (hereafter JM), Sept. 6, 1789, *PTJDE,* Canonic URL: http://rotunda.upress.virginia.edu.proxy.its.virginia.edu/founders/TSJN-01-15-02-0375-0003; Herbert E. Sloan, *Principle and Interest: Thomas Jefferson and the Problem of Debt* (New York: Oxford University Press, 1995). See chapter 3 below.

31. See Spahn, *Thomas Jefferson, Time, and History,* on the possibilities of rational foresight integral to TJ's progressive, linear conception of time.

32. TJ to Maria Cosway, Oct. 12, 1786, *PTJDE,* Canonic URL: http://rotunda.upress.virginia.edu.proxy.its.virginia.edu/founders/TSJN-01-10-02-0309.

33. David C. Hendrickson, *Peace Pact: The Lost World of the American Founding* (Lawrence: University Press of Kansas, 2003).

34. Peter S. Onuf, *The Origins of the Federal Republic: Jurisdictional Controversies in the United States, 1775–1787* (Philadelphia: University of Pennsylvania Press, 1983), 207–9.

35. "It really is an assembly of demigods," TJ wrote John Adams on Aug. 30, 1787. *PTJDE,* Canonic URL: http://rotunda.upress.virginia.edu.proxy.its.virginia.edu/founders/TSJN-01-12-02-0075.

36. Cecelia Kenyon, "Men of Little Faith: The Anti-Federalists on the Nature of Representative Government," *William and Mary Quarterly* (hereafter *WMQ*), 3rd ser., 12 (1955), 4–43. See also Saul Cornell, *The Other Founders: Anti-Federalism and the Dissenting Tradition in America, 1788–1828* (Chapel Hill: University of North Carolina Press for the Omohundro Institute of Early American History and Culture, 1999).

37. In *Fixing the Constitution* Jonathan Gienapp shows that "strict construction" of the constitutional text and the invocation of the framers' "original intent" were the products of constitutional contestation in the early 1790s, not essential or distinguishing attributes of one "party" or another.

38. Lance Banning, "Republican Ideology and the Triumph of the Constitution, 1789–1793," *WMQ,* 3rd ser., 31 (1974), 168–88.

39. JM, The Report of 1800, [Jan. 7, 1800], in *The Papers of James Madison Digital Edition,* ed. J. C. A. Stagg (Charlottesville: University of Virginia Press, Rotunda, 2010), Canonic URL: http://rotunda.upress.virginia.edu.proxy01.its.virginia.edu/founders/JSMN-01-17-02-0202. On democratic constitutionalism, see Larry D. Kramer, *The People Themselves: Popular*

Constitutionalism and Judicial Review (New York: Oxford University Press, 2004); and Gienapp, *Fixing the Constitution.*

40. TJ to "Henry Tompkinson" (Samuel Kercheval), July 12, 1816, *PTJDE,* Canonic URL: http://rotunda.upress.virginia.edu.proxy.its.virginia.edu/founders/TSJN-03-10-02-0128-0002.

41. See chapter 4 below.

42. Michal Jan Rozbicki, *Culture and Liberty in the Age of the American Revolution* (Charlottesville: University of Virginia Press, 2011).

43. Draft of Instructions to the Virginia Delegates, [July 1774]. See the discussion in Brian Steele, *Thomas Jefferson and American Nationhood* (New York: Cambridge University Press, 2012), 21–38.

44. TJ's "original Rough draught" of the Declaration, [June 11–July 4, 1776], *PTJDE,* Canonic URL: http://rotunda.upress.virginia.edu.proxy01.its.virginia.edu/founders/ TSJN-01-01-02-0176-0004. See the discussion in Onuf, *Jefferson's Empire,* 62–65.

45. Minutes of the Board of Visitors, University of Virginia, Mar. 4, 1825, in *Thomas Jefferson Writings,* 479.

46. Andrew McLaughlin, "The Background of American Federalism," *American Political Science Review* 12 (1918), 215–40; Jack P. Greene, *Peripheries and Center: Constitutional Development in the Extended Polities of the British Empire and the United States, 1607–1788* (Athens: University of Georgia Press, 1986).

47. Jack P. Greene, *The Constitutional Origins of the American Revolution* (New York: Cambridge University Press, 2011); John Phillip Reid, *The Constitutional History of the American Revolution,* 4 vols. (Madison: University of Wisconsin Press, 1986–93).

48. George Grenville [attributed to Thomas Whately], *The Regulations Lately Made Concerning the Colonies, and the Taxes Imposed upon them, Considered* (London, 1765), 109.

49. J. M. Bumsted, "'Things in the Womb of Time': Ideas of American Independence, 1633 to 1763," *WMQ,* 3rd ser., 31 (1974), 533–64; Grenville, *Regulations Lately Made.*

50. Douglas Bradburn, *The Citizenship Revolution: Politics and the Creation of the American Union, 1774–1804* (Charlottesville: University of Virginia Press, 2009).

51. Jerrilyn Greene Marston, *King and Congress: The Transfer of Political Legitimacy, 1774–1776* (Princeton, NJ: Princeton University Press, 1987); Onuf, *Origins of the Federal Republic,* 3–20.

52. Brian Steele, "Inventing Un-America," *Journal of American Studies* 47 (2013), 881–902.

53. Peter S. Onuf, "A Declaration of Independence for Diplomatic Historians," *Diplomatic History* 22 (1998), 71–83.

54. Peter S. Onuf, "Jefferson and Tocqueville on Liberty and Equality," in *Liberty and Equality: The American Conversation,* ed. S. Adam Seagrave (Lawrence: University Press of Kansas, 2015), 38–56. For a compelling interpretation of the civic culture Tocqueville encountered, see Kevin Butterfield, *The Making of Tocqueville's America: Law and Association in the Early United States* (Chicago: University of Chicago Press, 2015).

55. TJ to Joseph C. Cabell, Feb. 2, 1816, *PTJDE,* Canonic URL: http://rotunda.upress.virginia.edu.proxy01.its.virginia.edu/founders/TSJN-03-09-02-0286. See the discussion in Richard K. Matthews, *The Radical Politics of Thomas Jefferson: A Revisionist View* (Lawrence: University Press of Kansas, 1984), 15–16, 81–89.

56. TJ to Cabell, Feb. 2, 1816.

57. TJ to "Henry Tompkinson" (Kercheval), July 12, 1816.

58. TJ to Cabell, Feb. 2, 1816.

59. Ibid.

60. TJ to Thomas Law, June 13, 1814, *PTJDE,* Canonic URL: http://rotunda.upress.virginia.edu.proxy01.its.virginia.edu/founders/TSJN-03-07-02-0307.

61. TJ to "Henry Tompkinson" (Kercheval), July 12, 1816.

62. TJ, First Inaugural Address, Mar. 4, 1801.

63. Onuf, *Jefferson's Empire,* chap. 6.

64. TJ, First Inaugural Address, Mar. 4, 1801.

65. Ibid.

66. TJ to George Rogers Clark, Dec. 25, 1780, *PTJDE,* Canonic URL: http://rotunda.upress.virginia.edu.proxy01.its.virginia.edu/founders/TSJN-01-04-02-0295.

67. TJ to John Holmes, Apr. 22, 1820, in *Thomas Jefferson Writings,* 1434.

68. Ibid., 1435, 1434. "Are our slaves to be presented with freedom and a dagger?" TJ asked John Adams on Jan. 22, 1821. Founders Online, http://founders.archives.gov/documents/Jefferson/98-01-02-1789. On Jefferson and Missouri, see Onuf, *Jefferson's Empire,* 109–17.

69. TJ to Holmes, Apr. 22, 1820, 1434 (TJ's emphasis).

70. Alan Taylor, *The Internal Enemy: Slavery and War in Virginia, 1772–1832* (New York: Norton, 2013).

71. For this persistent obsession, see Jeffrey Zvengrowski, "'They Stood Like the Old Guard of Napoleon': Jefferson Davis and the Democratic Party, 1848–1871" (PhD diss., University of Virginia, 2015). See also Sam W. Haynes, *Unfinished Revolution: The Early American Republic in a British World* (Charlottesville: University of Virginia Press, 2010).

72. I am indebted to Christopher Tomlins, *Freedom Bound: Law, Labor, and Civic Identity in Colonizing English America, 1580–1865* (New York: Cambridge University Press, 2010). On settler constitutionalism, see also Craig Yirush, *Settlers, Liberty, and Empire: The Roots of Early American Political Theory, 1675–1775* (New York: Cambridge University Press, 2011).

73. Land reforms were crucial parts of a "system by which every fibre would be eradicated of antient or future aristocracy; and a foundation laid for a government truly republican," TJ wrote in his *Autobiography* (1821). *Thomas Jefferson Writings,* 44. See also Holly Brewer, "Entailing Aristocracy in Colonial Virginia: 'Ancient Feudal Restraints and Revolutionary Reform,'" *WMQ,* 3rd ser., 54 (1997), 207–46.

74. "Whenever there is in any country, uncultivated lands and unemployed poor, it is clear that the laws of property have been so far extended as to violate natural right. The earth is given as a common stock for man to labour and live on." TJ to JM, Oct. 28, 1785, *PTJDE,* Canonic URL: http://rotunda.upress.virginia.edu.proxy01.its.virginia.edu/founders/TSJN-01-08-02-0534. On the crucial importance of land to TJ's political economy, see Drew R. McCoy, *The Elusive Republic: Political Economy in Jeffersonian America* (Chapel Hill: University of North Carolina Press for the Omohundro Institute of Early American History and Culture, 1980).

75. TJ to James Heaton, May 20, 1826, in *Thomas Jefferson Writings,* 1516.

76. Benjamin Franklin, *Information to Those Who Would Remove to America* [before Mar. 1784], Founders Online, https://founders.archives.gov/documents/Franklin/01-41-02-0391.

77. TJ, First Inaugural Address, Mar. 4, 1801. On ward republics as "bulwarks" for the rights of slave owners, see Gordon-Reed and Onuf, *"Most Blessed of the Patriarchs,"* 291–95.

78. Abraham Lincoln, First Inaugural Address, Mar. 4, 1861, in *The Collected Works of Abraham Lincoln,* ed. Roy P. Basler, 8 vols. (New Brunswick, NJ: Rutgers University Press, 1953–55), 4:271.

79. TJ to Roger Weightman, June 24, 1826, Founders Online, http://founders.archives.gov/documents/Jefferson/98-01-02-6179.

CHAPTER TWO

1. Patrick Henry (hereafter PH) resolutions, May 29, 1765, in *Patrick Henry: Life, Correspondence, and Speeches,* by William Wirt Henry, 3 vols. (New York, 1891), 1:80–81. My account of these transactions—and of Henry's entire career—is indebted to Jon Kukla's definitive new biography, *Patrick Henry: Champion of Liberty* (New York: Simon & Schuster, 2017); on the Stamp Act, see 80–97. For a good short biography, see John A. Ragosta, *Patrick Henry: Proclaiming a Revolution* (New York: Routledge, 2017). See also Henry Mayer, *A Son of Thunder: Patrick Henry and the American Republic* (New York: Franklin Watts, 1986).

2. For the complete set of resolutions as printed in the *Maryland Gazette* (Annapolis), July 4, 1765, and many other newspapers, see Ragosta, *Patrick Henry: Proclaiming a Revolution,* documentary appendix.

3. Thomas Jefferson's Notes on Patrick Henry, before Apr. 12, 1812, in *The Papers of Thomas Jefferson Digital Edition* (hereafter *PTJDE*), ed. James P. McClure and J. Jefferson Looney (Charlottesville: University of Virginia Press, Rotunda, 2008–17), Canonic URL: http://rotunda.upress.virginia.edu.proxy01.its.virginia.edu/founders/TSJN-03-04-02-0496-0003. Hereafter Jefferson is referred to as TJ.

4. PH speech, June 25, 1788, in *The Documentary History of the Ratification of the Constitution Digital Edition* (hereafter *DHRCDE*), ed. John P. Kaminski, Gaspare J. Saladino, Richard Leffler, Charles H. Schoenleber, and Margaret A. Hogan (Charlottesville: University of Virginia Press, 2009), Canonic URL: http://rotunda.upress.virginia.edu.proxy01.its.virginia.edu/founders/RNCN-02-10-02-0002-0015-0001; TJ to Thomas Lomax, Mar. 12, 1799, *PTJDE,* Canonic URL: http://rotunda.upress.virginia.edu.proxy01.its.virginia.edu/founders/TSJN-01-31-02-0056.

5. Thomas Jefferson's Notes on Patrick Henry, before Apr. 12, 1812.

6. Reminiscences of Patrick Henry in the letters of TJ to Willian Wirt, December 1824, reprinted in *Patrick Henry and Thomas Jefferson,* ed. James M. Elson (Brookneal, VA: Patrick Henry Memorial Foundation, 1997), 60.

7. John Dunn, *Democracy: A History* (New York: Atlantic Monthly Press, 2005). See my essays "Federalism, Democracy, and Liberty in the New American Nation," in *Exclusionary Empire: English Liberty Overseas, 1600–1900,* ed. Jack P. Greene (New York: Cambridge Univer-

sity Press, 2009), 132–59; and "Thomas Jefferson and American Democracy," in *A Companion to Thomas Jefferson,* ed. Francis D. Cogliano (Malden, MA: Wiley-Blackwell, 2012), 397–418.

8. Jack P. Greene, *The Constitutional Origins of the American Revolution* (New York: Cambridge University Press, 2011); Greene, *Peripheries and Center: Constitutional Development in the Extended Polities of the British Empire and the United States, 1607–1788* (Athens: University of Georgia Press, 1986).

9. Minutes of the Board of Visitors, University of Virginia, Mar. 4, 1825, in *Thomas Jefferson Writings,* ed. Merrill D. Peterson (New York: Library of America, 1984), 479.

10. Montesquieu (Charles Secondat), *The Spirit of the Laws,* trans. and ed. Anne M. Cohler, Basia Carolyn Miller, and Harold Samuel Stone (Cambridge: Cambridge University Press, 1989), pt. 1, bk. 3, chap. 3, 22–24.

11. TJ to the Citizens of Washington, DC, Mar. 4, 1809, *PTJDE,* Canonic URL: http://rotunda.upress.virginia.edu.proxy01.its.virginia.edu/founders/TSJN-03-01-02-0006.

12. Jay Fliegelman, *Declaring Independence: Jefferson, Natural Language, & the Culture of Performance* (Stanford, CA: Stanford University Press, 1993), 94–107.

13. TJ to John Banister Jr., Oct. 15, 1785, Canonic URL: http://rotunda.upress.virginia.edu.proxy01.its.virginia.edu/founders/TSJN-01-08-02-0499. For further discussion, see Annette Gordon-Reed and Peter S. Onuf, *"Most Blessed of the Patriarchs": Thomas Jefferson and the Empire of the Imagination* (New York: Liveright, 2016), 130–31.

14. TJ to Abigail Adams, Feb. 22, 1787, *PTJDE,* Canonic URL: http://rotunda.upress.virginia.edu.proxy01.its.virginia.edu/founders/TSJN-01-11-02-0182; TJ to William Stephens Smith, Nov. 13, 1787, *PTJDE,* Canonic URL: http://rotunda.upress.virginia.edu.proxy01.its.virginia.edu/founders/TSJN-01-12-02-0348.

15. TJ to Maria Cosway, Oct. 12, 1786, *PTJDE,* Canonic URL: http://rotunda.upress.virginia.edu.proxy01.its.virginia.edu/founders/TSJN-01-10-02-0309.

16. William Wirt, *Sketches of the Life and Character of Patrick Henry,* 9th ed. (Philadelphia: Thomas Cowperthwait, 1841), 125. See also Mark Couvillon, *The Demosthenes of His Age: Accounts of Patrick Henry's Oratory by his Contemporaries* (Red Hill, VA: Patrick Henry Foundation, 2013); Lord Byron described Henry as "the forest-born Demosthenes" (28). On Henry's "persuasive skills," see Kukla, *Patrick Henry,* 19–24.

17. Wirt, *Life and Character of Henry,* 142.

18. See Henry Mayer's short essay on this theme, "Patrick Henry and Thomas Jefferson," in Elson, *Patrick Henry and Thomas Jefferson,* 1–6.

19. Thomas Jefferson's Notes on Patrick Henry, before Apr. 12, 1812.

20. TJ to Henry Lee, May 8, 1825, in *Thomas Jefferson Writings,* 1501.

21. Robert M. S. McDonald, "Thomas Jefferson's Changing Reputation as Author of the Declaration of Independence: The First Fifty Years," *Journal of the Early Republic* 19 (1999), 169–95; McDonald, *Confounding Father: Thomas Jefferson's Image in His Own Time* (Charlottesville: University of Virginia Press, 2016).

22. Wirt, *Life and Character of Henry,* 129; Kevin J. Hayes, *The Mind of a Patriot: Patrick Henry and the World of Ideas* (Charlottesville: University of Virginia Press, 2008); Kukla, *Patrick Henry,* chaps. 32–38 passim.

23. Benjamin Franklin, *Information to Those Who Would Remove to America* [before March 1784], Founders Online, https://founders.archives.gov/documents/Franklin/01-41-02-0391.

24. Peter S. Onuf, "Jefferson's Religion: Priestcraft, Enlightenment, and the Republican Revolution," in *The Mind of Thomas Jefferson* (Charlottesville: University of Virginia Press, 2007), 139–68. For an excellent discussion of Revolutionary deism, see Matthew Stewart, *Nature's God: The Heretical Origins of the American Republic* (New York: Norton, 2014).

25. On TJ's reform efforts in Virginia, see Dumas Malone, *Jefferson and His Time,* vol. 1, *Jefferson the Virginian* (Boston: Little, Brown, 1948), 247–85.

26. Bill for Establishing Religious Freedom and Bill for the More General Diffusion of Knowledge, both June 18, 1779, *PTJDE,* Canonic URLs: http://rotunda.upress.virginia.edu.proxy01.its.virginia.edu/founders/TSJN-01-02-02-0132-0004-0082 and http://rotunda.upress.virginia.edu.proxy01.its.virginia.edu/founders/TSJN-01-02-02-0132-0004-0079; TJ, *Autobiography* (1821), in *Thomas Jefferson Writings,* 44.

27. James Madison (hereafter JM), *Federalist,* no. 48 (Feb. 1, 1788), in *The Papers of James Madison Digital Edition* (hereafter *PJMDE*), ed. J. C. A. Stagg (Charlottesville: University of Virginia Press, Rotunda, 2010), Canonic URL: http://rotunda.upress.virginia.edu.proxy01.its.virginia.edu/founders/JSMN-01-10-02-0269.

28. TJ, *Notes on the State of Virginia,* query 17 ("Religions"), in *Thomas Jefferson Writings,* 287. My interpretation of *Notes* is indebted to Dustin Gish and Daniel Klinghard, *Thomas Jefferson and the Science of Republican Government: A Political Biography of "Notes on the State of Virginia"* (New York: Cambridge University Press, 2017).

29. For good discussions of this episode, see Francis D. Cogliano, *Emperor of Liberty: Thomas Jefferson's Foreign Policy* (New Haven, CT: Yale University Press, 2014), 11–41; and Michael Kranish, *Flight from Monticello: Thomas Jefferson at War* (New York: Oxford University Press, 2010).

30. "TJ's bitterness on this subject," editor Julian Boyd writes, "was unquestionably owing to his conviction that Patrick Henry himself aspired to this post of unlimited power and that Henry's initiative in the move to censure TJ's administration was part of a concerted plan to gain that end." Editorial note to Henry Young to William Davies, June 9, 1781, d. Staunton, *PTJDE,* Canonic URL: http://rotunda.upress.virginia.edu.proxy01.its.virginia.edu/founders/TSJN-01-06-02-0086.

31. TJ, *Notes on the State of Virginia,* query 13 ("Constitution"), in *Thomas Jefferson Writings,* 251–52.

32. Ibid., 251.

33. Ibid., 250.

34. Ibid., 252.

35. Kukla, *Patrick Henry,* 255–60.

36. TJ to James Monroe, May 20, 1782, *PTJDE,* Canonic URL: http://rotunda.upress.virginia.edu.proxy01.its.virginia.edu/founders/TSJN-01-06-02-0174. See also Malone, *Jefferson and His Time,* 1:394–96; and Kukla, *Patrick Henry,* 271–73.

37. Wirt, *Life and Character of Henry,* 421.

38. TJ to JM, Dec. 8, 1784, *PTJDE,* Canonic URL: http://rotunda.upress.virginia.edu.proxy01.its.virginia.edu/founders/TSJN-01-07-02-0402.

39. Jan Lewis, "'The Blessings of Domestic Society': Thomas Jefferson's Family and the Transformation of American Politics," in *Jeffersonian Legacies,* ed. Peter S. Onuf (Charlottesville: University of Virginia Press, 1993), 109–46; Gordon-Reed and Onuf, *"Most Blessed of the Patriarchs,"* 198–200.

40. Kukla, *Patrick Henry,* 272, 271. For a good discussion of evolving conceptions of constitutionalism and PH's understanding, see ibid., 208–16.

41. Samuel Meredith's Memorandum to William Wirt, 1805, in *Patrick Henry in His Speeches and Writings and in the Words of His Contemporaries,* ed. James M. Elson (Lynchburg, VA: Warwick House, 2007), app. B, 210.

42. Wirt, *Life and Character of Henry,* 90, 94.

43. Hardin Burnley, quoted in ibid., 386. For further discussion, see Kukla, *Patrick Henry,* 369–74.

44. PH speech, June 12, 1788, *DHRCDE,* Canonic URL: http://rotunda.upress.virginia.edu.proxy01.its.virginia.edu/founders/RNCN-02-10-02-0002-0002-0001.

45. PH speeches, June 4, 1788, *DHRCDE,* Canonic URLs: http://rotunda.upress.virginia.edu.proxy01.its.virginia.edu/founders/RNCN-02-09-02-0004-00060007-0001 and http://rotunda.upress.virginia.edu.proxy01.its.virginia.edu/founders/RNCN-02-09-02-0004-0006.

46. See A. G. Roeber, "'The Scrutiny of the Ill Natured Ignorant Vulgar': Lawyers and Print Culture in Virginia, 1716 to 1774," *Virginia Magazine of History and Biography* 91 (1983), 387–417. Thanks to Matt Hale for this citation. For a suggestive discussion of Rufus Choate's career, see Daniel Cohen, *Pillars of Salt, Monuments of Grace: New England Crime Literature and the Origins of American Popular Culture, 1674–1860* (Amherst: University of Massachusetts Press, 1993), 196–99, 243–45, and passim.

47. TJ to Wirt, Aug. 4, 1805, Founders Online, http://founders.archives.gov/documents/Jefferson/99-01-02-2187.

48. Thomas Jefferson's Notes on Patrick Henry, before Apr. 12, 1812.

49. TJ, *Notes on the State of Virginia,* query 17, ("Religions"), in *Thomas Jefferson Writings,* 287.

50. Quoted in Kukla, *Patrick Henry,* 320. In addition to Kukla's account of the ratification debate, ibid., 321–48, see Pauline Maier, *Ratification: The People Debate the Constitution, 1787–1788* (New York: Simon & Schuster, 2010), 255–319; and Mayer, *Son of Thunder,* 296–439.

51. PH speech, June 4, 1788, Canonic URL: http://rotunda.upress.virginia.edu.proxy01.its.virginia.edu/founders/RNCN-02-09-02-0004-0006-0001.

52. PH speech, June 24, 1788, *DHRCDE,* Canonic URL: http://rotunda.upress.virginia.edu.proxy01.its.virginia.edu/founders/RNCN-02-10-02-0002-0013-0001.

53. PH speech, June 4, 1788, Canonic URL: http://rotunda.upress.virginia.edu.proxy.its.virginia.edu/founders/RNCN-02-09-02-0004-0006-0001.

54. PH speech, June 7, 1788, *DHRCDE,* Canonic URL: http://rotunda.upress.virginia.edu.proxy.its.virginia.edu/founders/RNCN-02-09-02-0004-0009-0001.

55. TJ wrote Alexander Donald on Feb. 7, 1788: "I wish with all my soul that the nine first Conventions may accept the new Constitution, because this will secure to us the good it contains, which I think great & important, but I equally wish that the four latest conventions, whichever they be, may refuse to accede to it till a declaration of rights be annexed."

PTJDE, Canonic URL: http://rotunda.upress.virginia.edu.proxy01.its.virginia.edu/founders/TSJN-01-12-02-0602.

56. Lance Banning, "1788 and 1776: Patrick Henry, James Madison, the Constitution, and the Revolution," in *Toward a More Perfect Union: Six Essays on the Constitution,* ed. Neil L. York (Provo, UT: Brigham Young University, 1988), 59–89.

57. PH speech, June 5, 1788, *DHRCDE,* Canonic URL: http://rotunda.upress.virginia.edu.proxy01.its.virginia.edu/founders/RNCN-02-09-02-0004-0007-0001.

58. Ibid.

59. "There is in fact a manly and legitimate passion for equality that incites men to want to be strong and esteemed. This passion tends to elevate the small to the rank of the great. But in the human heart a depraved taste for equality is also found that leads the weak to want to bring the strong down to their level and that reduces men to preferring equality in servitude to inequality in liberty." Alexis de Tocqueville, *Democracy in America,* vol. 1 (1835), Online Library of Liberty, http://oll.libertyfund.org/titles/2285#Tocqueville_1532-01_EN_818.

60. PH speech, June 5, 1788.

61. PH speech, June 20, 1788, *DHRCDE,* Canonic URL: http://rotunda.upress.virginia.edu.proxy01.its.virginia.edu/founders/RNCN-02-10-02-0002-0009-0001.

62. Cecelia Kenyon, "Men of Little Faith: The Anti-Federalists on the Nature of Republican Government," *William and Mary Quarterly,* 3rd ser., 12 (1955), 3–43.

63. PH speech, June 9, 1788, *DHRCDE,* Canonic URL: http://rotunda.upress.virginia.edu.proxy01.its.virginia.edu/founders/RNCN-02-09-02-0004-0010-0001.

64. Ibid.

65. PH speech, June 5, 1788.

66. Ibid.

67. PH speech, June 23, 1788, *DHRCDE,* Canonic URL: http://rotunda.upress.virginia.edu.proxy01.its.virginia.edu/founders/RNCN-02-10-02-0002-0012-0001.

68. PH speech, June 5, 1788.

69. PH speech, June 9, 1788.

70. PH speech, June 25, 1788, *DHRCDE,* Canonic URL: http://rotunda.upress.virginia.edu.proxy01.its.virginia.edu/founders/RNCN-02-10-02-0002-0015-0001.

71. PH speech, June 4, 1788, Canonic URL: http://rotunda.upress.virginia.edu.proxy.its.virginia.edu/founders/RNCN-02-09-02-0004-0006-0001.

72. See the discussion in chapter 3.

73. According to David Meade Randolph's "Anecdote of Patrick Henry," PH told fellow Antifederalists that "the question had been fully discussed and settled, and, that as true and faithful republicans, they had all better go home! They should cherish it, and give it fair play—support it too, in order that the federal administration might be left to the untrammelled and free exercise of its functions." *DHRCDE,* Canonic URL: http://rotunda.upress.virginia.edu.proxy01.its.virginia.edu/founders/RNCN-02-10-02-0002-0017-0002-0004.

74. PH speech, June 5, 1788.

75. PH speech, June 14, 1788, *DHRCDE,* Canonic URL: http://rotunda.upress.virginia.edu.proxy01.its.virginia.edu/founders/RNCN -02-10-02-0002-0004-0001.

76. PH speech, June 9, 1788.

77. PH speech, June 5, 1788.

78. Ibid.

79. PH speech, June 12, 1788.

80. See the discussions in Kukla, *Patrick Henry,* 39–46; and James H. Kettner, *The Development of American Citizenship, 1608–1870* (Chapel Hill: University of North Carolina Press, 1978), 165–72.

81. PH speech, British Debt Cases, Nov. 24, 1791, in Wirt, *Life and Character of Henry,* 367.

82. Kukla, *Patrick Henry,* 24.

83. PH speech, June 9, 1788.

84. Harry Innes to TJ, Dec. 28, 1793, *PTJDE,* Canonic URL: http://rotunda.upress.virginia.edu.proxy01.its.virginia.edu/founders/TSJN-01-27-02-0561.

85. PH speech, Mar. 4, 1799, in William Wirt Henry, *Patrick Henry: Life, Correspondence, and Speeches,* 2:607–10.

86. TJ to John Taylor of Caroline, June 4, 1798, *PTJDE,* Canonic URL: http://rotunda.upress.virginia.edu.proxy01.its.virginia.edu/founders/TSJN-01-30-02-0280.

87. TJ, First Inaugural Address, Mar. 4, 1801, *PTJDE,* Canonic URL: http://rotunda.upress.virginia.edu.proxy01.its.virginia.edu/founders/TSJN-01-33-02-0116-0004.

88. Thomas Jefferson's Notes on Patrick Henry, before Apr. 12, 1812.

89. PH to Betsey Aylett, Red Hill, Aug. 20, 1796, in Wirt, *Life and Character of Henry,* 400.

90. Ibid., 402.

91. Armin Mattes, *Citizens of a Common Intellectual Homeland: The Transatlantic Origins of American Democracy and Nationhood, 1775–1840* (Charlottesville: University of Virginia Press, 2015); R. R. Palmer, *The Age of the Democratic Revolution: A Political History of Europe and America, 1760–1800,* 2 vols. (Princeton, NJ: Princeton University Press, 1959–64).

92. George Washington, Farewell Address, *American Daily Advertiser* (Philadelphia), Sept. 19, 1796, Washington Papers, http://gwpapers.virginia.edu/documents_gw/farewell/transcript.html#top. For further discussion of the address, see chapter 4.

93. PH to Aylett, Aug. 20, 1796, 401.

94. Washington, Farewell Address, Sept. 19, 1796.

95. Jeffrey L. Pasley, *"The Tyranny of Printers": Newspaper Politics in the Early American Republic* (Charlottesville: University of Virginia Press, 2001); Jeremy D. Bailey, *Thomas Jefferson and Executive Power* (New York: Cambridge University Press, 2007).

96. JM, *Federalist,* no. 10 (Nov. 22, 1787), *PJMDE,* Canonic URL: http://rotunda.upress.virginia.edu.proxy01.its.virginia.edu/founders/JSMN-01-10-02-0178.

97. TJ to Joseph Priestley, Mar. 21, 1801, *PTJDE,* Canonic URL: http://rotunda.upress.virginia.edu.proxy01.its.virginia.edu/founders/TSJN-01-33-02-0336.

98. TJ, First Inaugural Address, Mar. 4, 1801.

99. PH to Aylett, Aug. 20, 1796, 401.

100. Ibid.

CHAPTER THREE

1. Thomas Jefferson (hereafter TJ) to George Wythe, Aug. 13, 1786, in *The Papers of Thomas Jefferson Digital Edition* (hereafter *PTJDE*), ed. James P. McClure and J. Jefferson Looney (Charlottesville: University of Virginia Press, Rotunda, 2008–17), Canonic URL: http://rotunda.upress.virginia.edu.proxy01.its.virginia.edu/founders/TSJN-01-10-02-0162.

2. James Madison (hereafter JM), Vices of the Political System of the United States, [April–June 1787], in *The Papers of James Madison Digital Edition* (hereafter *PJMDE*), ed. J. C. A. Stagg (Charlottesville: University of Virginia Press, Rotunda, 2010), Canonic URL: http://rotunda.upress.virginia.edu.proxy01.its.virginia.edu/founders/JSMN-01-09-02-0187.

3. After TJ became part of the new federal administration, he reassured his old Antifederalist friend George Mason that "much has been gained" by the federal constitution, for the government of the Articles "was terminating in anarchy, as necessarily consequent to inefficiency." TJ to George Mason, June 13, 1790, *PTJDE,* Canonic URL: http://rotunda.upress.virginia.edu.proxy01.its.virginia.edu/founders/TSJN-01-16-02-0295. See also Peter S. Onuf, "Anarchy and the Crisis of the Union," in *"To Form a More Perfect Union": The Critical Ideas of the Constitution,* ed. Herman Belz, Ronald Hoffman, and Peter J. Albert (Charlottesville: University Press of Virginia, 1992), 272–302; and David C. Hendrickson, *Peace Pact: The Lost World of the American Founding* (Lawrence: University Press of Kansas, 2003).

4. Eliga Gould, *Among the Powers of the Earth: The American Revolution and the Making of a New World Empire* (Cambridge, MA: Harvard University Press, 2012).

5. Peter S. Onuf, "The 'Madison Problem' Revisited," *Law and History Review* 28 (2010), 515–25; Jeremy D. Bailey, *James Madison and Constitutional Imperfection* (New York: Cambridge University Press, 2015), 1–14. I am indebted to Andrew Burstein, Nancy Isenberg, the late Lance Banning, and George Van Cleve for my understanding of the relationship between Jefferson and Madison. See Burstein and Isenberg, *Madison and Jefferson* (New York: Random House, 2010); Banning, *The Sacred Fire of Liberty: James Madison and the Founding of the Federal Republic* (Ithaca, NY: Cornell University Press, 1995); Banning, *Jefferson and Madison: Three Conversations from the Founding* (Madison, WI: Madison House, 1995); and Van Cleve, *We Have Not a Government: The Articles of Confederation and the Road to the Constitution* (Chicago: University of Chicago Press, 2017).

6. Peter S. Onuf, *Jefferson's Empire: The Language of American Nationhood* (Charlottesville: University of Virginia Press, 2000); Brian Steele, *Thomas Jefferson and American Nationhood* (New York: Cambridge University Press, 2012).

7. TJ to JM, Dec. 20, 1787, *PTJDE,* Canonic URL: http://rotunda.upress.virginia.edu.proxy01.its.virginia.edu/founders/TSJN-01-12-02-0454.

8. See the excellent discussion in Burstein and Isenberg, *Madison and Jefferson,* 166–208.

9. JM, *Federalist,* no. 10 (Nov. 22, 1787), *PJMDE,* Canonic URL: http://rotunda.upress.virginia.edu.proxy01.its.virginia.edu/founders/JSMN-01-10-02-0178.

10. TJ to JM, July 31, 1788, *PTJDE,* Canonic URL: http://rotunda.upress.virginia.edu.proxy01.its.virginia.edu/founders/TSJN-01-13-02-0335.

11. JM to TJ, Feb. 4, 1790, *PJMDE,* Canonic URL: http://rotunda.upress.virginia.edu.proxy01.its.virginia.edu/founders/JSMN-01-13-02-0020.

12. TJ to William Stephens Smith, Nov. 13, 1787, *PTJDE,* Canonic URL: http://rotunda.upress.virginia.edu.proxy01.its.virginia.edu/founders/TSJN-01-12-02-0348. See also Conor Cruise O'Brien, *The Long Affair: Thomas Jefferson and the French Revolution, 1785–1800* (Chicago: University of Chicago Press, 1996), 149–50, where TJ is compared to Pol Pot; and Joseph J. Ellis, *American Sphinx: The Character of Thomas Jefferson* (New York: Knopf, 1997), 150, where he is compared to Mao and Lenin.

13. "If men were angels, no government would be necessary. If angels were to govern men, neither external nor internal controls on government would be necessary." JM, *Federalist,* no. 51 (Feb. 6, 1788), *PJMDE,* Canonic URL: http://rotunda.upress.virginia.edu.proxy01.its.virginia.edu/founders/JSMN-01-10-02-0279. See the discussion in Lance Banning, "Some Second Thoughts on Virtue and the Course of Revolutionary Thinking," in *Conceptual Change and the Constitution,* ed. Terence Ball and J. G. A. Pocock (Lawrence: University Press of Kansas, 1988), 194–212; and Alan Gibson, "The Tenth Federalist Revisited—Again," unpublished paper in my possession.

14. Brian Steele, "Inventing Un-America," *Journal of American Studies* 47 (2013), 881–902.

15. TJ, *Notes on the State of Virginia,* ed. William Peden (Chapel Hill: University of North Carolina Press, 1955), query 18 ("Manners"), 162–63. See also Steele, *Jefferson and American Nationhood,* 53–90; and Annette Gordon-Reed and Peter S. Onuf, *"Most Blessed of the Patriarchs": Thomas Jefferson and the Empire of the Imagination* (New York: Liveright, 2016), 137–54.

16. Lance Banning, "The Practicable Sphere of a Republic: James Madison, the Constitutional Convention, and the Emergence of Revolutionary Federalism," in *Beyond Confederation: Origins of the Constitution and American National Identity,* ed. Richard Beeman, Stephen Botein, and Edward C. Carter II (Chapel Hill: University of North Carolina Press for the Omohundro Institute of Early American History and Culture, 1987), 162–87, at 178.

17. JM, *Federalist,* no. 10 (Nov. 22, 1787); Montesquieu (Charles Secondat), *The Spirit of the Laws,* trans. and ed. Anne Cohler, Basia Carolyn Miller, and Harold Samuel Stone (Cambridge: Cambridge University Press, 1989), pt. 1, chap. 9; David Hume, "Idea of a Perfect Commonwealth," in Hume, *Essays Moral, Political, and Literary,* ed. Eugene Miller (Indianapolis: Liberty, 1985), 512–29. See also Douglas Adair's influential essays "The Tenth Federalist Revisited," *William and Mary Quarterly* (hereafter *WMQ*), 3rd ser., 8 (1951), 48–67, and "'That Politics may be Reduced to a Science': David Hume, James Madison, and the Tenth Federalist," *Huntington Library Quarterly* 20 (1957), 343–60; and Mark Spencer's excellent commentary in "Hume and Madison on Faction," *WMQ,* 3rd ser., 59 (2002), 869–96. The most comprehensive and compelling reading of JM's famous essay is Gibson, "Tenth Federalist Revisited—Again."

18. Colleen Sheehan, "Madison v. Hamilton: The Battle over Republicanism and the Role of Public Opinion," *American Political Science Review* 98 (2004), 405–24.

19. Albert Furtwangler, *The Authority of Publius: A Reading of the Federalist Papers* (Ithaca, NY: Cornell University Press, 1984), chap. 5. Michael P. Zuckert, in his influential essay "Federalism and the Founding: Toward a Reinterpretation of the Constitutional Convention,"

Review of Politics 48 (1986), 166–210, writes that JM's argument for the extended republic met with "resounding silence at the Constitutional Convention" (192).

20. Alan Gibson, "Madison's 'Great Desideratum': Impartial Administration and the Extended Republic," *American Political Thought* 1 (2012), 181–207. See also Michael P. Zuckert, "A System without Precedent: Federalism in the American Constitution," in *The Framing and Ratification of the Constitution,* ed. Leonard W. Levy and Dennis J. Mahoney (New York: Macmillan, 1987), 144–45; and Alison L. Lacroix, "The Authority for Federalism: Madison's Negative and the Origins of Federal Ideology," *Law and History Review* 28 (2010), 451–505.

21. JM, speech of June 8, 1787, Power of the Legislature to Negative State Laws, *PJMDE,* Canonic URL: http://rotunda.upress.virginia.edu.proxy01.its.virginia.edu/founders/JSMN-01-10-02-0025. JM elaborated in a speech on June 28, Rule of Representation in the First Branch of the Legislature: "The negative proposed on the State laws, will make it an essential branch of the State Legislatures." *PJMDE,* Canonic URL: http://rotunda.upress.virginia.edu.proxy01.its.virginia.edu/founders/JSMN-01-10-02-004.

22. JM to TJ, March 19, 1787 (my emphasis), *PJMDE,* Canonic URL: http://rotunda.upress.virginia.edu.proxy01.its.virginia.edu/founders/JSMN-01-09-02-0169. See the excellent discussion in Charles F. Hobson, "The Negative on State Laws: James Madison, the Constitution, and the Crisis of Republican Government," *WMQ,* 3rd ser., 36 (1979), 215–35.

23. JM to Edmund Randolph, Apr. 8, 1787, *PJMDE,* Canonic URL: http://rotunda.upress.virginia.edu.proxy01.its.virginia.edu/founders/JSMN-01-09-02-0197; see also JM to George Washington [hereafter GW], Apr. 16, 1787, *PJMDE,* Canonic URL: http://rotunda.upress.virginia.edu.proxy01.its.virginia.edu/founders/JSMN-010-9-02-0208. On colonial appeals to the Privy Council, see Mary Sarah Bilder, *The Transatlantic Constitution: Colonial Legal Culture and the Empire* (Cambridge, MA: Harvard University Press, 2004).

24. TJ, Notes of Proceedings in the Continental Congress [June 7–Aug. 1, 1776], *PTJDE,* Canonic URL: http://rotunda.upress.virginia.edu.proxy01.its.virginia.edu/founders/TSJN-01-01-02-0160. On the protection covenant, see James H. Kettner, *The Development of American Citizenship, 1608–1870* (Chapel Hill: University of North Carolina Press, 1978), 165–72.

25. Van Cleve, *We Have Not a Government,* chap. 9. Van Cleve characterizes JM as "politically tone deaf" (92).

26. Parliament's Declaratory Act, Mar. 18, 1766, Avalon Project, Yale Law School, http://avalon.law.yale.edu/18th_century/declaratory_act_1766.asp.

27. Brendan McConville, *The King's Three Faces: The Rise and Fall of Royal America* (Chapel Hill: University of North Carolina Press for the Omohundro Institute of Early American History and Culture, 2006); Eric Nelson, *The Royalist Revolution: Monarchy and the American Founding* (Cambridge, MA: Harvard University Press, 2014).

28. JM, "Consolidation," *National Gazette,* Dec. 3, 1791, *PJMDE,* Canonic URL: http://rotunda.upress.virginia.edu.proxy01.its.virginia.edu/founders/JSMN-01-14-02-0122.

29. Edmund S. Morgan, *Inventing the People: The Rise of Popular Sovereignty in England and America* (New York: Norton, 1988).

30. JM, Vices of the Political System [April–June 1787].

31. Michael Zuckert argues that the framers avoided discussing the "locus of sovereignty" as much as possible; JM's conception of the "compound republic"—like Anglo-American conceptions of the imperial constitution—was "incompatible with the abstract doctrine of sovereignty." Zuckert, "Federalism and the Founding," 185–86. For a provocative discussion of the sovereignty question in the broader context of Anglo-American history, see Zuckert, "System without Precedent," 134–37.

32. Calvin H. Johnson, *Righteous Anger at the Wicked States: The Meaning of the Founders' Constitution* (New York: Cambridge University Press, 2005). For a persuasive rejoinder, see Alan Gibson's commentary in *Law and Politics Book Review* 20 (2010), 644–54, http://www.lpbr.net/2010/12/righteous-anger-at-wicked-states.html.

33. JM to TJ, Oct. 24, 1787, *PJMDE,* Canonic URL: http://rotunda.upress.virginia.edu.proxy01.its.virginia.edu/founders/JSMN-01-10-02-0151.

34. JM to GW, Apr. 16, 1787.

35. JM to Randolph, Apr. 8, 1787.

36. JM, speech of June 28, 1787, Rule of Representation. JM repeatedly compared states to counties in arguing for proportional representation. See the discussion in Mary Sarah Bilder, *Madison's Hand: Revising the Constitutional Convention* (Cambridge, MA: Harvard University Press, 2015), 96–101.

37. "Were it practicable for the genl. Govt. to extend its care to every requisite object without the cooperation of the State Govts. the people would not be less free as members of one great Republic than as members of thirteen small ones." JM speech, June 21, 1787, Relationship between Federal and State Governments, *PJMDE,* Canonic URL: http://rotunda.upress.virginia.edu.proxy01.its.virginia.edu/founders/JSMN-01-10-02-0038.

38. David Brearly speech, June 9, 1787, in Robert Yates Notes on Debates, in *The Records of the Federal Convention of 1787,* ed. Max Farrand, 3 vols. (New Haven, CT: Yale University Press, 1911), 1:182, http://oll.libertyfund.org/titles/farrand-the-records-of-the-federal-convention-of-1787-vol-1?q=%22boundaries+be+erased%22#. See the discussion in Peter S. Onuf, *The Origins of the Federal Republic: Jurisdictional Controversies in the United States, 1775–1787* (Philadelphia: University of Pennsylvania Press, 1983), 194–95.

39. JM to TJ, Oct. 24, 1787.

40. Ibid.

41. TJ to JM, June 20, 1787, *PTJDE,* Canonic URL: http://rotunda.upress.virginia.edu.proxy01.its.virginia.edu/founders/TSJN-01-11-02-0411.

42. "Our jealousy is only put to sleep by the unlimited confidence we all repose in the person [Washington] to whom we all look as our president." TJ to Edward Carrington, May 27, 1788, *PTJDE,* Canonic URL: http://rotunda.upress.virginia.edu.proxy01.its.virginia.edu/founders/TSJN-01-13-02-0120. See also Kathleen Bartoloni-Tuazon, *For Fear of an Elective King: George Washington and the Presidential Title Controversy of 1789* (Ithaca, NY: Cornell University Press, 2014).

43. TJ to JM, Dec. 20, 1787.

44. On attachments, see Emily Pears, "Chords of Affection: A Theory of National Political Attachments in the American Founding," *American Political Thought* 6 (2017), 1–29.

45. JM, *Federalist,* no. 10 (Nov. 22, 1787).

46. JM, *Federalist,* no. 39 (Jan. 16, 1788), *PJMDE,* Canonic URL: http://rotunda.upress.virginia.edu.proxy01.its.virginia.edu/founders/JSMN-01-10-02-0234. At the Convention, JM impatiently dismissed the "partly federal, and partly national" formulation, first introduced by Oliver Ellsworth. JM, Rule of Representation in the Senate [July 14, 1787], *PJMDE,* Canonic URL: http://rotunda.upress.virginia.edu.proxy01.its.virginia.edu/founders/JSMN-01-10-02-0059.

47. On interpretative ambiguity, see JM, *Federalist,* no. 37 (Jan. 11, 1788), *PJMDE,* Canonic URL: http://rotunda.upress.virginia.edu.proxy01.its.virginia.edu/founders/JSMN-01-10-02-0227.

48. Bailey, *Madison and Constitutional Imperfection,* 28–37 and passim.

49. JM, *Federalist,* no. 51 (Feb. 6, 1788).

50. For a provocative discussion of how, according to JM, "the people of the states" constituted themselves as "a single 'people of America'" in their respective ratifying conventions," see S. Adam Seagrave, "Madison's Tightrope: The Federal Union and the Madisonian Foundations of Legitimate Government," *Polity* 47 (2015), 249–72, at 259.

51. JM, *Federalist,* no. 51 (Feb. 6, 1788).

52. JM, *Federalist,* no. 10 (Nov. 22, 1787).

53. JM to TJ, Oct. 24, 1787.

54. JM, *Federalist,* no. 55 (Feb. 13, 1788), *PJMDE,* Canonic URL: http://rotunda.upress.virginia.edu.proxy01.its.virginia.edu/founders/JSMN-01-10-02-0292: "I am unable to conceive that the state legislatures which must feel so many motives to watch, and which possess so many means of counteracting the federal legislature, would fail either to detect or to defeat a conspiracy of the latter against the liberties of their common constituents." See Banning, "Practicable Sphere of a Republic."

55. JM, *Federalist,* no. 48 (Feb. 1, 1788), *PJMDE,* Canonic URL: http://rotunda.upress.virginia.edu.proxy01.its.virginia.edu/founders/JSMN-01-10-02-0269; JM to TJ, Oct. 17, 1788, *PJMDE,* Canonic URL: http://rotunda.upress.virginia.edu.proxy01.its.virginia.edu/founders/JSMN-01-11-02-0218: "Repeated violations of these parchment barriers have been committed by overbearing majorities in every State," especially in Virginia. See the discussion in Banning, *Sacred Fire of Liberty,* 274–90; Banning, *Jefferson and Madison,* 1–26; and Burstein and Isenberg, *Madison and Jefferson,* 195–99. On JM's conception of the Constitution as a bill of rights, see Jonathan Gienapp, *Fixing the Constitution: Constitutional Imagination at the American Founding* (Cambridge, MA: Harvard University Press, forthcoming).

56. Mary Sarah Bilder makes a strong case for Jefferson's influence over JM at this time in *Madison's Hand,* chap. 10.

57. TJ to Katherine Sprowle Douglas, July 5, 1785, *PTJDE,* Canonic URL: http://rotunda.upress.virginia.edu.proxy01.its.virginia.edu/founders/TSJN-01-08-02-0199; TJ to Wythe, Aug. 13, 1786.

58. Lord Sheffield [John Holroyd], *Observations on the Commerce of the American States* (London: J. DeBrett, 1784); Charles R. Ritcheson, *Aftermath of Revolution: British Policy Toward the United States, 1783–1795* (Dallas: Southern Methodist University Press, 1969).

59. Louise Burnham Dunbar, *A Study of "Monarchical" Tendencies in the United States, 1776 to 1801* (Urbana: University of Illinois Press, 1922); Cathy D. Matson and Peter S. Onuf, *A Union of Interests: Political and Economic Thought in Revolutionary America* (Lawrence: University Press of Kansas, 1990), 86–90.

60. GW to JM, Nov. 5, 1786, *PJMDE,* Canonic URL: http://rotunda.upress.virginia.edu.proxy01.its.virginia.edu/founders/JSMN-01-09-02-0070.

61. Seagrave, "Madison's Tightrope."

62. TJ to Joseph Jones, Aug. 14, 1787, *PTJDE,* Canonic URL: http://rotunda.upress.virginia.edu.proxy01.its.virginia.edu/founders/TSJN-01-12-02-0038.

63. "All Europe is made to believe we are a lawless banditti, in a state of absolute anarchy, cutting one another's throats, and plundering without distinction." TJ to Maria Cosway, Oct. 12, 1786, *PTJDE,* Canonic URL: http://rotunda.upress.virginia.edu.proxy01.its.virginia.edu/founders/TSJN-01-10-02-0309; see also TJ to Wythe, Aug. 13, 1786.

64. Gordon-Reed and Onuf, *"Most Blessed of the Patriarchs,"* 107–15.

65. Joyce Appleby, "America as a Model for the French Radical Reformers of 1789," *WMQ,* 3rd ser., 28 (1971), 267–86; Philippe Ziesche, *Cosmopolitan Patriots: Americans in Paris in the Age of Revolution* (Charlottesville: University of Virginia Press, 2010).

66. TJ to JM, Dec. 20, 1787. The best recent account of the insurgency is Leonard L. Richards, *Shays's Rebellion: The American Revolution's Final Battle* (Philadelphia: University of Pennsylvania Press, 2002).

67. TJ to Smith, Nov. 13, 1787.

68. TJ to Charles Bellini, Sept. 30, 1785, *PTJDE,* Canonic URL: http://rotunda.upress.virginia.edu.proxy01.its.virginia.edu/founders/TSJN-01-08-02-0448.

69. TJ to Cosway, Oct. 12, 1786.

70. TJ, *Notes on the State of Virginia,* ed. Peden, query 19 ("Manufactures"), 164–65.

71. Jean M. Yarbrough, *American Virtues: Thomas Jefferson on the Character of a Free People* (Lawrence: University Press of Kansas, 1998).

72. TJ to Cosway, Oct. 12, 1786.

73. TJ to Smith, Nov. 13, 1787.

74. TJ to JM, Jan. 30, 1787, *PTJDE,* Canonic URL: http://rotunda.upress.virginia.edu.proxy.its.virginia.edu/founders/TSJN-01-11-02-0095.

75. TJ to Carrington, Jan. 16, 1787, *PTJDE,* Canonic URL: http://rotunda.upress.virginia.edu.proxy01.its.virginia.edu/founders/TSJN-01-11-02-0047.

76. Richard D. Brown, "Shays's Rebellion and the Ratification of the Federal Constitution in Massachusetts," in Beeman, Botein, and Carter, *Beyond Confederation,* 113–27.

77. TJ, *Notes on the State of Virginia,* ed. Peden, query 17 ("Religion"), 161.

78. TJ to Smith, Nov. 13, 1787.

79. TJ to John Jay, Sept. 22, 1787, *PTJDE,* Canonic URL: http://rotunda.upress.virginia.edu.proxy01.its.virginia.edu/founders/TSJN-01-12-02-0159.

80. TJ to Carrington, Jan. 16, 1787. On conjectural history, see Nicholas Onuf and Peter S. Onuf, *Nations, Markets, and War: Modern History and the American Civil War* (Charlottesville: University of Virginia Press, 2006), 42–48.

81. Richard K. Matthews, *The Radical Politics of Thomas Jefferson: A Revisionist View* (Lawrence: University Press of Kansas, 1984); O'Brien, *Long Affair;* Ellis, *American Sphinx.*

82. TJ to John Adams, Aug. 30, 1787, *PTJDE,* Canonic URL: http://rotunda.upress.virginia.edu.proxy01.its.virginia.edu/founders/TSJN-01-12-02-0075.

83. TJ to Le Comte Diodati, Aug. 3, 1789, *PTJDE,* Canonic URL: http://rotunda.upress.virginia.edu.proxy01.its.virginia.edu/founders/TSJN-01-15-02-0317. See also the discussions in Ziesche, *Cosmopolitan Patriots,* 15–38.

84. TJ to GW, May 2, 1788, *PTJDE,* Canonic URL: http://rotunda.upress.virginia.edu.proxy01.its.virginia.edu/founders/TSJN-01-13-02-0059.

85. TJ to John Adams, Jan. 11, 1816, *PTJDE,* Canonic URL: http://rotunda.upress.virginia.edu.proxy01.its.virginia.edu/founders/TSJN-03-09-02-0219.

86. TJ to Joel Barlow, June 20, 1792, *PTJDE,* Canonic URL: http://rotunda.upress.virginia.edu.proxy01.its.virginia.edu/founders/TSJN-01-24-02-0092.

87. JM, *Federalist,* no. 49 (Feb. 2, 1788), *PJMDE,* Canonic URL: http://rotunda.upress.virginia.edu.proxy01.its.virginia.edu/founders/JSMN-01-10-02-0270.

88. TJ to JM, Sept. 6, 1789, *PTJDE,* Canonic URL: http://rotunda.upress.virginia.edu.proxy01.its.virginia.edu/founders/TSJN-01-15-02-0375-0003.

89. Burstein and Isenberg, *Madison and Jefferson,* 204–7.

90. JM to TJ, Feb. 4, 1790, *PJMDE,* Canonic URL: http://rotunda.upress.virginia.edu.proxy01.its.virginia.edu/founders/JSMN-01-13-02-0020.

91. The authoritative discussions of this letter are Herbert Sloan, "The Earth Belongs in Usufruct to the Living," in *Jeffersonian Legacies,* ed. Peter S. Onuf (Charlottesville: University of Virginia Press, 1993), and Sloan, *Principle and Interest: Thomas Jefferson and the Problem of Debt* (New York: Oxford University Press, 1995). See also Banning, *Jefferson and Madison,* 27–55.

92. TJ to JM, Sept. 6, 1789.

93. JM to TJ, Feb. 4, 1790.

94. Ibid.

95. Woody Holton, "'Divide et Impera': *Federalist 10* in a Wider Sphere," *WMQ,* 3rd ser., 62 (2005), 175–212.

96. For a provocative account of how meanings were fixed in and by words in American constitutionalism, see Gienapp, *Fixing the Constitution.*

97. TJ to JM, Sept. 6, 1789.

98. According to Thomas Paine's classic formulation, "Society is produced by our wants, and government by our wickedness; the former promotes our happiness *positively* by uniting our affections, the latter *negatively* by restraining our vices. The one encourages intercourse, the other creates distinctions. The first a patron, the last a punisher." Paine, *Common Sense* (Philadelphia: W. & T. Bradford, 1776; Project Gutenberg, 2008), https://www.gutenberg.org/files/147/147-h/147-h.htm.

99. TJ to James Monroe, May 5, 1793, *PTJDE,* Canonic URL: http://rotunda.upress.virginia.edu.proxy01.its.virginia.edu/founders/TSJN-01-25-02-0603. See also the excellent discussion in Banning, *Jefferson and Madison,* 57–102.

100. TJ to JM, June 29, 1792, *PTJDE,* Canonic URL: http://rotunda.upress.virginia.edu.proxy01.its.virginia.edu/founders/TSJN-01-24-02-0134.

101. In his "*Observations* on . . . reading history," May 19, 1731, the young Benjamin Franklin noted that "the great affairs of the world, the wars, revolutions, etc., are carried on and affected by parties" and called for the formation of a "United Party for Virtue," including "the virtuous and good men of all nations." *Benjamin Franklin's Autobiography,* ed. William B. Cairns (New York: Longmans, Green, 1905), 99–100. I am indebted to Matt Hale for this citation.

102. For a good overview of this tumultuous period, see Burstein and Isenberg, *Madison and Jefferson,* 211–348. See also Lance Banning, *The Jeffersonian Persuasion: Evolution of a Party Ideology* (Ithaca, NY: Cornell University Press, 1978); and Banning, *Sacred Fire of Liberty.*

103. John Page to TJ, June 21, 1798, *PTJDE,* Canonic URL: http://rotunda.upress.virginia.edu.proxy01.its.virginia.edu/founders/TSJN-01-30-02-0304.

104. Thomas Cooper to TJ, Oct. 25, 1802, *PTJDE,* Canonic URL: http://rotunda.upress.virginia.edu.proxy01.its.virginia.edu/founders/TSJN-01-38-02-0510-0001.

105. For a close reading of JM's *National Gazette* essays, see Colleen Sheehan, *James Madison and the Spirit of Republican Self-Government* (New York: Cambridge University Press, 2009). See also Sheehan's analysis of JM's 1791 "Notes on Government," drafted in preparation for the *National Gazette* essays, in *The Mind of James Madison: The Legacy of Classical Republicanism* (New York: Cambridge University Press, 2015). See also Alan Gibson, "Veneration and Vigilance: James Madison and Public Opinion, 1785–1800," *Review of Politics* 67 (2005), 5–35; and Todd Estes, *The Jay Treaty Debate, Public Opinion, and the Evolution of Early American Political Culture* (Amherst: University of Massachusetts Press, 2006).

106. On the early history of public opinion in the United States, see the excellent analysis in Mark G. Schmeller, *Invisible Sovereign: Imagining Public Opinion from the Revolution to Reconstruction* (Baltimore: Johns Hopkins University Press, 2016), esp. 7–59. I am indebted to Bailey, *Madison and Constitutional Imperfection,* 59–113. See also Bailey, "From 'Floating Ardor' to the 'Union of Sentiment': Jefferson on the Relationship between Public Opinion and the Executive," in *A Companion to Thomas Jefferson,* ed. Francis D. Cogliano (Malden, MA: Wiley-Blackwell, 2012), 184–98.

107. JM, "A Candid State of Parties," *National Gazette,* Sept. 22, 1792, *PJMDE,* Canonic URL: http://rotunda.upress.virginia.edu.proxy01.its.virginia.edu/founders/JSMN-01-14-02-0334.

108. JM, "Charters," *National Gazette,* Jan. 18, 1792, *PJMDE,* Canonic URL: http://rotunda.upress.virginia.edu.proxy01.its.virginia.edu/founders/JSMN-01-14-02-0172.

109. JM, "Public Opinion," *National Gazette,* ca. Dec. 19, 1791, *PJMDE,* Canonic URL: http://rotunda.upress.virginia.edu.proxy01.its.virginia.edu/founders/JSMN-01-14-02-0145. "FORCE is always on the side of the governed," David Hume wrote, "and the governors gave nothing to support them but opinion." Hume, "Of the First Principles of Government," in *Essays Moral, Political, and Literary,* 32–36. On this "maxim," see the discussion in Schmeller, *Invisible Sovereign,* 17–18.

110. JM, "British Government," *National Gazette,* Jan. 28, 1792, *PJMDE,* Canonic URL: http://rotunda.upress.virginia.edu.proxy01.its.virginia.edu/founders/JSMN-01-14-02-0180.

111. JM, "Spirit of Governments," *National Gazette,* Feb. 18, 1792, *PJMDE,* Canonic URL: http://rotunda.upress.virginia.edu.proxy01.its.virginia.edu/founders/JSMN-01-14-02-0203.

112. JM, "Government of the United States," *National Gazette,* Feb. 4, 1792, *PJMDE,* Canonic URL: http://rotunda.upress.virginia.edu.proxy01.its.virginia.edu/founders/JSMN-01-14-02-0190.

113. JM, "Candid State of Parties." Subsequent quotations are from this essay.

114. Ibid.

115. TJ to John Taylor of Caroline, June 4, 1798, *PTJDE,* Canonic URL: http://rotunda.upress.virginia.edu.proxy01.its.virginia.edu/founders/TSJN-01-30-02-0280.

116. On "constitutional time," see David J. Siemers, *Ratifying the Republic: Antifederalists and Federalists in Constitutional Time* (Stanford, CA: Stanford University Press, 2002).

117. JM, "Universal Peace," *National Gazette,* Jan. 31, 1792, *PJMDE,* Canonic URL: http://rotunda.upress.virginia.edu.proxy01.its.virginia.edu/founders/JSMN-01-14-02-0185.

118. TJ to Edmund Pendleton, Feb. 14, 1799, *PTJDE,* Canonic URL: http://rotunda.upress.virginia.edu.proxy01.its.virginia.edu/founders/TSJN-01-31-02-0024.

119. TJ to Joseph Priestley, Mar. 21, 1801, *PTJDE,* Canonic URL: http://rotunda.upress.virginia.edu.proxy01.its.virginia.edu/founders/TSJN-01-33-02-0336.

120. TJ, First Inaugural Address, Mar. 4, 1801, *PTJDE,* Canonic URL: http://rotunda.upress.virginia.edu.proxy01.its.virginia.edu/founders/TSJN-01-33-02-0116-0004.

121. TJ, Second Inaugural Address, Mar. 4, 1805, in *Thomas Jefferson Writings,* ed. Merrill D. Peterson (New York: Library of America, 1984), 522–23.

CHAPTER FOUR

1. Thomas Jefferson (hereafter TJ), First Inaugural Address, Mar. 4, 1801, in *The Papers of Thomas Jefferson Digital Edition* (hereafter *PTJDE*), ed. James P. McClure and J. Jefferson Looney (Charlottesville: University of Virginia Press, Rotunda, 2008–17), Canonic URL: http://rotunda.upress.virginia.edu.proxy01.its.virginia.edu/founders/TSJN-01-33-02-0116-0004.

2. Annette Gordon-Reed and Peter S. Onuf, *"Most Blessed of the Patriarchs": Thomas Jefferson and the Empire of the Imagination* (New York: Liveright, 2016), 138–56.

3. Matthew Rainbow Hale, "Regenerating the World: The French Revolution, Civic Festivals, and the Forging of Modern American Democracy, 1793–1795," *Journal of American History* 103 (2017), 891–920.

4. TJ to Joseph Priestley, Mar. 21, 1801, *PTJDE,* Canonic URL: http://rotunda.upress.virginia.edu.proxy01.its.virginia.edu/founders/TSJN-01-33-02-0336.

5. Francis D. Cogliano, *Thomas Jefferson: Reputation and Legacy* (Charlottesville: University of Virginia Press, 2009); Douglas Adair, *Fame and the Founding Fathers: Essays,* ed. Trevor Colbourn (New York: Norton, 1974).

6. James D. Drake, *The Nation's Nature: How Continental Presumptions Gave Rise to the United States of America* (Charlottesville: University of Virginia Press, 2011).

7. Brian Steele, "Inventing Un-America," *Journal of American Studies* 47 (2013), 881–902.

8. George Washington (hereafter GW) to Thomas Johnson, July 20, 1770, in *The Papers of George Washington Digital Edition* (hereafter *PGWDE*) (Charlottesville: University of Virginia Press, Rotunda, 2008), Canonic URL: http://rotunda.upress.virginia.edu.proxy01.its.virginia.edu/founders/GEWN-02-08-02-0239. It was important to avoid the perception, GW wrote, that improving Potomac navigation was a "partial Scheme." The best account of GW's vision of improvement is John Lauritz Larson, *Internal Improvement: National Public Works and the Promise of Popular Government in the Early United States* (Chapel Hill: University of North Carolina Press, 2001), 22–32. See also Edward J. Larson, *George Washington, Nationalist* (Charlottesville: University of Virginia Press, 2016), 23–43.

9. Thomas Slaughter, *The Whiskey Rebellion: Frontier Epilogue to the American Revolution* (New York: Oxford University Press, 1986), 68–80.

10. For a brilliant study of land speculation and state-making in this period, see Michael Blaakman, "Speculation Nation: Land and Mania in the Revolutionary American Republic, 1776–1803" (PhD diss., Yale University, 2016).

11. GW to the State Governors, June 8, 1783, George Washington's Mount Vernon, http://www.mountvernon.org/education/primary-sources-2/article/circular-to-the-states-george-washington-to-the-states-june-8-1783/.

12. GW to Gilbert du Motier, Marquis de Lafayette, Aug. 15, 1786, *PGWDE,* Canonic URL: http://rotunda.upress.virginia.edu.proxy01.its.virginia.edu/founders/GEWN-04-04-02-0200.

13. Stuart Leibiger, *George Washington, James Madison, and the Creation of the American Republic* (Charlottesville: University of Virginia Press, 1999), 61–70; see chap. 3 for a good discussion of GW's anxieties about the union.

14. GW to Henry Lee Jr., Sept. 22, 1788, *PGWDE,* Canonic URL: http://rotunda.upress.virginia.edu.proxy01.its.virginia.edu/founders/GEWN-04-06-02-0469.

15. GW, First Inaugural Address, Apr. 30, 1789, *PGWDE,* Canonic URL: http://rotunda.upress.virginia.edu.proxy01.its.virginia.edu/founders/GEWN-05-02-02-0130-0003.

16. Quoted in Jon Kukla, *Patrick Henry: Champion of Liberty* (New York: Simon & Schuster, 2017), 320; Patrick Henry speech, June 5, 1788, in *The Documentary History of the Ratification of the Constitution Digital Edition,* ed. John P. Kaminski, Gaspare J. Saladino, Richard Leffler, Charles H. Schoenleber, and Margaret A. Hogan (Charlottesville: University of Virginia Press, 2009), Canonic URL: http://rotunda.upress.virginia.edu.proxy01.its.virginia.edu/founders/RNCN-02-09-02-0004-0007-0001.

17. Eliga Gould, *Among the Powers of the Earth: The American Revolution and the Making of a New World Empire* (Cambridge, MA: Harvard University Press, 2012).

18. Emer de Vattel, *The Law of Nations, Or, Principles of the Law of Nature, Applied to the Conduct and Affairs of Nations and Sovereigns,* ed. Béla Kapossy and Richard Whitmore (Indianapolis: Liberty Fund, 2008), bk. 2, chap. 4, "Of the Right to Security, and the Effects of the Sovereignty and Independence of nations," http://oll.libertyfund.org/titles/vattel-the-law-of-nations-lf-ed.

19. Citizen-soldiers could not win the war, but they played a critical role in the broader politicization that made victory possible. John W. Shy, "The Military Conflict Considered as a Revolutionary War," in *A People Numerous and Armed: Reflections on the Military Struggle for American Independence,* rev. ed. (Ann Arbor: University of Michigan Press, 1990), 213–44.

20. Charles Royster, *A Revolutionary People at War: The Continental Army and American Character, 1775–1783* (Chapel Hill: University of North Carolina Press, 1979), 25–53. On Congress's assumption of the Crown's prerogative powers in war and diplomacy, see Jerrilyn Greene Marston, *King and Congress: The Transfer of Political Legitimacy, 1774–1776* (Princeton, NJ: Princeton University Press, 1987).

21. Josiah Quincy to GW, Mar. 21, 1776, *PGWDE,* Canonic URL: http://rotunda.upress.virginia.edu.proxy01.its.virginia.edu/founders/GEWN-03-03-02-0377.

22. David Finney to GW, Mar. 25, 1789, *PGWDE,* Canonic URL: http://rotunda.upress.virginia.edu.proxy01.its.virginia.edu/founders/GEWN-05-01-02-0339.

23. His self-restraint was legendary: "I could only be a crowned Washington," an admiring Napoleon Bonaparte exclaimed. Quoted in Don Higginbotham, *George Washington: Uniting a Nation* (Lanham, MD: Rowman & Littlefield, 2002), 18.

24. Glenn A. Phelps, *George Washington and American Constitutionalism* (Lawrence: University Press of Kansas, 1993), 23–61.

25. GW, General Orders, Mar. 1, 1778, *PGWDE,* Canonic URL: http://rotunda.upress.virginia.edu.proxy01.its.virginia.edu/founders/GEWN-03-14-02-0001.

26. For the young Washington's early military career, see Stephen Brumwell, *George Washington: Gentleman Warrior* (New York: Quercus, 2012).

27. See James Hrdlicka, "War and Constitution-Making in Revolutionary Massachusetts, 1754–1788" (PhD diss., University of Virginia, 2016); and Fred Anderson, *A People's Army: Massachusetts Soldiers and Society in the Seven Years' War* (Chapel Hill: University of North Carolina Press for the Omohundro Institute of Early American History and Culture, 1984).

28. Royster, *Revolutionary People at War,* 54–126.

29. Joanne B. Freeman, *Affairs of Honor: National Politics in the New Republic* (New Haven, CT: Yale University Press, 2001).

30. GW was persuaded "that nothing but the zeal of those Gentlemen who live with me and act in this capacity for the great American Cause and personal attachment to me, has induced them to undergo the trouble and confinement they have experienced since they have become Members of my Family." GW to John Hancock, Apr. 23, 1776, *PGWDE,* Canonic URL: http://rotunda.upress.virginia.edu.proxy01.its.virginia.edu/founders/GEWN-03-04-02-0096.

31. GW to Benjamin Harrison, Dec. 18[–30] 1778, *PGWDE,* Canonic URL: http://rotunda.upress.virginia.edu.proxy01.its.virginia.edu/founders/GEWN-03-18-02-0510.

32. GW to Gov. Joseph Reed, Apr. 8[–9], 1779, *PGWDE,* Canonic URL: http://rotunda.upress.virginia.edu.proxy01.its.virginia.edu/founders/GEWN-03-20-02-0009.

33. GW, General Orders, Mar. 1, 1778.

34. Garry Wills, *Cincinnatus: George Washington and the Enlightenment* (Garden City, NY: Doubleday, 1984).

35. I am indebted here to Brian Steele, "'General Washington Did Not Harbor One Principle of Federalism': Thomas Jefferson Remembers George Washington," in *Sons of the Father: George Washington and His Protégés,* ed. Robert M. S. McDonald (Charlottesville: University of Virginia Press, 2013), 72–98.

36. See James Roger Sharp, *American Politics in the Early Republic: The New Nation in Crisis* (New Haven, CT: Yale University Press, 1993).

37. George Washington, Farewell Address, *American Daily Advertiser* (Philadelphia), Sept. 19, 1796, Washington Papers, http://gwpapers.virginia.edu/documents_gw/farewell/transcript.html#top. See the discussion in Stanley Elkins and Eric McKitrick, *The Age of Federalism* (New York: Oxford University Press, 1993), 489–97.

38. Todd Estes, *The Jay Treaty Debate, Public Opinion, and the Evolution of Early American Political Culture* (Amherst: University of Massachusetts Press, 2006), 57–90.

39. Ralph Ketcham, *Presidents Above Party: The First American Presidency, 1789–1829* (Chapel Hill: University of North Carolina Press, 1984).

40. Freeman, *Affairs of Honor,* 6–10.

41. Lance Banning, *The Jeffersonian Persuasion: Evolution of a Party Ideology* (Ithaca, NY: Cornell University Press, 1978).

42. Lance Banning, "Republican Ideology and the Triumph of the Constitution, 1789–1793," *William and Mary Quarterly,* 3rd ser., 31 (1974), 168–88.

43. Richard Hofstadter, *The Idea of a Party System: The Rise of Legitimate Opposition in the United States, 1780–1840* (Berkeley: University of California Press, 1969).

44. Henry Lee, *Funeral Oration, on the Death of General Washington* (Philadelphia, 1800), 16.

45. GW, General Orders, Head Quarters, New York, July 9, 1776, *PGWDE,* Canonic URL: http://rotunda.upress.virginia.edu.proxy01.its.virginia.edu/founders/GEWN-03-05-02-0176.

46. See David Armitage, *The Declaration of Independence: A Global History* (Cambridge, MA: Harvard University Press, 2007).

47. Dumas Malone, *Jefferson and His Time,* vol. 1, *Jefferson the Virginian* (Boston: Little, Brown, 1948), 235–46.

48. TJ was not alone in neglecting the constitution of the union. See Jack N. Rakove, *The Beginnings of National Politics: An Interpretive History of the Continental Congress* (New York: Knopf, 1979).

49. The best account of GW's conception of sovereignty is George William Van Cleve, *We Have Not a Government: The Articles of Confederation and the Road to the Constitution* (Chicago: University of Chicago Press, 2017).

50. Gordon S. Wood, *The Creation of the American Republic, 1776–1787* (Chapel Hill: University of North Carolina Press, 1969), 344–90.

51. In *Federalist,* no. 15 (Dec. 1, 1787), "Publius" (Alexander Hamilton) characteristically chided Antifederalists for "cherish[ing] with blind devotion the political monster of an imperium in imperio." *The Papers of Alexander Hamilton Digital Edition,* ed. Harold C. Syrett (Charlottesville: University of Virginia Press, Rotunda, 2011), Canonic URL: http://rotunda.upress.virginia.edu.proxy01.its.virginia.edu/founders/ARHN-01-04-02-0168.

52. Higginbotham, *George Washington: Uniting a Nation;* Kenneth Bowling, "George Washington's Vision for the United States," unpublished paper in my possession; Edward J. Larson, *George Washington, Nationalist;* Van Cleve, *We Have Not a Government.*

53. Don Higginbotham, "War and State-Making in Revolutionary America," in *Empire and Nation: The American Revolution in the Atlantic World,* ed. Eliga H. Gould and Peter S. Onuf (Baltimore: Johns Hopkins University Press, 2005), 54–71.

54. Jack P. Greene, *The Constitutional Origins of the American Revolution* (New York: Cambridge University Press, 2011).

55. On the Anglophobic sources of American identity, see Peter S. Onuf, "American Exceptionalism and National Identity," *American Political Thought* 1 (2012), 77–100; and Onuf, "Imperialism and Nationalism in the Early American Republic," in *Empire's Twin: U.S. Anti-Imperialism from the Founding Era to the Age of Terrorism,* ed. Ian Tyrell and Jay Sexton (Ithaca, NY: Cornell University Press, 2015), 21–40.

56. Henry Wiencek, *An Imperfect God: George Washington, His Slaves, and the Creation of America* (New York: Farrar, Straus & Giroux, 2003); Mary V. Thompson, "'The Only Unavoidable Subject of Regret': George Washington and Slavery," http://www.mountvernon.org/sites/mountvernon.org/files/The%20only%20Unavoidable%20Subject%20°f%20Regret_JS%20edits.pdf; Dorothy Twohig, "'That Species of Property': Washington's Role in the Controversy Over Slavery," Washington Papers, http://gwpapers.virginia.edu/history/articles/species/.

57. I am indebted to Matthew Crow, *Thomas Jefferson, Legal History, and the Art of Recollection* (New York: Cambridge University Press, 2017); see also David Thomas Konig's important forthcoming study, *Nature's Advocate: Thomas Jefferson and the Republic of Law.* On the importance of history to American constitutionalism, see Trevor Colbourn, *The Lamp of Experience: Whig History and the Intellectual Origins of the American Revolution* (1965; reprint, Indianapolis: Liberty Fund, 1998), 193–225, http://oll.libertyfund.org/titles/colbourn-the-lamp-of-experience.

58. See Peter S. Onuf, "Jefferson's Religion: Priestcraft, Enlightenment, and the Republican Revolution," in *The Mind of Thomas Jefferson* (Charlottesville: University of Virginia Press, 2007), 139–68. For an excellent study of deism more generally, see Matthew Stewart, *Nature's God: The Heretical Origins of the American Republic* (New York: Norton, 2014).

59. Minutes of the Board of Visitors, University of Virginia, Mar. 4, 1825, in *Thomas Jefferson Writings,* ed. Merrill D. Peterson (New York: Library of America, 1984), 479.

60. Pauline Maier, *American Scripture: Making the Declaration of Independence* (New York: Knopf, 1997).

61. TJ to George Rogers Clark, Dec. 25, 1780, *PTJDE,* Canonic URL: http://rotunda.upress.virginia.edu.proxy01.its.virginia.edu/founders/TSJN-01-04-02-0295. See also TJ to GW, Dec. 28, 1793, for *French* use of term in instructions to Genet, *PGWDE,* Canonic URL: http://rotunda.upress.virginia.edu.proxy01.its.virginia.edu/founders/GEWN-05-14-02-0395.

62. TJ to JM, Apr. 27, 1809, *PTJDE,* Canonic URL: http://rotunda.upress.virginia.edu.proxy01.its.virginia.edu/founders/TSJN-03-01-02-0140.

63. Peter S. Onuf, "The Expanding Union," in *Devising Liberty: Preserving and Creating Freedom in the New American Republic,* ed. David Thomas Konig (Stanford, CA: Stanford

University Press, 1995), 50–80. On the new nation's "geographical predestination," see Albert K. Weinberg, *Manifest Destiny: A Study of Nationalist Expansionism in American History* (Baltimore: Johns Hopkins University Press, 1935), 43–71.

64. Draft of Instructions to the Virginia Delegates in the Continental Congress (MS Text of *A Summary View, &c.*) [July 1774], *PTJDE,* Canonic URL: http://rotunda.upress.virginia.edu.proxy01.its.virginia.edu/founders/TSJN-01-01-02-0090.

65. TJ to John Randolph, Nov. 29, 1775, *PTJDE,* Canonic URL: http://rotunda.upress.virginia.edu.proxy01.its.virginia.edu/founders/TSJN-01-01-02-0141.

66. See the insightful discussion in Francis D. Cogliano, *Emperor of Liberty: Thomas Jefferson's Foreign Policy* (New Haven, CT: Yale University Press, 2014), 1–6 and passim.

67. Reginald C. Stuart, *The Half-Way Pacifist: Thomas Jefferson's View of War* (Toronto: University of Toronto Press, 1978).

68. TJ to Benjamin Franklin, Aug. 13, 1777, *PTJDE,* Canonic URL: http://rotunda.upress.virginia.edu.proxy01.its.virginia.edu/founders/TSJN-01-02-02-0022.

69. Edmund S. Morgan, *Inventing the People: The Rise of Popular Sovereignty in England and America* (New York: Norton, 1988).

70. TJ to George Wythe, Sept. 16, 1787 (my emphasis), *PTJDE,* Canonic URL: http://rotunda.upress.virginia.edu.proxy01.its.virginia.edu/founders/TSJN-01-12-02-0128. See also TJ to the Georgia legislature, Jan. 15, 1802: "State-sovereignties, as recognised by the constitution, are an integral and essential part of our great political fabric." *PTJDE,* Canonic URL: http://rotunda.upress.virginia.edu.proxy01.its.virginia.edu/founders/TSJN-01-36-02-0229.

71. TJ, Thoughts on the Bankruptcy Bill [ca. Dec. 10, 1792], *PTJDE,* Canonic URL: http://rotunda.upress.virginia.edu.proxy01.its.virginia.edu/founders/TSJN-01-24-02-0707.

72. On TJ's federalism, see Peter S. Onuf, *Jefferson's Empire: The Language of American Nationhood* (Charlottesville: University of Virginia Press, 2000), 109–46.

73. TJ, Second Inaugural Address, Mar. 4, 1805, in *Thomas Jefferson Writings,* 519.

74. Jeremy D. Bailey, *Thomas Jefferson and Executive Power* (New York: Cambridge University Press, 2007). For a brilliant discussion of the tension between executive power and constitutional constraints, see James E. Lewis Jr., *The Burr Conspiracy: Uncovering the Story of an Early American Crisis* (Princeton, NJ: Princeton University Press, 2017), 246–71.

75. Leonard Sadosky, *Revolutionary Negotiations: Indians, Empires, and Diplomats in the Founding of America* (Charlottesville: University of Virginia Press, 2009).

76. James Horn, Jan Ellen Lewis, and Peter S. Onuf, eds., *The Revolution of 1800: Democracy, Race, and the New Republic* (Charlottesville: University of Virginia Press, 2002).

77. "The revolution of 1800 . . . was as real a revolution in the principles of our government as that of 76." TJ to Spencer Roane, Sept. 6, 1819, Founders Online, https://founders.archives.gov/?q=%20Recipient%3A%22Roane%2C%20Spencer%22&s=2111311111&sa=&r=3&sr=Roa. "The Judiciary is the dangerous corps of sappers and miners. because they are in place for life and beyond responsibility." TJ to Ethan A. Brown, Feb. 18, 1821, Founders Online, https://founders.archives.gov/?q=%22sappers%20and%20miners%22%20Author%3A%22Jefferson%2C%20Thomas%22&s=2111311111&sa.

78. TJ, First Inaugural Address, Mar. 4, 1801.

79. "The republicans are the *nation,*" TJ wrote the newspaper editor William Duane on March 28, 1811: "I will not say our *party,* the term is false and degrading." *PTJDE,* Canonic URL: http://rotunda.upress.virginia.edu.proxy01.its.virginia.edu/founders/TSJN-03-03-02-0378.

80. TJ, First Inaugural Address, Mar. 4, 1801.

81. Onuf, "Imperialism and Nationalism," 21–40.

82. Max M. Edling, *A Hercules in the Cradle: War, Money, and the American State, 1783–1867* (Chicago: University of Chicago Press, 2014), 81–107. For an excellent new biography of Gallatin, see Gregory May, *Financial Founder: Albert Gallatin and the Strange Undoing of Alexander Hamilton's Vision for America* (Washington, DC: Regnery, forthcoming).

83. Jack Ericson Eblen, *The First and Second United States Empires: Governors and Territorial Government, 1784–1912* (Pittsburgh: University of Pittsburgh Press, 1968).

84. TJ to Priestley, Mar. 21, 1801.

85. Montesquieu (Charles Secondat), *The Spirit of the Laws,* trans. and ed. Anne Cohler, Basia Carolyn Miller, and Harold Samuel Stone (Cambridge: Cambridge University Press, 1989), pt. 1, chap. 9; see the discussion in chapter 3 of this book.

86. Jeffrey L. Pasley, *"The Tyranny of Printers": Newspaper Politics in the Early American Republic* (Charlottesville: University of Virginia Press, 2001); Peter S. Onuf and Leonard J. Sadosky, *Jeffersonian America* (Malden, MA: Blackwell, 2002).

87. TJ to Priestley, Mar. 21, 1801.

88. Max M. Edling, *A Revolution in Favor of Government: Origins of the U.S. Constitution and the Making of the American State* (New York: Oxford University Press, 2003).

89. Peter S. Onuf, "Thomas Jefferson and the Expanding Union," in *Mind of Thomas Jefferson,* 109–20.

90. Peter S. Onuf, *Statehood and Union: A History of the Northwest Ordinance* (1989; rev. ed., University of Notre Dame Press, 2018); Onuf, "Democracy, Empire and the 1816 Indiana Constitution," *Indiana Magazine of History* 111 (2015), 5–29.

91. Christopher Tomlins, *Freedom Bound: Law, Labor, and Civic Identity in Colonizing English America, 1580–1865* (New York: Cambridge University Press, 2010).

92. Colonizers could deploy the technology of colonization to create a racially homogenous republic. See Nicholas Guyatt, *Bind Us Apart: How the First American Liberals Invented Racial Segregation* (New York: Basic Books, 2016); and Robert Parkinson, *The Common Cause: Creating Race and Nation in the American Revolution* (Chapel Hill: University of North Carolina Press, 2016).

93. See S. Max Edelson's brilliant new study, *The New Map of Empire: How Britain Imagined America before Independence* (Cambridge, MA: Harvard University Press, 2017).

94. Onuf, "Expanding Union," 50–80.

95. On federal state-making I am indebted to Edling, *Revolution in Favor of Government;* Brian Balogh, *A Government Out of Sight: The Mystery of National Authority in Nineteenth-Century America* (New York: Cambridge University Press, 2009); and Michael Kammen, *A Machine That Would Go of Itself: The Constitution in American Culture* (New York: Knopf, 1986). See also the essays collected in Peter Thompson and Peter S. Onuf, *State and Citizen: British America and the Early United States* (Charlottesville: University of Virginia Press, 2013).

96. On the crucial role of provincial elites in mobilizing the people, see R. R. Palmer, *The Age of the Democratic Revolution: A Political History of Europe and America, 1760–1800,* vol. 1, *The Challenge* (Princeton, NJ: Princeton University Press, 1959), 185–235.

97. Konig, *Nature's Advocate.*

98. TJ, *Notes on the State of Virginia,* ed. William Peden (Chapel Hill: University of North Carolina Press, 1954), query 19 ("Manufactures"), 164–65. On TJ and land reform in Virginia, see Malone, *Jefferson and His Time,* 1:247–60.

99. Robert M. C. McDonald, *Confounding Father: Thomas Jefferson's Image in His Own Time* (Charlottesville: University of Virginia Press, 2016).

100. Jay Fliegelman, *Declaring Independence: Jefferson, Natural Language, & the Culture of Performance* (Stanford, CA: Stanford University Press, 1993), 164–67.

101. On the multiplicity of American Declarations, see Maier, *American Scripture.*

102. Maurizio Valsania, *The Limits of Optimism: Thomas Jefferson's Dualistic Enlightenment* (Charlottesville: University of Virginia Press, 2011).

103. Richard D. Brown, *Knowledge Is Power: The Diffusion of Information in Early America, 1700–1865* (New York: Oxford University Press, 1989).

104. Gordon-Reed and Onuf, *"Most Blessed of the Patriarchs,"* 169–207.

105. Jean M. Yarbrough, *American Virtues: Thomas Jefferson on the Character of a Free People* (Lawrence: University Press of Kansas, 1998).

106. According to Locke, whatever man "removes out of the state that nature hath provided, and left it in, he hath mixed his labour with, and joined to it something that is his own, and thereby makes it his property." John Locke, *Second Treatise of Government* (1690), chap. 5, "Of Property," sec. 27 (Project Gutenberg, 2010), https://www.gutenberg.org/files/7370/7370-h/7370-h.htm#CHAPTER_V.

107. Hosea 8:7.

108. Lewis, *Burr Conspiracy,* 118–47.

109. *Historical Account of the Washington Monument, in Capitol Square, Richmond, Va., with Biographical Sketches of Thomas Jefferson, John Marshall, Patrick Henry, George Mason, Thomas Nelson, and Andrew Lewis* (Richmond, 1869), https://archive.org/details/historicalaccounoonyew.

110. Peter B. Knupfer, *The Union as It Is: Constitutional Unionism and Sectional Compromise, 1787–1861* (Chapel Hill: University of North Carolina Press, 1991); François Furstenberg, *In the Name of the Father: Washington's Legacy, Slavery, and the Making of a Nation* (New York: Penguin, 2006).

111. Nicholas Onuf and Peter S. Onuf, *Nations, Markets, and War: Modern History and the American Civil War* (Charlottesville: University of Virginia Press, 2006).

112. TJ to Joseph C. Cabell, Feb. 2, 1816, *PTJDE,* Canonic URL: http://rotunda.upress.virginia.edu.proxy01.its.virginia.edu/founders/TSJN-03-09-02-0286.

113. TJ to John Holmes, Apr. 22, 1820, in *Thomas Jefferson Writings,* 1435. For further discussion, see Onuf, *Jefferson's Empire,* 109–17.

114. TJ to John Holmes, Apr. 22, 1820.

Index

Abbreviations: PH (Patrick Henry), TJ (Thomas Jefferson), GW (George Washington)